Cram101 Textbook Outlines to accompany:

Fundamentals of Multinational Finance

Moffett and Stonehill and Eiteman, 1st Edition

An Academic Internet Publishers (AIPI) publication (c) 2007.

Cram101 and Cram101.com are AIPI publications and services. All notes, highlights, reviews, and practice tests are prepared by AIPI for use in AIPI publications, all rights reserved.

You have a discounted membership at www.Cram101.com with this book.

Get all of the practice tests for the chapters of this textbook, and access in-depth reference material for writing essays and papers. Here is an example from a Cram101 Biology text:

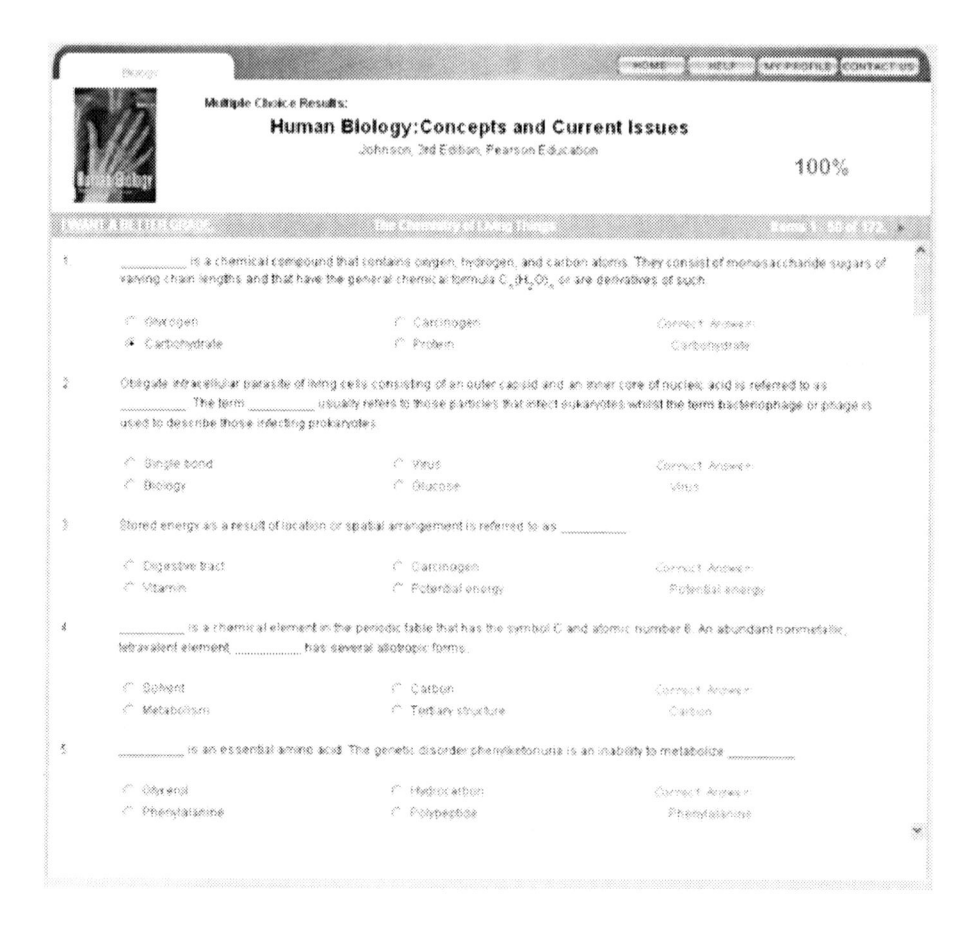

When you need problem solving help with math, stats, and other disciplines, www.Cram101.com will walk through the formulas and solutions step by step.

With Cram101.com online, you also have access to extensive reference material.

You will nail those essays and papers. Here is an example from a Cram101 Biology text:

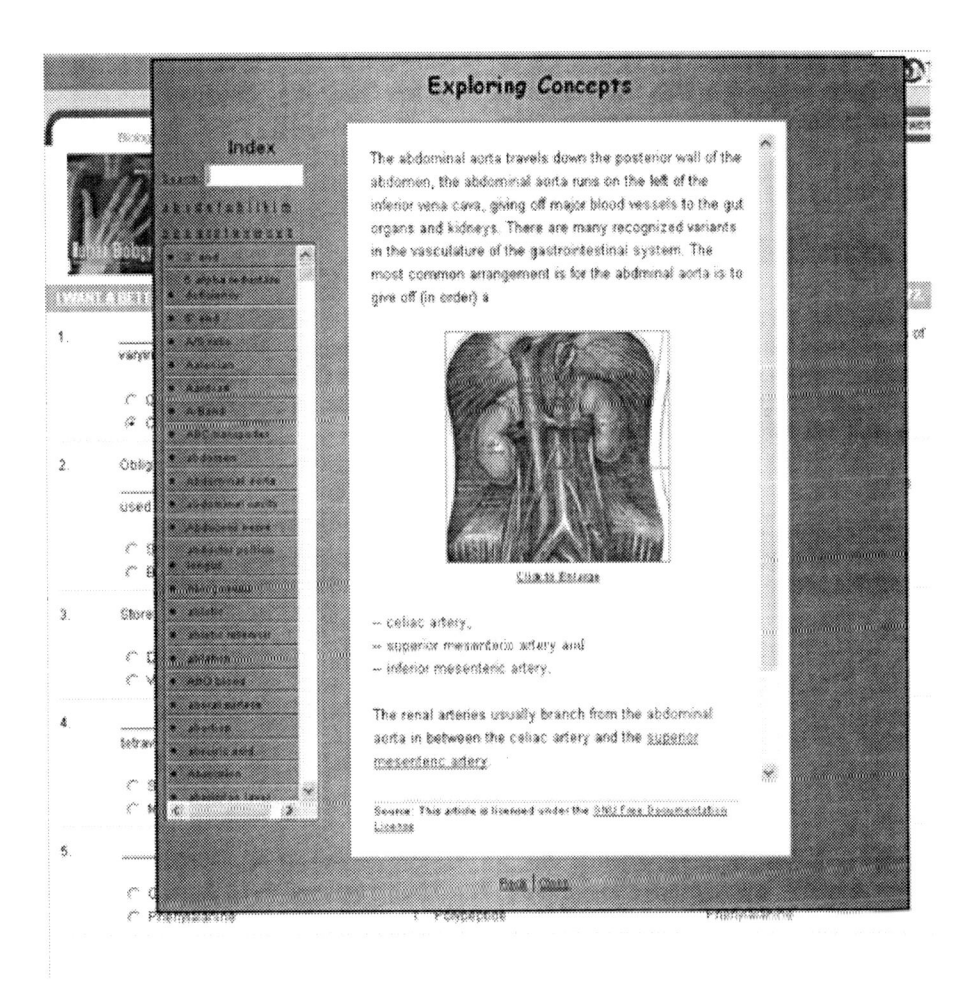

Visit **www.Cram101.com**, click Sign Up at the top of the screen, and enter DK73DW in the promo code box on the registration screen. Access to www.Cram101.com is normally $9.95, but because you have purchased this book, your access fee is only $4.95. Sign up and stop highlighting textbooks forever.

Learning System

Cram101 Textbook Outlines is a learning system. The notes in this book are the highlights of your textbook, you will never have to highlight a book again.

How to use this book. Take this book to class, it is your notebook for the lecture. The notes and highlights on the left hand side of the pages follow the outline and order of the textbook. All you have to do is follow along while your intructor presents the lecture. Circle the items emphasized in class and add other important information on the right side. With Cram101 Textbook Outlines you'll spend less time writing and more time listening. Learning becomes more efficient.

Cram101.com Online

Increase your studying efficiency by using Cram101.com's practice tests and online reference material. It is the perfect complement to Cram101 Textbook Outlines. Use self-teaching matching tests or simulate in-class testing with comprehensive multiple choice tests, or simply use Cram's true and false tests for quick review. Cram101.com even allows you to enter your in-class notes for an integrated studying format combining the textbook notes with your class notes.

Visit **www.Cram101.com**, click Sign Up at the top of the screen, and enter **DK73DW1669** in the promo code box on the registration screen. Access to www.Cram101.com is normally $9.95, but because you have purchased this book, your access fee is only $4.95. Sign up and stop highlighting textbooks forever.

Copyright © 2007 by Academic Internet Publishers, Inc. All rights reserved. "Cram101"® and "Never Highlight a Book Again!"® are registered trademarks of Academic Internet Publishers, Inc. The Cram101 Textbook Outline series is printed in the United States. ISBN: 1-4288-0915-5

Fundamentals of Multinational Finance
Moffett and Stonehill and Eiteman, 1st

CONTENTS

1. The Globalization Process 2
2. History of Foreign Exchange Rates 22
3. The Balance of Payments 40
4. International Parity Conditions 56
5. Foreign Exchange Rate Determination 72
6. The Foreign Exchange Market 92
7. Foreign Currency Derivatives 108
8. Transaction Exposure 126
9. Operating Exposure 142
10. Translation Exposure 162
11. Global Cost and Availability of Capital 174
12. Sourcing Equity Globally 196
13. Financial Structure and International Debt 212
14. Interest Rate and Currency Swaps 236
15. Foreign Direct Investment Theory and Strategy 252
16. Multinational Capital Budgeting 262
17. Adjusting for Risk in Foreign Investment 284
18. Cross-Border Mergers, Acquisitions, and Valuation 310
19. International Portfolio Theory and Diversification 338
20. Multinational Tax Management 350
21. Repositioning Funds 366
22. Working Capital Management in the MNE 386
23. International Trade Finance 412

Chapter 1. The Globalization Process

Firm	An organization that employs resources to produce a good or service for profit and owns and operates one or more plants is referred to as a firm.
Financial plan	The financial plan section of a business plan consists of three financial statements (the income statement, the cash flow projection, and the balance sheet) and a brief analysis of these three statements.
Complexity	The technical sophistication of the product and hence the amount of understanding required to use it is referred to as complexity. It is the opposite of simplicity.
Globalization	The increasing world-wide integration of markets for goods, services and capital that attracted special attention in the late 1990s is called globalization.
Corporation	A legal entity chartered by a state or the Federal government that is distinct and separate from the individuals who own it is a corporation. This separation gives the corporation unique powers which other legal entities lack.
Operation	A standardized method or technique that is performed repetitively, often on different materials resulting in different finished goods is called an operation.
Domestic	From or in one's own country. A domestic producer is one that produces inside the home country. A domestic price is the price inside the home country. Opposite of 'foreign' or 'world.'.
International trade	The export of goods and services from a country and the import of goods and services into a country is referred to as the international trade.
Competitive advantage	A business is said to have a competitive advantage when its unique strengths, often based on cost, quality, time, and innovation, offer consumers a greater percieved value and there by differtiating it from its competitors.
Sustainable competitive advantage	A strength, relative to competitors, in the markets served and the products offered is referred to as the sustainable competitive advantage.
Market	A market is, as defined in economics, a social arrangement that allows buyers and sellers to discover information and carry out a voluntary exchange of goods or services.
Competitor	Other organizations in the same industry or type of business that provide a good or service to the same set of customers is referred to as a competitor.
Capital	Capital generally refers to financial wealth, especially that used to start or maintain a business. In classical economics, capital is one of four factors of production, the others being land and labor and entrepreneurship.
Manufacturing	Production of goods primarily by the application of labor and capital to raw materials and other intermediate inputs, in contrast to agriculture, mining, forestry, fishing, and services a manufacturing.
Service	Service refers to a "non tangible product" that is not embodied in a physical good and that typically effects some change in another product, person, or institution. Contrasts with good.
Inputs	The inputs used by a firm or an economy are the labor, raw materials, electricity and other resources it uses to produce its outputs.
Buyer	A buyer refers to a role in the buying center with formal authority and responsibility to select the supplier and negotiate the terms of the contract.
Equity capital	Equity capital refers to money raized from within the firm or through the sale of ownership in the firm.
Investment	Investment refers to spending for the production and accumulation of capital and additions to inventories. In a financial sense, buying an asset with the expectation of making a return.

Chapter 1. The Globalization Process

Chapter 1. The Globalization Process

Equity	Equity is the name given to the set of legal principles, in countries following the English common law tradition, which supplement strict rules of law where their application would operate harshly, so as to achieve what is sometimes referred to as "natural justice."
Exporting	Selling products to another country is called exporting.
Free trade area	Free trade area refers to a group of countries that adopt free trade on trade among group members, while not necessarily changing the barriers that each member country has on trade with the countries outside the group.
Free trade	Free trade refers to a situation in which there are no artificial barriers to trade, such as tariffs and quotas. Usually used, often only implicitly, with frictionless trade, so that it implies that there are no barriers to trade of any kind.
Financial management	The job of managing a firm's resources so it can meet its goals and objectives is called financial management.
Management	Management characterizes the process of leading and directing all or part of an organization, often a business, through the deployment and manipulation of resources. Early twentieth-century management writer Mary Parker Follett defined management as "the art of getting things done through people."
Export	In economics, an export is any good or commodity, shipped or otherwise transported out of a country, province, town to another part of the world in a legitimate fashion, typically for use in trade or sale.
Affiliates	Local television stations that are associated with a major network are called affiliates. Affiliates agree to preempt time during specified hours for programming provided by the network and carry the advertising contained in the program.
Intellectual capital	Intellectual capital makes an organization worth more than its balance sheet value. For many years, intellectual capital and goodwill meant the same thing. Today, intellectual capital management is far broader. It seeks to explain how knowledge, collaboration, and process-engagement create decisions and actions that lead to cost allocations, productivity, and finally financial performance.
Joint venture	Joint venture refers to an undertaking by two parties for a specific purpose and duration, taking any of several legal forms.
Licensing	Licensing is a form of strategic alliance which involves the sale of a right to use certain proprietary knowledge (so called intellectual property) in a defined way.
Contract	A contract is a "promise" or an "agreement" that is enforced or recognized by the law. In the civil law, a contract is considered to be part of the general law of obligations.
Asset	An item of property, such as land, capital, money, a share in ownership, or a claim on others for future payment, such as a bond or a bank deposit is an asset.
Enterprise	Enterprise refers to another name for a business organization. Other similar terms are business firm, sometimes simply business, sometimes simply firm, as well as company, and entity.
Foreign exchange risk	Foreign exchange risk refers to a form of risk that refers to the possibility of experiencing a drop in revenue or an increase in cost in an international transaction due to a change in foreign exchange rates. Importers, exporters, investors, and multinational firms alike are exposed to this risk.
Foreign exchange	In finance, foreign exchange means currencies, such as U.S. Dollars and Euros. These are traded on foreign exchange markets.
Exchange	The trade of things of value between buyer and seller so that each is better off after the trade is called the exchange.
Credit	Credit refers to a recording as positive in the balance of payments, any transaction that gives rise to a payment into the country, such as an export, the sale of an asset, or borrowing from abroad.

Chapter 1. The Globalization Process

Chapter 1. The Globalization Process

Currency risk	Currency risk is a form of risk that arises from the change in price of one currency against another. Whenever investors or companies have assets or business operations across national borders, they face currency risk if their positions are not hedged.
Financial manager	Managers who make recommendations to top executives regarding strategies for improving the financial strength of a firm are referred to as a financial manager.
Exchange rate	Exchange rate refers to the price at which one country's currency trades for another, typically on the exchange market.
Financial instrument	Formal or legal documents in writing, such as contracts, deeds, wills, bonds, leases, and mortgages is referred to as a financial instrument.
Derivative	A derivative is a generic term for specific types of investments from which payoffs over time are derived from the performance of assets (such as commodities, shares or bonds), interest rates, exchange rates, or indices (such as a stock market index, consumer price index (CPI) or an index of weather conditions).
Instrument	Instrument refers to an economic variable that is controlled by policy makers and can be used to influence other variables, called targets. Examples are monetary and fiscal policies used to achieve external and internal balance.
Transaction exposure	Transaction exposure refers to foreign exchange gains and losses resulting from actual international transactions. These may be hedged through the foreign exchange market, the money market, or the currency futures market.
Competitiveness	Competitiveness usually refers to characteristics that permit a firm to compete effectively with other firms due to low cost or superior technology, perhaps internationally.
Cash flow	In finance, cash flow refers to the amounts of cash being received and spent by a business during a defined period of time, sometimes tied to a specific project. Most of the time they are being used to determine gaps in the liquid position of a company.
Translation exposure	The foreign-located assets and liabilities of a multinational corporation, which are denominated in foreign currency units, and are exposed to losses and gains due to changing exchange rates is called accounting or translation exposure.
Financial statement	Financial statement refers to a summary of all the transactions that have occurred over a particular period.
Foreign subsidiary	A company owned in a foreign country by another company is referred to as foreign subsidiary.
Accounting	A system that collects and processes financial information about an organization and reports that information to decision makers is referred to as accounting.
Subsidiary	A company that is controlled by another company or corporation is a subsidiary.
Creditor	A person to whom a debt or legal obligation is owed, and who has the right to enforce payment of that debt or obligation is referred to as creditor.
Capital budgeting	Capital budgeting is the planning process used to determine a firm's long term investments such as new machinery, replacement machinery, new plants, new products, and research and development projects.
Operating agreement	Operating agreement refers to an agreement entered into among members that governs the affairs and business of the LLC and the relations among members, managers, and the LLC.
Strategic alliance	Strategic alliance refers to a long-term partnership between two or more companies established to help each company build competitive market advantages.
Emerging markets	The term emerging markets is commonly used to describe business and market activity in industrializing or emerging regions of the world. It is sometimes loosely used as a replacement for emerging economies,

Chapter 1. The Globalization Process

Chapter 1. The Globalization Process

	but really signifies a business phenomenon that is not fully described by or constrained to geography or economic strength; such countries are considered to be in a transitional phase between developing and developed status.
Emerging market	The term emerging market is commonly used to describe business and market activity in industrializing or emerging regions of the world.
Extension	Extension refers to an out-of-court settlement in which creditors agree to allow the firm more time to meet its financial obligations. A new repayment schedule will be developed, subject to the acceptance of creditors.
Acquisition	A company's purchase of the property and obligations of another company is an acquisition.
Valuation	In finance, valuation is the process of estimating the market value of a financial asset or liability. They can be done on assets (for example, investments in marketable securities such as stocks, options, business enterprises, or intangible assets such as patents and trademarks) or on liabilities (e.g., Bonds issued by a company).
Diversification	Investing in a collection of assets whose returns do not always move together, with the result that overall risk is lower than for individual assets is referred to as diversification.
Portfolio	In finance, a portfolio is a collection of investments held by an institution or a private individual. Holding but not always a portfolio is part of an investment and risk-limiting strategy called diversification. By owning several assets, certain types of risk (in particular specific risk) can be reduced.
Distribution	Distribution in economics, the manner in which total output and income is distributed among individuals or factors.
Shareholder	A shareholder is an individual or company (including a corporation) that legally owns one or more shares of stock in a joined stock company.
Dividend	Amount of corporate profits paid out for each share of stock is referred to as dividend.
Working capital	The dollar difference between total current assets and total current liabilities is called working capital.
Scope	Scope of a project is the sum total of all projects products and their requirements or features.
Accounts receivable	Accounts receivable is one of a series of accounting transactions dealing with the billing of customers which owe money to a person, company or organization for goods and services that have been provided to the customer. This is typically done in a one person organization by writing an invoice and mailing or delivering it to each customer.
Accounts payable	A written record of all vendors to whom the business firm owes money is referred to as accounts payable.
Working capital management	Working capital management refers to the financing and management of the current assets of the firm. The financial manager determines the mix between temporary and permanent 'current assets' and the nature of the financing arrangement.
Business unit	The lowest level of the company which contains the set of functions that carry a product through its life span from concept through manufacture, distribution, sales and service is a business unit.
Inventory	Tangible property held for sale in the normal course of business or used in producing goods or services for sale is an inventory.
Revenue	Revenue is a U.S. business term for the amount of money that a company receives from its activities, mostly from sales of products and/or services to customers.
Expense	In accounting, an expense represents an event in which an asset is used up or a liability is incurred. In terms of the accounting equation, expenses reduce owners' equity.

Chapter 1. The Globalization Process

Chapter 1. The Globalization Process

Economic development	Increase in the economic standard of living of a country's population, normally accomplished by increasing its stocks of physical and human capital and improving its technology is an economic development.
Host country	The country in which the parent-country organization seeks to locate or has already located a facility is a host country.
Procurement	Procurement is the acquisition of goods or services at the best possible total cost of ownership, in the right quantity, at the right time, in the right place for the direct benefit or use of the governments, corporations, or individuals generally via, but not limited to a contract.
Integration	Economic integration refers to reducing barriers among countries to transactions and to movements of goods, capital, and labor, including harmonization of laws, regulations, and standards. Integrated markets theoretically function as a unified market.
Logistics	Those activities that focus on getting the right amount of the right products to the right place at the right time at the lowest possible cost is referred to as logistics.
Marketing	Promoting and selling products or services to customers, or prospective customers, is referred to as marketing.
Supply	Supply is the aggregate amount of any material good that can be called into being at a certain price point; it comprises one half of the equation of supply and demand. In classical economic theory, a curve representing supply is one of the factors that produce price.
Corporate governance	Corporate governance is the set of processes, customs, policies, laws and institutions affecting the way a corporation is directed, administered or controlled.
Shareholder wealth maximization	Shareholder wealth maximization refers to maximizing the wealth of the firm's shareholders through achieving the highest possible value for the firm in the marketplace. It is the overriding objective of the firm and should influence all decisions.
Market share	That fraction of an industry's output accounted for by an individual firm or group of firms is called market share.
Diversified portfolio	Diversified portfolio refers to a portfolio that includes a variety of assets whose prices are not likely all to change together. In international economics, this usually means holding assets denominated in different currencies.
Systematic risk	Movements in a stock portfolio's value that are attributable to macroeconomic forces affecting all firms in an economy, rather than factors specific to an individual firm are referred to as systematic risk.
Shares	Shares refer to an equity security, representing a shareholder's ownership of a corporation. Shares are one of a finite number of equal portions in the capital of a company, entitling the owner to a proportion of distributed, non-reinvested profits known as dividends and to a portion of the value of the company in case of liquidation.
Senior management	Senior management is generally a team of individuals at the highest level of organizational management who have the day-to-day responsibilities of managing a corporation.
Board of directors	The group of individuals elected by the stockholders of a corporation to oversee its operations is a board of directors.
Long run	In economic models, the long run time frame assumes no fixed factors of production. Firms can enter or leave the marketplace, and the cost (and availability) of land, labor, raw materials, and capital goods can be assumed to vary.
Human resources	Human resources refers to the individuals within the firm, and to the portion of the firm's organization that deals with hiring, firing, training, and other personnel issues.

Go to Cram101.com for the Practice Tests for this Chapter.

Chapter 1. The Globalization Process

Chapter 1. The Globalization Process

Financial report	Financial report refers to a written statement-also called an accountant's certificate, accountant's opinion, or audit report-prepared by an independent accountant or auditor after an audit.
Market position	Market position is a measure of the position of a company or product on a market.
Administration	Administration refers to the management and direction of the affairs of governments and institutions; a collective term for all policymaking officials of a government; the execution and implementation of public policy.
Technology	The body of knowledge and techniques that can be used to combine economic resources to produce goods and services is called technology.
Corporate Strategy	Corporate strategy is concerned with the firm's choice of business, markets and activities and thus it defines the overall scope and direction of the business.
Financial risk	The risk related to the inability of the firm to meet its debt obligations as they come due is called financial risk.
Stakeholder	A stakeholder is an individual or group with a vested interest in or expectation for organizational performance. Usually stakeholders can either have an effect on or are affected by an organization.
Capitalism	Capitalism refers to an economic system in which capital is mostly owned by private individuals and corporations. Contrasts with communism.
Mission statement	Mission statement refers to an outline of the fundamental purposes of an organization.
Debt capital	Debt capital refers to funds raized through various forms of borrowing to finance a company that must be repaid.
Agent	A person who makes economic decisions for another economic actor. A hired manager operates as an agent for a firm's owner.
Appreciation	Appreciation refers to a rise in the value of a country's currency on the exchange market, relative either to a particular other currency or to a weighted average of other currencies. The currency is said to appreciate. Opposite of 'depreciation.' Appreciation can also refer to the increase in value of any asset.
Profit	Profit refers to the return to the resource entrepreneurial ability; total revenue minus total cost.
Interest	In finance and economics, interest is the price paid by a borrower for the use of a lender's money. In other words, interest is the amount of paid to "rent" money for a period of time.
Stockholder	A stockholder is an individual or company (including a corporation) that legally owns one or more shares of stock in a joined stock company. The shareholders are the owners of a corporation. Companies listed at the stock market strive to enhance shareholder value.
Trend	Trend refers to the long-term movement of an economic variable, such as its average rate of increase or decrease over enough years to encompass several business cycles.
Stock option	A stock option is a specific type of option that uses the stock itself as an underlying instrument to determine the option's pay-off and therefore its value.
Option	A contract that gives the purchaser the option to buy or sell the underlying financial instrument at a specified price, called the exercise price or strike price, within a specific period of time.
Stock	In financial terminology, stock is the capital raized by a corporation, through the issuance and sale of shares.
Takeover	A takeover in business refers to one company (the acquirer) purchasing another (the target). Such events resemble mergers, but without the formation of a new company.
Aid	Assistance provided by countries and by international institutions such as the World Bank to developing

Chapter 1. The Globalization Process

Chapter 1. The Globalization Process

	countries in the form of monetary grants, loans at low interest rates, in kind, or a combination of these is called aid. Aid can also refer to assistance of any type rendered to benefit some group or individual.
Bid	A bid price is a price offered by a buyer when he/she buys a good. In the context of stock trading on a stock exchange, the bid price is the highest price a buyer of a stock is willing to pay for a share of that given stock.
Nepotism	Nepotism means favoring relatives or personal friends because of their relationship rather than because of their abilities.
Operational goals	Specific, measurable results expected from departments, work groups, and individuals within the organization are called operational goals.
Shareholder value	For a publicly traded company, shareholder value is the part of its capitalization that is equity as opposed to long-term debt. In the case of only one type of stock, this would roughly be the number of outstanding shares times current shareprice.
Stock market	An organized marketplace in which common stocks are traded. In the United States, the largest stock market is the New York Stock Exchange, on which are traded the stocks of the largest U.S. companies.
Income distribution	A description of the fractions of a population that are at various levels of income. The larger these differences in income, the 'worse' the income distribution is usually said to be, the smaller the 'better.'
Capital gain	Capital gain refers to the gain in value that the owner of an asset experiences when the price of the asset rises, including when the currency in which the asset is denominated appreciates.
Gain	In finance, gain is a profit or an increase in value of an investment such as a stock or bond. Gain is calculated by fair market value or the proceeds from the sale of the investment minus the sum of the purchase price and all costs associated with it.
Assessment	Collecting information and providing feedback to employees about their behavior, communication style, or skills is an assessment.
Analyst	Analyst refers to a person or tool with a primary function of information analysis, generally with a more limited, practical and short term set of goals than a researcher.
Intangible assets	Assets that have special rights but not physical substance are referred to as intangible assets.
Intangible asset	An intangible assets is defined as an asset that is not physical in nature. The most common types are trade secrets (e.g., customer lists and know-how), copyrights, patents, trademarks, and goodwill.
Brand	A name, symbol, or design that identifies the goods or services of one seller or group of sellers and distinguishes them from the goods and services of competitors is a brand.
Economic environment	The economic environment represents the external conditions under which people are engaged in, and benefit from, economic activity. It includes aspects of economic status, paid employment, and finances.
Positioning	The art and science of fitting the product or service to one or more segments of the market in such a way as to set it meaningfully apart from competition is called positioning.
Balance	In banking and accountancy, the outstanding balance is the amount of money owned, (or due), that remains in a deposit account (or a loan account) at a given date, after all past remittances, payments and withdrawal have been accounted for. It can be positive (then, in the balance sheet of a firm, it is an asset) or negative (a liability).
Fund	Independent accounting entity with a self-balancing set of accounts segregated for the purposes of carrying on specific activities is referred to as a fund.

Chapter 1. The Globalization Process

Chapter 1. The Globalization Process

Tradeoff	The sacrifice of some or all of one economic goal, good, or service to achieve some other goal, good, or service is a tradeoff.
Parent company	Parent company refers to the entity that has a controlling influence over another company. It may have its own operations, or it may have been set up solely for the purpose of owning the Subject Company.
Hedging	A technique for avoiding a risk by making a counteracting transaction is referred to as hedging.
Management team	A management team is directly responsible for managing the day-to-day operations (and profitability) of a company.
Mistake	In contract law a mistake is incorrect understanding by one or more parties to a contract and may be used as grounds to invalidate the agreement. Common law has identified three different types of mistake in contract: unilateral mistake, mutual mistake, and common mistake.
Multinational enterprise	Multinational enterprise refers to a firm, usually a corporation, that operates in two or more countries.
Economic forces	Forces that affect the availability, production, and distribution of a society's resources among competing users are referred to as economic forces.
Greenfield investment	In foreign investment, direct investment in new facilities or the expansion of existing facilities is Greenfield investment.
Licensing agreement	Detailed and comprehensive written agreement between the licensor and licensee that sets forth the express terms of their agreement is called a licensing agreement.
Labor union	A group of workers organized to advance the interests of the group is called a labor union.
Statute	A statute is a formal, written law of a country or state, written and enacted by its legislative authority, perhaps to then be ratified by the highest executive in the government, and finally published.
Labor	People's physical and mental talents and efforts that are used to help produce goods and services are called labor.
Union	A worker association that bargains with employers over wages and working conditions is called a union.
Capital market	A financial market in which long-term debt and equity instruments are traded is referred to as a capital market. The capital market includes the stock market and the bond market.
Policy	Similar to a script in that a policy can be a less than completely rational decision-making method. Involves the use of a pre-existing set of decision steps for any problem that presents itself.
Interlocking directorate	Interlocking directorate refers to a situation where one or more members of the board of directors of a corporation are also on the board of directors of a competing corporation; illegal under the Clayton
Productive assets	Productive assets refers to assets used to operate the business; frequently called long-term assets. They are property such as land, livestock, and trees that produce income.
Leveraged buyout	An attempt by employees, management, or a group of investors to purchase an organization primarily through borrowing is a leveraged buyout.
Buyout	A buyout is an investment transaction by which the entire or a controlling part of the stock of a company is sold. A firm buysout the stake of the company to strengthen its influence on the company's decision making body. A buyout can take the forms of a leveraged buyout or a management buyout.
Conglomerate	A conglomerate is a large company that consists of divisions of often seemingly unrelated businesses.
Voting shares	Voting shares are shares that give the stockholder the right to vote on matters of corporate policy making as well as who will compose the members of the board of directors.
Incorporation	Incorporation is the forming of a new corporation. The corporation may be a business, a non-profit

Go to Cram101.com for the Practice Tests for this Chapter.

Chapter 1. The Globalization Process

Chapter 1. The Globalization Process

	organization or even a government of a new city or town.
Common stock	Common stock refers to the basic, normal, voting stock issued by a corporation; called residual equity because it ranks after preferred stock for dividend and liquidation distributions.
Securities and exchange commission	Securities and exchange commission refers to U.S. government agency that determines the financial statements that public companies must provide to stockholders and the measurement rules that they must use in producing those statements.
Security	Security refers to a claim on the borrower future income that is sold by the borrower to the lender. A security is a type of transferable interest representing financial value.
Fortune magazine	Fortune magazine is America's longest-running business magazine. Currently owned by media conglomerate Time Warner, it was founded in 1930 by Henry Luce. It is known for its regular features ranking companies by revenue.
Industry	A group of firms that produce identical or similar products is an industry. It is also used specifically to refer to an area of economic production focused on manufacturing which involves large amounts of capital investment before any profit can be realized, also called "heavy industry".
Stock exchange	A stock exchange is a corporation or mutual organization which provides facilities for stock brokers and traders, to trade company stocks and other securities.
Peak	Peak refers to the point in the business cycle when an economic expansion reaches its highest point before turning down. Contrasts with trough.
Privatization	A process in which investment bankers take companies that were previously owned by the government to the public markets is referred to as privatization.
Auction	A preexisting business model that operates successfully on the Internet by announcing an item for sale and permitting multiple purchasers to bid on them under specified rules and condition is an auction.
Sprint	The Sprint Corporation was founded in 1899 by Cleyson Leroy Brown under the name of the "Brown Telephone Company" in the small town of Abilene, Kansas. The company was a landline telephone company that operated as a competitor to the Bell System.
Regulation	Regulation refers to restrictions state and federal laws place on business with regard to the conduct of its activities.
Competitive market	A market in which no buyer or seller has market power is called a competitive market.
Fragmentation	Fragmentation refers to the splitting of production processes into separate parts that can be done in different locations, including in different countries.
Holding company	A corporation whose purpose or function is to own or otherwise hold the shares of other corporations either for investment or control is called holding company.
Pension fund	Amounts of money put aside by corporations, nonprofit organizations, or unions to cover part of the financial needs of members when they retire is a pension fund.
Pension	A pension is a steady income given to a person (usually after retirement). Pensions are typically payments made in the form of a guaranteed annuity to a retired or disabled employee.
Holding	The holding is a court's determination of a matter of law based on the issue presented in the particular case. In other words: under this law, with these facts, this result.
Venture capital	Venture capital is capital provided by outside investors for financing of new, growing or struggling businesses. Venture capital investments generally are high risk investments but offer the potential for above average returns.
Partnership	In the common law, a partnership is a type of business entity in which partners share with each other

Go to Cram101.com for the Practice Tests for this Chapter.

Chapter 1. The Globalization Process

	the profits or losses of the business undertaking in which they have all invested.
Citibank	In April of 2006, Citibank struck a deal with 7-Eleven to put its ATMs in over 5,500 convenience stores in the U.S. In the same month, it also announced it would sell all of its Buffalo and Rochester New York branches and accounts to M&T Bank.
Leadership	Management merely consists of leadership applied to business situations; or in other words: management forms a sub-set of the broader process of leadership.
Incentive	An incentive is any factor (financial or non-financial) that provides a motive for a particular course of action, or counts as a reason for preferring one choice to the alternatives.
Expected return	Expected return refers to the return on an asset expected over the next period.
Consolidation	The combination of two or more firms, generally of equal size and market power, to form an entirely new entity is a consolidation.
Speculation	The purchase or sale of an asset in hopes that its price will rise or fall respectively, in order to make a profit is called speculation.
Controller	Controller refers to the financial executive primarily responsible for management accounting and financial accounting. Also called chief accounting officer.
Confirmed	When the seller's bank agrees to assume liability on the letter of credit issued by the buyer's bank the transaction is confirmed. The term means that the credit is not only backed up by the issuing foreign bank, but that payment is also guaranteed by the notifying American bank.
Discount rate	Discount rate refers to the rate, per year, at which future values are diminished to make them comparable to values in the present. Can be either subjective or objective.
Discount	The difference between the face value of a bond and its selling price, when a bond is sold for less than its face value it's referred to as a discount.

Chapter 2. History of Foreign Exchange Rates

Fixed exchange rate	A fixed exchange rate, sometimes is a type of exchange rate regime wherein a currency's value is matched to the value of another single currency or to a basket of other currencies, or to another measure of value, such as gold.
Exchange rate	Exchange rate refers to the price at which one country's currency trades for another, typically on the exchange market.
Exchange	The trade of things of value between buyer and seller so that each is better off after the trade is called the exchange.
Firm	An organization that employs resources to produce a good or service for profit and owns and operates one or more plants is referred to as a firm.
Foreign exchange	In finance, foreign exchange means currencies, such as U.S. Dollars and Euros. These are traded on foreign exchange markets.
International monetary system	International monetary system is a network of international commercial and government institutions that determine currency exchange rates.
Market value	Market value refers to the price of an asset agreed on between a willing buyer and a willing seller; the price an asset could demand if it is sold on the open market.
Accounting	A system that collects and processes financial information about an organization and reports that information to decision makers is referred to as accounting.
Cash flow	In finance, cash flow refers to the amounts of cash being received and spent by a business during a defined period of time, sometimes tied to a specific project. Most of the time they are being used to determine gaps in the liquid position of a company.
Market	A market is, as defined in economics, a social arrangement that allows buyers and sellers to discover information and carry out a voluntary exchange of goods or services.
Policy	Similar to a script in that a policy can be a less than completely rational decision-making method. Involves the use of a pre-existing set of decision steps for any problem that presents itself.
Gain	In finance, gain is a profit or an increase in value of an investment such as a stock or bond. Gain is calculated by fair market value or the proceeds from the sale of the investment minus the sum of the purchase price and all costs associated with it.
Foreign exchange risk	Foreign exchange risk refers to a form of risk that refers to the possibility of experiencing a drop in revenue or an increase in cost in an international transaction due to a change in foreign exchange rates. Importers, exporters, investors, and multinational firms alike are exposed to this risk.
Management	Management characterizes the process of leading and directing all or part of an organization, often a business, through the deployment and manipulation of resources. Early twentieth-century management writer Mary Parker Follett defined management as "the art of getting things done through people."
Balance of payments	Balance of payments refers to a list, or accounting, of all of a country's international transactions for a given time period, usually one year.
Capital flow	International capital movement is referred to as capital flow.
Capital	Capital generally refers to financial wealth, especially that used to start or maintain a business. In classical economics, capital is one of four factors of production, the others being land and labor and entrepreneurship.
Balance	In banking and accountancy, the outstanding balance is the amount of money owned, (or due), that remains in a deposit account (or a loan account) at a given date, after all past

Chapter 2. History of Foreign Exchange Rates

Chapter 2. History of Foreign Exchange Rates

	remittances, payments and withdrawal have been accounted for. It can be positive (then, in the balance sheet of a firm, it is an asset) or negative (a liability).
Commodity markets	Commodity markets are markets where raw or primary products are exchanged. These raw commodities are traded on regulated exchanges, in which they are bought and sold in standardized Contracts.
Money market	The money market, in macroeconomics and international finance, refers to the equilibration of demand for a country's domestic money to its money supply; market for short-term financial instruments.
Instrument	Instrument refers to an economic variable that is controlled by policy makers and can be used to influence other variables, called targets. Examples are monetary and fiscal policies used to achieve external and internal balance.
Commodity	Could refer to any good, but in trade a commodity is usually a raw material or primary product that enters into international trade, such as metals or basic agricultural products.
Security	Security refers to a claim on the borrower future income that is sold by the borrower to the lender. A security is a type of transferable interest representing financial value.
Estate	An estate is the totality of the legal rights, interests, entitlements and obligations attaching to property. In the context of wills and probate, it refers to the totality of the property which the deceased owned or in which some interest was held.
Managed exchange rate	Managed exchange rate refers to the most prevalent exchange-rate system today. In this system, a country occasionally intervenes to stabilize its currency but there is no fixed or announced parity.
Exchange rate regime	Exchange rate regime refers to the rules under which a country's exchange rate is determined, especially the way the monetary or other government authorities do or do not intervene in the exchange market.
Currency exchange rate	The rate between two currencies that specifies how much one country's currency is worth expressed in terms of the other country's currency is the currency exchange rate.
Par value	The central value of a pegged exchange rate, around which the actual rate is permitted to fluctuate within set bounds is a par value.
Valuation	In finance, valuation is the process of estimating the market value of a financial asset or liability. They can be done on assets (for example, investments in marketable securities such as stocks, options, business enterprises, or intangible assets such as patents and trademarks) or on liabilities (e.g., Bonds issued by a company).
Spot exchange rate	The exchange rate at which a foreign exchange dealer will convert one currency into another that particular day is the spot exchange rate.
Devaluation	Lowering the value of a nation's currency relative to other currencies is called devaluation.
Depreciation	Depreciation is an accounting and finance term for the method of attributing the cost of an asset across the useful life of the asset. Depreciation is a reduction in the value of a currency in floating exchange rate.
Depreciate	A nation's currency is said to depreciate when exchange rates change so that a unit of its currency can buy fewer units of foreign currency.
Eurocurrencies	A variant of the Eurobond, which are foreign currencies deposited in banks outside the home country is an eurocurrencies.
Eurocurrency	Eurocurrency is the term used to describe deposits residing in banks that are located outside the borders of the country that issues the currency the deposit is denominated in.

Chapter 2. History of Foreign Exchange Rates

Chapter 2. History of Foreign Exchange Rates

Domestic	From or in one's own country. A domestic producer is one that produces inside the home country. A domestic price is the price inside the home country. Opposite of 'foreign' or 'world.'.
Common currency	A situation where several countries form a monetary union with a single currency and a unified central bank is referred to as common currency.
Union	A worker association that bargains with employers over wages and working conditions is called a union.
Euro	The common currency of a subset of the countries of the EU, adopted January 1, 1999 is called euro.
Medium of exchange	Medium of exchange refers to any item sellers generally accept and buyers generally use to pay for a good or service; money; a convenient means of exchanging goods and services without engaging in barter.
Store of value	To act as a store of value, a commodity, a form of money, or financial capital must be able to be reliably saved, stored, and retrieved - and be predictably useful when it is so retrieved.
Gold standard	The gold standard is a monetary system in which the standard economic unit of account is a fixed weight of gold.
International trade	The export of goods and services from a country and the import of goods and services into a country is referred to as the international trade.
Trade balance	Balance of trade in terms of exports versus imports is called trade balance.
Supply	Supply is the aggregate amount of any material good that can be called into being at a certain price point; it comprises one half of the equation of supply and demand. In classical economic theory, a curve representing supply is one of the factors that produce price.
Authority	Authority in agency law, refers to an agent's ability to affect his principal's legal relations with third parties. Also used to refer to an actor's legal power or ability to do something. In addition, sometimes used to refer to a statute, case, or other legal source that justifies a particular result.
Trade flow	The quantity or value of a country's bilateral trade with another country is called trade flow.
Supply and demand	The partial equilibrium supply and demand economic model originally developed by Alfred Marshall attempts to describe, explain, and predict changes in the price and quantity of goods sold in competitive markets.
Export	In economics, an export is any good or commodity, shipped or otherwise transported out of a country, province, town to another part of the world in a legitimate fashion, typically for use in trade or sale.
Flexible exchange rate	Exchange rates with a fixed parity against one or more currencies with frequent revaluation's is referred to as a flexible exchange rate.
Speculation	The purchase or sale of an asset in hopes that its price will rise or fall respectively, in order to make a profit is called speculation.
Asset	An item of property, such as land, capital, money, a share in ownership, or a claim on others for future payment, such as a bond or a bank deposit is an asset.
Open market	In economics, the open market is the term used to refer to the environment in which bonds are bought and sold.
Forward exchange	When two parties agree to exchange currency and execute a deal at some specific date in the

Chapter 2. History of Foreign Exchange Rates

	future, we have forward exchange.
Exchange market	Exchange market refers to the market on which national currencies are bought and sold.
Gross National Product	Gross National Product is the total value of final goods and services produced in a year by a country's nationals (including profits from capital held abroad).
Great Depression	The period of severe economic contraction and high unemployment that began in 1929 and continued throughout the 1930s is referred to as the Great Depression.
Depression	Depression refers to a prolonged period characterized by high unemployment, low output and investment, depressed business confidence, falling prices, and widespread business failures. A milder form of business downturn is a recession.
Central Bank	Central bank refers to the institution in a country that is normally responsible for managing the supply of the country's money and the value of its currency on the foreign exchange market.
International Monetary Fund	The International Monetary Fund is the international organization entrusted with overseeing the global financial system by monitoring exchange rates and balance of payments, as well as offering technical and financial assistance when asked.
Bretton Woods	A 1944 conference in which representatives of 40 countries met to design a new international monetary system is referred to as the Bretton Woods conference.
World Bank	The World Bank is a group of five international organizations responsible for providing finance and advice to countries for the purposes of economic development and poverty reduction, and for encouraging and safeguarding international investment.
Fund	Independent accounting entity with a self-balancing set of accounts segregated for the purposes of carrying on specific activities is referred to as a fund.
Aid	Assistance provided by countries and by international institutions such as the World Bank to developing countries in the form of monetary grants, loans at low interest rates, in kind, or a combination of these is called aid. Aid can also refer to assistance of any type rendered to benefit some group or individual.
Economic development	Increase in the economic standard of living of a country's population, normally accomplished by increasing its stocks of physical and human capital and improving its technology is an economic development.
Deficit	The deficit is the amount by which expenditure exceed revenue.
Special drawing right	Special drawing right refers to what was originally intended within the IMF as a sort of international money for use among central banks pegging their exchange rates. The special drawing right is a transferable right to acquire another country's currency.
Foreign exchange reserves	Foreign exchange reserves are the foreign currency deposits held by national banks of different nations. These are assets of governments which are held in different reserve currencies such as the dollar, euro and yen.
Reserve asset	Any asset that is used as international reserves, including a national currency, precious metal such as gold is referred to as a reserve asset.
Unit of account	Unit of account refers to a basic function of money, providing a unit of measurement for defining, recording, and comparing value.
Service	Service refers to a "non tangible product" that is not embodied in a physical good and that typically effects some change in another product, person, or institution. Contrasts with good.
Reserve currency	A reserve currency is a currency which is held in significant quantities by many governments

Chapter 2. History of Foreign Exchange Rates

	and institutions as part of their foreign exchange reserves.
Capital Outflow	Capital outflow is an economic term describing capital flowing out of (or leaving) a particular economy. Outflowing capital can be caused by any number of economic or political reasons but can often originate from instability in either sphere.
Foreign exchange market	A market for converting the currency of one country into that of another country is called foreign exchange market. It is by far the largest market in the world, in terms of cash value traded, and includes trading between large banks, central banks, currency speculators, multinational corporations, governments, and other financial markets and institutions.
Volatility	Volatility refers to the extent to which an economic variable, such as a price or an exchange rate, moves up and down over time.
Interest rate	The rate of return on bonds, loans, or deposits. When one speaks of 'the' interest rate, it is usually in a model where there is only one.
Interest	In finance and economics, interest is the price paid by a borrower for the use of a lender's money. In other words, interest is the amount of paid to "rent" money for a period of time.
Currency board	A currency board is a system, popular in emerging economies, in which the exchange rate of a local currency and a foreign currency can be controlled by law.
Currency union	A group of countries that agree to peg their exchange rates and to coordinate their monetary policies so as to avoid the need for currency realignments is called a currency union.
Legal tender	Legal tender is payment that, by law, cannot be refused in settlement of a debt denominated in the same currency.
Tender	An unconditional offer of payment, consisting in the actual production in money or legal tender of a sum not less than the amount due.
De facto	De facto, in fact, actual. Often used in contrast to de jure to refer to a real state of affairs.
Basket	A basket is an economic term for a group of several securities created for the purpose of simultaneous buying or selling. Baskets are frequently used for program trading.
Margin	A deposit by a buyer in stocks with a seller or a stockbroker, as security to cover fluctuations in the market in reference to stocks that the buyer has purchased but for which he has not paid is a margin. Commodities are also traded on margin.
Pegged exchange rate	A pegged exchange rate, is a type of exchange rate regime wherein a currency's value is matched to the value of another single currency or to a basket of other currencies, or to another measure of value, such as gold.
Crawling peg	The crawling peg is an exchange rate that is pegged, but for which the par value is changed frequently in a pre-announced fashion in response to changes in a country's balance of payments.
Intervention	Intervention refers to an activity in which a government buys or sells its currency in the foreign exchange market in order to affect its currency's exchange rate.
Foreign exchange intervention	An international 'financial transaction in which a central bank buys or sells currency to influence foreign exchange rates a foreign exchange intervention.
Economic growth	Economic growth refers to the increase over time in the capacity of an economy to produce goods and services and to improve the well-being of its citizens.
Inflation	An increase in the overall price level of an economy, usually as measured by the CPI or by the implicit price deflator is called inflation.

Chapter 2. History of Foreign Exchange Rates

Economy	The income, expenditures, and resources that affect the cost of running a business and household are called an economy.
Fiscal policy	Fiscal policy refers to any macroeconomic policy involving the levels of government purchases, transfers, or taxes, usually implicitly focused on domestic goods, residents, or firms.
International reserves	International reserves refers to the assets denominated in foreign currency, plus gold, held by a central bank, sometimes for the purpose of intervening in the exchange market to influence or peg the exchange rate.
Fixed exchange rate regime	A regime in which central banks buy and sell their own currencies to keep their exchange rates fixed at a certain level is referred to as fixed exchange rate regime.
Holding	The holding is a court's determination of a matter of law based on the issue presented in the particular case. In other words: under this law, with these facts, this result.
Full employment	Full employment refers to the unemployment rate at which there is no cyclical unemployment of the labor force; equal to between 4 and 5 percent in the United States because some frictional and structural unemployment is unavoidable.
Economic policy	Economic policy refers to the actions that governments take in the economic field. It covers the systems for setting interest rates and government deficit as well as the labor market, national ownership, and many other areas of government.
Recession	A significant decline in economic activity. In the U.S., recession is approximately defined as two successive quarters of falling GDP, as judged by NBER.
Integration	Economic integration refers to reducing barriers among countries to transactions and to movements of goods, capital, and labor, including harmonization of laws, regulations, and standards. Integrated markets theoretically function as a unified market.
Economics	The social science dealing with the use of scarce resources to obtain the maximum satisfaction of society's virtually unlimited economic wants is an economics.
Rate of exchange	Rate of exchange refers to the price paid in one's own money to acquire 1 unit of a foreign currency; the rate at which the money of one nation is exchanged for the money of another nation.
Money supply	There are several formal definitions, but all include the quantity of currency in circulation plus the amount of demand deposits. The money supply, together with the amount of real economic activity in a country, is an important determinant of price.
Dollarization	Dollarization refers to the official adoption by a country other than the United States of the U.S. dollar as its local currency.
Business Week	Business Week is a business magazine published by McGraw-Hill. It was first published in 1929 under the direction of Malcolm Muir, who was serving as president of the McGraw-Hill Publishing company at the time. It is considered to be the standard both in industry and among students.
Argument	The discussion by counsel for the respective parties of their contentions on the law and the facts of the case being tried in order to aid the jury in arriving at a correct and just conclusion is called argument.
Economic integration	Occurs when two or more nations join to form a free-trade zone are called economic integration. As economic integration increases, the barriers of trade between markets diminishes.
Financial market	In economics, a financial market is a mechanism which allows people to trade money for securities or commodities such as gold or other precious metals. In general, any commodity

Chapter 2. History of Foreign Exchange Rates

Chapter 2. History of Foreign Exchange Rates

	market might be considered to be a financial market, if the usual purpose of traders is not the immediate consumption of the commodity, but rather as a means of delaying or accelerating consumption over time.
Seignorage	The revenue a govenment receives by issuing money is a seignorage.
Profit	Profit refers to the return to the resource entrepreneurial ability; total revenue minus total cost.
Emerging market	The term emerging market is commonly used to describe business and market activity in industrializing or emerging regions of the world.
Bank run	A bank run is a type of financial crisis. It is a panic which occurs when a large number of customers of a bank fear it is insolvent and withdraw their deposits.
Financial institution	A financial institution acts as an agent that provides financial services for its clients. Financial institutions generally fall under financial regulation from a government authority.
Bank failure	A situation in which a bank cannot satisfy its obligations to pay its depositors and other creditors and so goes out of business is called bank failure.
Closing	The finalization of a real estate sales transaction that passes title to the property from the seller to the buyer is referred to as a closing. Closing is a sales term which refers to the process of making a sale. It refers to reaching the final step, which may be an exchange of money or acquiring a signature.
Emerging markets	The term emerging markets is commonly used to describe business and market activity in industrializing or emerging regions of the world. It is sometimes loosely used as a replacement for emerging economies, but really signifies a business phenomenon that is not fully described by or constrained to geography or economic strength; such countries are considered to be in a transitional phase between developing and developed status.
Leadership	Management merely consists of leadership applied to business situations; or in other words: management forms a sub-set of the broader process of leadership.
Maastricht Treaty	Treaty agreed to in 1991, but not ratified until January 1, 1994, that committed the 12 member states of the European Community to a closer economic and political union is the Maastricht Treaty.
Convergence	The blending of various facets of marketing functions and communication technology to create more efficient and expanded synergies is a convergence.
Gross domestic product	Gross domestic product refers to the total value of new goods and services produced in a given year within the borders of a country, regardless of by whom.
Government debt	The total of government obligations in the form of bonds and shorter-term borrowings. Government debt held by the public excludes bonds held by quasi-governmental agencies such as the central bank.
Federal reserve system	The central banking authority responsible for monetary policy in the United States is called federal reserve system or the Fed.
Federal Reserve	The Federal Reserve System was created via the Federal Reserve Act of December 23rd, 1913. All national banks were required to join the system and other banks could join. The Reserve Banks opened for business on November 16th, 1914. Federal Reserve Notes were created as part of the legislation, to provide an elastic supply of currency.
Single market	A single market is a customs union with common policies on product regulation, and freedom of movement of all the four factors of production (goods, services, capital and labor).
Currency area	Currency area refers to a group of countries that share a common currency. Originally defined

Chapter 2. History of Foreign Exchange Rates

Chapter 2. History of Foreign Exchange Rates

	by Mundell as a group that has fixed exchange rates among their national currencies.
Core	A core is the set of feasible allocations in an economy that cannot be improved upon by subset of the set of the economy's consumers (a coalition). In construction, when the force in an element is within a certain center section, the core, the element will only be under compression.
Openness	Openness refers to the extent to which an economy is open, often measured by the ratio of its trade to GDP.
Economic forces	Forces that affect the availability, production, and distribution of a society's resources among competing users are referred to as economic forces.
Alignment	Term that refers to optimal coordination among disparate departments and divisions within a firm is referred to as alignment.
Economic environment	The economic environment represents the external conditions under which people are engaged in, and benefit from, economic activity. It includes aspects of economic status, paid employment, and finances.
Transparency	Transparency refers to a concept that describes a company being so open to other companies working with it that the once-solid barriers between them become see-through and electronic information is shared as if the companies were one.
Transaction cost	A transaction cost is a cost incurred in making an economic exchange. For example, most people, when buying or selling a stock, must pay a commission to their broker; that commission is a transaction cost of doing the stock deal.
Currency risk	Currency risk is a form of risk that arises from the change in price of one currency against another. Whenever investors or companies have assets or business operations across national borders, they face currency risk if their positions are not hedged.
Foundation	A Foundation is a type of philanthropic organization set up by either individuals or institutions as a legal entity (either as a corporation or trust) with the purpose of distributing grants to support causes in line with the goals of the foundation.
Purchasing power	The amount of goods that money will buy, usually measured by the CPI is referred to as purchasing power.
Purchasing	Purchasing refers to the function in a firm that searches for quality material resources, finds the best suppliers, and negotiates the best price for goods and services.
Monetary policy	The use of the money supply and/or the interest rate to influence the level of economic activity and other policy objectives including the balance of payments or the exchange rate is called monetary policy.
Inflating	Inflating refers to determining real gross domestic product by increasing the dollar value of the nominal gross domestic product produced in a year in which prices are lower than those in a base year.
Yield	The interest rate that equates a future value or an annuity to a given present value is a yield.
Tradeoff	The sacrifice of some or all of one economic goal, good, or service to achieve some other goal, good, or service is a tradeoff.
Cooperative	A business owned and controlled by the people who use it, producers, consumers, or workers with similar needs who pool their resources for mutual gain is called cooperative.
Discretionary policy	The setting of monetary and fiscal targets by policymakers, based on their best judgments is referred to as discretionary policy.

Chapter 2. History of Foreign Exchange Rates

Citibank	In April of 2006, Citibank struck a deal with 7-Eleven to put its ATMs in over 5,500 convenience stores in the U.S. In the same month, it also announced it would sell all of its Buffalo and Rochester New York branches and accounts to M&T Bank.
Technology	The body of knowledge and techniques that can be used to combine economic resources to produce goods and services is called technology.
Monetary union	An arrangement by which several nations adopt a common currency as a unit of account and medium of exchange. The European Monetary Union is scheduled to adopt the 'Euro' as the common currency in 1999.
Adoption	In corporation law, a corporation's acceptance of a pre-incorporation contract by action of its board of directors, by which the corporation becomes liable on the contract, is referred to as adoption.
Future value	Future value measures what money is worth at a specified time in the future assuming a certain interest rate. This is used in time value of money calculations.
Interest payment	The payment to holders of bonds payable, calculated by multiplying the stated rate on the face of the bond by the par, or face, value of the bond. If bonds are issued at a discount or premium, the interest payment does not equal the interest expense.
Bond	Bond refers to a debt instrument, issued by a borrower and promising a specified stream of payments to the purchaser, usually regular interest payments plus a final repayment of principal.
Coupon	In finance, a coupon is "attached" to a bond, either physically (as with old bonds) or electronically. Each coupon represents a predetermined payment promized to the bond-holder in return for his or her loan of money to the bond-issuer. .
Sinking fund	A sinking fund is a method by which an organization sets aside money over time to retire its indebtedness. More specifically, it is a fund into which money can be deposited, so that over time its preferred stock, debentures or stocks can be retired.
Public debt	Public debt refers to the total amount owed by the Federal government to the owners of government securities; equal to the sum of past government budget deficits less government budget surpluses.
Bearer	A person in possession of a negotiable instrument that is payable to him, his order, or to whoever is in possession of the instrument is referred to as bearer.
State bank	State bank refers to a commercial bank authorized by a state government to engage in the business of banking.
Credit	Credit refers to a recording as positive in the balance of payments, any transaction that gives rise to a payment into the country, such as an export, the sale of an asset, or borrowing from abroad.
Amortization	Systematic and rational allocation of the acquisition cost of an intangible asset over its useful life is referred to as amortization.
Conversion	Conversion refers to any distinct act of dominion wrongfully exerted over another's personal property in denial of or inconsistent with his rights therein. That tort committed by a person who deals with chattels not belonging to him in a manner that is inconsistent with the ownership of the lawful owner.

Chapter 2. History of Foreign Exchange Rates

Chapter 3. The Balance of Payments

Competitiveness	Competitiveness usually refers to characteristics that permit a firm to compete effectively with other firms due to low cost or superior technology, perhaps internationally.
Interest rate	The rate of return on bonds, loans, or deposits. When one speaks of 'the' interest rate, it is usually in a model where there is only one.
Exchange rate	Exchange rate refers to the price at which one country's currency trades for another, typically on the exchange market.
Exchange	The trade of things of value between buyer and seller so that each is better off after the trade is called the exchange.
Domestic	From or in one's own country. A domestic producer is one that produces inside the home country. A domestic price is the price inside the home country. Opposite of 'foreign' or 'world.'.
Industry	A group of firms that produce identical or similar products is an industry. It is also used specifically to refer to an area of economic production focused on manufacturing which involves large amounts of capital investment before any profit can be realized, also called "heavy industry".
Interest	In finance and economics, interest is the price paid by a borrower for the use of a lender's money. In other words, interest is the amount of paid to "rent" money for a period of time.
Policy	Similar to a script in that a policy can be a less than completely rational decision-making method. Involves the use of a pre-existing set of decision steps for any problem that presents itself.
Financial transaction	A financial transaction involves a change in the status of the finances of two or more businesses or individuals.
Gross domestic product	Gross domestic product refers to the total value of new goods and services produced in a given year within the borders of a country, regardless of by whom.
Price level	The overall level of prices in a country, as usually measured empirically by a price index, but often captured in theoretical models by a single variable is a price level.
Variable	A variable is something measured by a number; it is used to analyze what happens to other things when the size of that number changes.
Fiscal policy	Fiscal policy refers to any macroeconomic policy involving the levels of government purchases, transfers, or taxes, usually implicitly focused on domestic goods, residents, or firms.
Economic policy	Economic policy refers to the actions that governments take in the economic field. It covers the systems for setting interest rates and government deficit as well as the labor market, national ownership, and many other areas of government.
Host country	The country in which the parent-country organization seeks to locate or has already located a facility is a host country.
Foreign exchange control	The control a government may exercise over the quantity of foreign currency demanded by its citizens and firms and over the rates of exchange in order to limit its out-payments to its in-payments is referred to as foreign exchange control.
Exchange control	Rationing of foreign exchange, typically used when the exchange rate is fixed and the central bank is unable or unwilling to enforce the rate by exchange-market intervention is an exchange control.
Foreign exchange	In finance, foreign exchange means currencies, such as U.S. Dollars and Euros. These are traded on foreign exchange markets.

Go to **Cram101.com** for the Practice Tests for this Chapter.

Chapter 3. The Balance of Payments

Chapter 3. The Balance of Payments

Cash disbursement	Cash disbursement is a transaction that is posted to a cardholder's credit card account in which the cardholder receives cash at an ATM, or cash or travelers checks at a branch of a member financial institution or at a qualified and approved agent of a member financial institution.
Dividend	Amount of corporate profits paid out for each share of stock is referred to as dividend.
License	A license in the sphere of Intellectual Property Rights (IPR) is a document, contract or agreement giving permission or the 'right' to a legally-definable entity to do something (such as manufacture a product or to use a service), or to apply something (such as a trademark), with the objective of achieving commercial gain.
Firm	An organization that employs resources to produce a good or service for profit and owns and operates one or more plants is referred to as a firm.
Market potential	Market potential refers to maximum total sales of a product by all firms to a segment during a specified time period under specified environmental conditions and marketing efforts of the firms.
Short run	Short run refers to a period of time that permits an increase or decrease in current production volume with existing capacity, but one that is too short to permit enlargement of that capacity itself (eg, the building of new plants, training of additional workers, etc.).
Market	A market is, as defined in economics, a social arrangement that allows buyers and sellers to discover information and carry out a voluntary exchange of goods or services.
Trade deficit	The amount by which imports exceed exports of goods and services is referred to as trade deficit.
Deficit	The deficit is the amount by which expenditure exceed revenue.
Investment	Investment refers to spending for the production and accumulation of capital and additions to inventories. In a financial sense, buying an asset with the expectation of making a return.
Export	In economics, an export is any good or commodity, shipped or otherwise transported out of a country, province, town to another part of the world in a legitimate fashion, typically for use in trade or sale.
Parent company	Parent company refers to the entity that has a controlling influence over another company. It may have its own operations, or it may have been set up solely for the purpose of owning the Subject Company.
Honda	With more than 14 million internal combustion engines built each year, Honda is the largest engine-maker in the world. In 2004, the company began to produce diesel motors, which were both very quiet whilst not requiring particulate filters to pass pollution standards. It is arguable, however, that the foundation of their success is the motorcycle division.
Corporation	A legal entity chartered by a state or the Federal government that is distinct and separate from the individuals who own it is a corporation. This separation gives the corporation unique powers which other legal entities lack.
Subsidiary	A company that is controlled by another company or corporation is a subsidiary.
Profit	Profit refers to the return to the resource entrepreneurial ability; total revenue minus total cost.
Corporate bond	A Corporate bond is a bond issued by a corporation, as the name suggests. The term is usually applied to longer term debt instruments, generally with a maturity date falling at least 12 months after their issue date (the term "commercial paper" being sometimes used for instruments with a shorter maturity).

Go to Cram101.com for the Practice Tests for this Chapter.

Chapter 3. The Balance of Payments

Chapter 3. The Balance of Payments

Broker	In commerce, a broker is a party that mediates between a buyer and a seller. A broker who also acts as a seller or as a buyer becomes a principal party to the deal.
Bond	Bond refers to a debt instrument, issued by a borrower and promising a specified stream of payments to the purchaser, usually regular interest payments plus a final repayment of principal.
Balance of payments	Balance of payments refers to a list, or accounting, of all of a country's international transactions for a given time period, usually one year.
Balance	In banking and accountancy, the outstanding balance is the amount of money owned, (or due), that remains in a deposit account (or a loan account) at a given date, after all past remittances, payments and withdrawal have been accounted for. It can be positive (then, in the balance sheet of a firm, it is an asset) or negative (a liability).
Accounting	A system that collects and processes financial information about an organization and reports that information to decision makers is referred to as accounting.
Cash flow	In finance, cash flow refers to the amounts of cash being received and spent by a business during a defined period of time, sometimes tied to a specific project. Most of the time they are being used to determine gaps in the liquid position of a company.
Aid	Assistance provided by countries and by international institutions such as the World Bank to developing countries in the form of monetary grants, loans at low interest rates, in kind, or a combination of these is called aid. Aid can also refer to assistance of any type rendered to benefit some group or individual.
Investment banker	Investment banker refers to a financial organization that specializes in selling primary offerings of securities. Investment bankers can also perform other financial functions, such as advising clients, negotiating mergers and takeovers, and selling secondary offerings.
Disequilibrium	Inequality or imbalance of supply and demand is referred to as disequilibrium.
Supply and demand	The partial equilibrium supply and demand economic model originally developed by Alfred Marshall attempts to describe, explain, and predict changes in the price and quantity of goods sold in competitive markets.
Trade balance	Balance of trade in terms of exports versus imports is called trade balance.
Supply	Supply is the aggregate amount of any material good that can be called into being at a certain price point; it comprises one half of the equation of supply and demand. In classical economic theory, a curve representing supply is one of the factors that produce price.
Cash flow statement	A cash flow statement is a financial report that shows incoming and outgoing money during a particular period (often monthly or quarterly). The statement shows how changes in balance sheet and income accounts affected cash and cash equivalents and breaks the analysis down according to operating, investing, and financing activities.
Balance sheet	A statement of the assets, liabilities, and net worth of a firm or individual at some given time often at the end of its "fiscal year," is referred to as a balance sheet.
Liability	A liability is a present obligation of the enterprise arizing from past events, the settlement of which is expected to result in an outflow from the enterprise of resources embodying economic benefits.
Asset	An item of property, such as land, capital, money, a share in ownership, or a claim on others for future payment, such as a bond or a bank deposit is an asset.
Service	Service refers to a "non tangible product" that is not embodied in a physical good and that typically effects some change in another product, person, or institution. Contrasts with good.

Chapter 3. The Balance of Payments

Chapter 3. The Balance of Payments

Barter	Barter is a type of trade where goods or services are exchanged for a certain amount of other goods or services; no money is involved in the transaction.
Stock	In financial terminology, stock is the capital raized by a corporation, through the issuance and sale of shares.
Government bond	A government bond is a bond issued by a national government denominated in the country's own currency. Bonds issued by national governments in foreign currencies are normally referred to as sovereign bonds.
Mistake	In contract law a mistake is incorrect understanding by one or more parties to a contract and may be used as grounds to invalidate the agreement. Common law has identified three different types of mistake in contract: unilateral mistake, mutual mistake, and common mistake.
Bookkeeping	The recording of business transactions is called bookkeeping.
Current account	Current account refers to a country's international transactions arising from current flows, as opposed to changes in stocks which are part of the capital account. Includes trade in goods and services plus inflows and outflows of transfers. A current account is a deposit account in the UK and countries with a UK banking heritage.
Comparative advantage	The ability to produce a good at lower cost, relative to other goods, compared to another country is a comparative advantage.
Theory of comparative advantage	Ricardo's theory that specialization and free trade will benefit all trading partners, even those that may be absolutely less efficient producers are theory of comparative advantage.
Exporter	A firm that sells its product in another country is an exporter.
Investment income	Investment income refers to consisting of virtually the same elements as portfolio income, a measure by which to justify a deduction for interest on investment indebtedness. Income derived from investments.
Net income	Net income is equal to the income that a firm has after subtracting costs and expenses from the total revenue. Expenses will typically include tax expense.
Grant	Grant refers to an intergovernmental transfer of funds. Since the New Deal, state and local governments have become increasingly dependent upon federal grants for an almost infinite variety of programs.
Fixed asset	Fixed asset, also known as property, plant, and equipment (PP&E), is a term used in accountancy for assets and property which cannot easily be converted into cash. This can be compared with current assets such as cash or bank accounts, which are described as liquid assets. In most cases, only tangible assets are referred to as fixed.
Private sector	The households and business firms of the economy are referred to as private sector.
International trade	The export of goods and services from a country and the import of goods and services into a country is referred to as the international trade.
Core	A core is the set of feasible allocations in an economy that cannot be improved upon by subset of the set of the economy's consumers (a coalition). In construction, when the force in an element is within a certain center section, the core, the element will only be under compression.
Manufacturing	Production of goods primarily by the application of labor and capital to raw materials and other intermediate inputs, in contrast to agriculture, mining, forestry, fishing, and services a manufacturing.
Economic growth	The percentage change in the quantity of goods and services produced from one year to the

Chapter 3. The Balance of Payments

rate	next is referred to as economic growth rate.
Economic growth	Economic growth refers to the increase over time in the capacity of an economy to produce goods and services and to improve the well-being of its citizens.
Demand factor	A demand factor is a factor that determines consumers' willingness and ability to pay for goods and services.
Buyer	A buyer refers to a role in the buying center with formal authority and responsibility to select the supplier and negotiate the terms of the contract.
Economy	The income, expenditures, and resources that affect the cost of running a business and household are called an economy.
Financial assets	Financial assets refer to monetary claims or obligations by one party against another party. Examples are bonds, mortgages, bank loans, and equities.
Financial account	This is the term used in the balance of payments statistics, since sometime in the 1990s, for what used to be called the 'capital account are referred to as financial account.
Capital account	The capital account is one of two primary components of the balance of payments. It tracks the movement of funds for investments and loans into and out of a country.
Capital	Capital generally refers to financial wealth, especially that used to start or maintain a business. In classical economics, capital is one of four factors of production, the others being land and labor and entrepreneurship.
Acquisition	A company's purchase of the property and obligations of another company is an acquisition.
Portfolio investment	Portfolio investment refers to the acquisition of portfolio capital. Usually refers to such transactions across national borders and/or across currencies.
Direct investment	Direct investment refers to a domestic firm actually investing in and owning a foreign subsidiary or division.
Portfolio	In finance, a portfolio is a collection of investments held by an institution or a private individual. Holding but not always a portfolio is part of an investment and risk-limiting strategy called diversification. By owning several assets, certain types of risk (in particular specific risk) can be reduced.
Operation	A standardized method or technique that is performed repetitively, often on different materials resulting in different finished goods is called an operation.
Maturity	Maturity refers to the final payment date of a loan or other financial instrument, after which point no further interest or principal need be paid.
Capital flow	International capital movement is referred to as capital flow.
Capital inflow	Capital inflow refers to a net flow of capital, real and/or financial, into a country, in the form of increased purchases of domestic assets by foreigners and/or reduced holdings of foreign assets by domestic residents.
Foreign direct investment	Foreign direct investment refers to the buying of permanent property and businesses in foreign nations.
Voting shares	Voting shares are shares that give the stockholder the right to vote on matters of corporate policy making as well as who will compose the members of the board of directors.
Shares	Shares refer to an equity security, representing a shareholder's ownership of a corporation. Shares are one of a finite number of equal portions in the capital of a company, entitling the owner to a proportion of distributed, non-reinvested profits known as dividends and to a portion of the value of the company in case of liquidation.

Chapter 3. The Balance of Payments

Treasury bills	Short-term obligations of the federal government are treasury bills. They are like zero coupon bonds in that they do not pay interest prior to maturity; instead they are sold at a discount of the par value to create a positive yield to maturity.
Debt security	Type of security acquired by loaning assets is called a debt security.
Security	Security refers to a claim on the borrower future income that is sold by the borrower to the lender. A security is a type of transferable interest representing financial value.
Capital surplus	Capital surplus refers to a balance sheet account. Balance sheet item under shareholders' equity. Increases by the value above an original par value per share that newly issued shares are sold for.
Debtor nation	Debtor nation refers to a country whose assets owned abroad are worth less than the assets within the country that are owned by foreigners. Contrasts with creditor nation.
Equity investment	Equity investment generally refers to the buying and holding of shares of stock on a stock market by individuals and funds in anticipation of income from dividends and capital gain as the value of the stock rises.
Debt crisis	Debt crisis refers to a situation in which a country, usually an LDC, finds itself unable to service its debts.
Equity	Equity is the name given to the set of legal principles, in countries following the English common law tradition, which supplement strict rules of law where their application would operate harshly, so as to achieve what is sometimes referred to as "natural justice."
Treasury security	A treasury security is a government bond issued by the United States Department of the Treasury through the Bureau of the Public Debt. They are the debt financing instruments of the U.S. Federal government, and are often referred to simply as Treasuries.
Emerging markets	The term emerging markets is commonly used to describe business and market activity in industrializing or emerging regions of the world. It is sometimes loosely used as a replacement for emerging economies, but really signifies a business phenomenon that is not fully described by or constrained to geography or economic strength; such countries are considered to be in a transitional phase between developing and developed status.
Emerging market	The term emerging market is commonly used to describe business and market activity in industrializing or emerging regions of the world.
Current Account deficit	Current account deficit occurs when a country imports more goods and services than it exports.
Official reserves	The reserves of foreign-currency-denominated assets that a central bank holds, sometimes as backing for its own currency, but usually only for the purpose of possible future exchange market intervention are official reserves.
Authority	Authority in agency law, refers to an agent's ability to affect his principal's legal relations with third parties. Also used to refer to an actor's legal power or ability to do something. In addition, sometimes used to refer to a statute, case, or other legal source that justifies a particular result.
Fixed exchange rate	A fixed exchange rate, sometimes is a type of exchange rate regime wherein a currency's value is matched to the value of another single currency or to a basket of other currencies, or to another measure of value, such as gold.
Excess supply	Supply minus demand. Thus a country's supply of exports of a homogeneous good is its excess supply of that good.
Capital mobility	The ability of capital to move internationally. The degree of capital mobility depends on government policies restricting or taxing capital inflows and/or outflows, plus the risk that

Chapter 3. The Balance of Payments

Chapter 3. The Balance of Payments

	investors in one country associate with assets in another.
Capital Outflow	Capital outflow is an economic term describing capital flowing out of (or leaving) a particular economy. Outflowing capital can be caused by any number of economic or political reasons but can often originate from instability in either sphere.
Contribution	In business organization law, the cash or property contributed to a business by its owners is referred to as contribution.
Gain	In finance, gain is a profit or an increase in value of an investment such as a stock or bond. Gain is calculated by fair market value or the proceeds from the sale of the investment minus the sum of the purchase price and all costs associated with it.
Property	Assets defined in the broadest legal sense. Property includes the unrealized receivables of a cash basis taxpayer, but not services rendered.
Floating exchange rate	A system under which the exchange rate for converting one currency into another is continuously adjusted depending on the laws of supply and demand is referred to as a floating exchange rate.
Gold standard	The gold standard is a monetary system in which the standard economic unit of account is a fixed weight of gold.
Openness	Openness refers to the extent to which an economy is open, often measured by the ratio of its trade to GDP.
Capital market	A financial market in which long-term debt and equity instruments are traded is referred to as a capital market. The capital market includes the stock market and the bond market.
Depression	Depression refers to a prolonged period characterized by high unemployment, low output and investment, depressed business confidence, falling prices, and widespread business failures. A milder form of business downturn is a recession.
Bretton Woods	A 1944 conference in which representatives of 40 countries met to design a new international monetary system is referred to as the Bretton Woods conference.
Exchange rate regime	Exchange rate regime refers to the rules under which a country's exchange rate is determined, especially the way the monetary or other government authorities do or do not intervene in the exchange market.
Fixed exchange rate regime	A regime in which central banks buy and sell their own currencies to keep their exchange rates fixed at a certain level is referred to as fixed exchange rate regime.
Capital movement	Capital inflow and/or outflow is referred to as capital movement.
Capital flight	Large financial capital outflows from a country prompted by fear of default or, especially, by fear of devaluation is called capital flight.
Convertible currency	Convertible currency refers to a currency that can legally be exchanged for another or for gold.
Economics	The social science dealing with the use of scarce resources to obtain the maximum satisfaction of society's virtually unlimited economic wants is an economics.
Debt service	The payments made by a borrower on their debt, usually including both interest payments and partial repayment of principal, are called debt service.
Bearer	A person in possession of a negotiable instrument that is payable to him, his order, or to whoever is in possession of the instrument is referred to as bearer.
Purchase of assets	Purchase of assets refers to a method of financial recording for mergers, in which the difference between the purchase price and the adjusted book value is recognized as goodwill.

Chapter 3. The Balance of Payments

Chapter 3. The Balance of Payments

	Under new rulings by the FASB, goodwill does not need to be written off under normal circumstances.
Money laundering	When illegal money is made to appear legal by passing it through a bank or legal business, we have money laundering.
Credit	Credit refers to a recording as positive in the balance of payments, any transaction that gives rise to a payment into the country, such as an export, the sale of an asset, or borrowing from abroad.
Debit	Debit refers to recording as negative in the balance of payments, any transaction that gives rise to a payment out of the country, such as an import, the purchase of an asset, or lending to foreigners. Opposite of credit.
Stock exchange	A stock exchange is a corporation or mutual organization which provides facilities for stock brokers and traders, to trade company stocks and other securities.
Mutual fund	A mutual fund is a form of collective investment that pools money from many investors and invests the money in stocks, bonds, short-term money market instruments, and/or other securities. In a mutual fund, the fund manager trades the fund's underlying securities, realizing capital gains or loss, and collects the dividend or interest income.
Fund	Independent accounting entity with a self-balancing set of accounts segregated for the purposes of carrying on specific activities is referred to as a fund.
Foreign corporation	Foreign corporation refers to a corporation incorporated in one state doing business in another state. A corporation doing business in a jurisdiction in which it was not formed.
United Nations	An international organization created by multilateral treaty in 1945 to promote social and economic cooperation among nations and to protect human rights is the United Nations.
World Bank	The World Bank is a group of five international organizations responsible for providing finance and advice to countries for the purposes of economic development and poverty reduction, and for encouraging and safeguarding international investment.
Devaluation	Lowering the value of a nation's currency relative to other currencies is called devaluation.
Analyst	Analyst refers to a person or tool with a primary function of information analysis, generally with a more limited, practical and short term set of goals than a researcher.
Composition	An out-of-court settlement in which creditors agree to accept a fractional settlement on their original claim is referred to as composition.

Chapter 4. International Parity Conditions

Economic theory	Economic theory refers to a statement of a cause-effect relationship; when accepted by all economists, an economic principle.
Interest rate	The rate of return on bonds, loans, or deposits. When one speaks of 'the' interest rate, it is usually in a model where there is only one.
Exchange rate	Exchange rate refers to the price at which one country's currency trades for another, typically on the exchange market.
Price level	The overall level of prices in a country, as usually measured empirically by a price index, but often captured in theoretical models by a single variable is a price level.
Exchange	The trade of things of value between buyer and seller so that each is better off after the trade is called the exchange.
Interest	In finance and economics, interest is the price paid by a borrower for the use of a lender's money. In other words, interest is the amount of paid to "rent" money for a period of time.
Core	A core is the set of feasible allocations in an economy that cannot be improved upon by subset of the set of the economy's consumers (a coalition). In construction, when the force in an element is within a certain center section, the core, the element will only be under compression.
Service	Service refers to a "non tangible product" that is not embodied in a physical good and that typically effects some change in another product, person, or institution. Contrasts with good.
Market	A market is, as defined in economics, a social arrangement that allows buyers and sellers to discover information and carry out a voluntary exchange of goods or services.
Competitive market	A market in which no buyer or seller has market power is called a competitive market.
Conversion	Conversion refers to any distinct act of dominion wrongfully exerted over another's personal property in denial of or inconsistent with his rights therein. That tort committed by a person who deals with chattels not belonging to him in a manner that is inconsistent with the ownership of the lawful owner.
Spot exchange rate	The exchange rate at which a foreign exchange dealer will convert one currency into another that particular day is the spot exchange rate.
Relative price	Relative price refers to the price of one thing in terms of another; i.e., the ratio of two prices.
Basket	A basket is an economic term for a group of several securities created for the purpose of simultaneous buying or selling. Baskets are frequently used for program trading.
Price index	A measure of the average prices of a group of goods relative to a base year. A typical price index for a vector of quantities q and prices pb, pg in the base and given years respectively would be I = 100 Pgq / Pbq.
Spot rate	Spot rate refers to the rate at which the currency is traded for immediate delivery. It is the existing cash price.
Differential rate	A difference in wage rate paid for the same work performed under differing conditions is a differential rate.
Inflation	An increase in the overall price level of an economy, usually as measured by the CPI or by the implicit price deflator is called inflation.
Long run	In economic models, the long run time frame assumes no fixed factors of production. Firms can enter or leave the marketplace, and the cost (and availability) of land, labor, raw

Chapter 4. International Parity Conditions

Chapter 4. International Parity Conditions

	materials, and capital goods can be assumed to vary.
Inflation rate	The percentage increase in the price level per year is an inflation rate. Alternatively, the inflation rate is the rate of decrease in the purchasing power of money.
Effective exchange rate index	Effective exchange rate index refers to an index reflecting the value of a basket of representative foreign currencies.
Base period	Base period refers to the time period used for comparative analysis; the basis for indexing, e.g., of price change. A base period may be a month, year or average of years.
Weighted average	The weighted average unit cost of the goods available for sale for both cost of goods sold and ending inventory.
Purchasing power	The amount of goods that money will buy, usually measured by the CPI is referred to as purchasing power.
Purchasing	Purchasing refers to the function in a firm that searches for quality material resources, finds the best suppliers, and negotiates the best price for goods and services.
Purchasing power parity	purchasing power parity is a theory based on the law of one price which says that the long-run equilibrium exchange rate of two currencies is the rate that equalizes the currencies' purchasing power.
Production	The creation of finished goods and services using the factors of production: land, labor, capital, entrepreneurship, and knowledge.
Expense	In accounting, an expense represents an event in which an asset is used up or a liability is incurred. In terms of the accounting equation, expenses reduce owners' equity.
Euro	The common currency of a subset of the countries of the EU, adopted January 1, 1999 is called euro.
BMW	BMW is an independent German company and manufacturer of automobiles and motorcycles. BMW is the world's largest premium carmaker and is the parent company of the BMW MINI and Rolls-Royce car brands, and, formerly, Rover.
Export	In economics, an export is any good or commodity, shipped or otherwise transported out of a country, province, town to another part of the world in a legitimate fashion, typically for use in trade or sale.
Firm	An organization that employs resources to produce a good or service for profit and owns and operates one or more plants is referred to as a firm.
Appreciation	Appreciation refers to a rise in the value of a country's currency on the exchange market, relative either to a particular other currency or to a weighted average of other currencies. The currency is said to appreciate. Opposite of 'depreciation.' Appreciation can also refer to the increase in value of any asset.
Price elasticity	The responsiveness of the market to change in price is called price elasticity. If price elasticity is low, a large change in price will lead to a small change in supply.
Price elasticity of demand	Price elasticity of demand refers to the ratio of the percentage change in quantity demanded of a product or resource to the percentage change in its price; a measure of the responsiveness of buyers to a change in the price of a product or resource.
Elasticity	In economics, elasticity is the ratio of the incremental percentage change in one variable with respect to an incremental percentage change in another variable. Elasticity is usually expressed as a positive number (i.e., an absolute value) when the sign is already clear from context.

Chapter 4. International Parity Conditions

Chapter 4. International Parity Conditions

Quantity demanded	The amount of a good or service that buyers desire to purchase at a particular price during some period is a quantity demanded.
Inelastic	Inelastic refers to having an elasticity less than one. For a price elasticity of demand, this means that expenditure falls as price falls. For an income elasticity, it means that expenditure share falls with income.
Price inelastic	Having a price elasticity of less than one is referred to as price inelastic. Price inelastic indicates a lower consumer sensitivity to price changes.
Revenue	Revenue is a U.S. business term for the amount of money that a company receives from its activities, mostly from sales of products and/or services to customers.
Nominal interest rate	The interest rate actually observed in the market, in contrast to the real interest rate is a nominal interest rate.
Real rate of return	The adjusted after-inflation return on an investment, calculated by subtracting the current rate of inflation from the rate of return is called the real rate of return.
Rate of return	A rate of return is a comparison of the money earned (or lost) on an investment to the amount of money invested.
Fisher effect	Fisher effect refers to the outcome that when expected inflation occurs, interest rates will rise; named after economist Irving Fisher.
Real rate of interest	The real rate of interest is the percentage increase in purchasing power that the borrower pays to the lender for the privilege of borrowing. It is the nominal rate of interest minus the inflation rate.
Nominal rate of interest	The nominal rate of interest is the percentage by which the money the borrower pays back exceeds the money that he borrowed, making no adjustment for any fall in the purchasing power of this money that results from inflation.
Fund	Independent accounting entity with a self-balancing set of accounts segregated for the purposes of carrying on specific activities is referred to as a fund.
Consideration	Consideration in contract law, a basic requirement for an enforceable agreement under traditional contract principles, defined in this text as legal value, bargained for and given in exchange for an act or promise. In corporation law, cash or property contributed to a corporation in exchange for shares, or a promise to contribute such cash or property.
Treasury bills	Short-term obligations of the federal government are treasury bills. They are like zero coupon bonds in that they do not pay interest prior to maturity; instead they are sold at a discount of the par value to create a positive yield to maturity.
Security	Security refers to a claim on the borrower future income that is sold by the borrower to the lender. A security is a type of transferable interest representing financial value.
Financial risk	The risk related to the inability of the firm to meet its debt obligations as they come due is called financial risk.
Market value	Market value refers to the price of an asset agreed on between a willing buyer and a willing seller; the price an asset could demand if it is sold on the open market.
Maturity	Maturity refers to the final payment date of a loan or other financial instrument, after which point no further interest or principal need be paid.
Bond	Bond refers to a debt instrument, issued by a borrower and promising a specified stream of payments to the purchaser, usually regular interest payments plus a final repayment of principal.
Creditworthiness	Creditworthiness indicates whether a borrower has in the past made loan payments when due.

Chapter 4. International Parity Conditions

Chapter 4. International Parity Conditions

Private sector	The households and business firms of the economy are referred to as private sector.
Issuer	The company that borrows money from investors by issuing bonds is referred to as issuer. They are legally responsible for the obligations of the issue and for reporting financial conditions, material developments and any other operational activities as required by the regulations of their jurisdictions.
Capital market	A financial market in which long-term debt and equity instruments are traded is referred to as a capital market. The capital market includes the stock market and the bond market.
Capital	Capital generally refers to financial wealth, especially that used to start or maintain a business. In classical economics, capital is one of four factors of production, the others being land and labor and entrepreneurship.
Industry	A group of firms that produce identical or similar products is an industry. It is also used specifically to refer to an area of economic production focused on manufacturing which involves large amounts of capital investment before any profit can be realized, also called "heavy industry".
Foreign exchange risk	Foreign exchange risk refers to a form of risk that refers to the possibility of experiencing a drop in revenue or an increase in cost in an international transaction due to a change in foreign exchange rates. Importers, exporters, investors, and multinational firms alike are exposed to this risk.
Foreign exchange	In finance, foreign exchange means currencies, such as U.S. Dollars and Euros. These are traded on foreign exchange markets.
Risk premium	In finance, the risk premium can be the expected rate of return above the risk-free interest rate.
Premium	Premium refers to the fee charged by an insurance company for an insurance policy. The rate of losses must be relatively predictable: In order to set the premium (prices) insurers must be able to estimate them accurately.
Forward rate	Forward rate refers to the forward exchange rate, this is the exchange rate on a forward market transaction.
Forward exchange	When two parties agree to exchange currency and execute a deal at some specific date in the future, we have forward exchange.
Rate of exchange	Rate of exchange refers to the price paid in one's own money to acquire 1 unit of a foreign currency; the rate at which the money of one nation is exchanged for the money of another nation.
Forward premium	The difference between a forward exchange rate and the spot exchange rate, expressed as an annualized percentage return on buying foreign currency spot and selling it forward is a forward premium.
Discount	The difference between the face value of a bond and its selling price, when a bond is sold for less than its face value it's referred to as a discount.
Foreign exchange market	A market for converting the currency of one country into that of another country is called foreign exchange market. It is by far the largest market in the world, in terms of cash value traded, and includes trading between large banks, central banks, currency speculators, multinational corporations, governments, and other financial markets and institutions.
Interest Rate Parity	The Interest Rate Parity is the basic identity that relates interest rates and exchange rates. The identity is theoretical, and usually follows from assumptions imposed in economics models.
Exchange market	Exchange market refers to the market on which national currencies are bought and sold.

Go to **Cram101.com** for the Practice Tests for this Chapter.

Chapter 4. International Parity Conditions

Money market	The money market, in macroeconomics and international finance, refers to the equilibration of demand for a country's domestic money to its money supply; market for short-term financial instruments.
Transaction cost	A transaction cost is a cost incurred in making an economic exchange. For example, most people, when buying or selling a stock, must pay a commission to their broker; that commission is a transaction cost of doing the stock deal.
Investment	Investment refers to spending for the production and accumulation of capital and additions to inventories. In a financial sense, buying an asset with the expectation of making a return.
Instrument	Instrument refers to an economic variable that is controlled by policy makers and can be used to influence other variables, called targets. Examples are monetary and fiscal policies used to achieve external and internal balance.
Principal	In agency law, one under whose direction an agent acts and for whose benefit that agent acts is a principal.
Arbitrage	An arbitrage is a combination of nearly simultaneous transactions designed to profit from an existing discrepancy among prices, exchange rates, and/or interest rates on different markets without assuming risk.
Profit	Profit refers to the return to the resource entrepreneurial ability; total revenue minus total cost.
Disequilibrium	Inequality or imbalance of supply and demand is referred to as disequilibrium.
Eurocurrencies	A variant of the Eurobond, which are foreign currencies deposited in banks outside the home country is an eurocurrencies.
Eurocurrency	Eurocurrency is the term used to describe deposits residing in banks that are located outside the borders of the country that issues the currency the deposit is denominated in.
Yield	The interest rate that equates a future value or an annuity to a given present value is a yield.
Gain	In finance, gain is a profit or an increase in value of an investment such as a stock or bond. Gain is calculated by fair market value or the proceeds from the sale of the investment minus the sum of the purchase price and all costs associated with it.
Currency risk	Currency risk is a form of risk that arises from the change in price of one currency against another. Whenever investors or companies have assets or business operations across national borders, they face currency risk if their positions are not hedged.
Depreciate	A nation's currency is said to depreciate when exchange rates change so that a unit of its currency can buy fewer units of foreign currency.
Bank failure	A situation in which a bank cannot satisfy its obligations to pay its depositors and other creditors and so goes out of business is called bank failure.
Capital controls	Capital controls refer to restrictions on cross-border capital flows that segment different stock markets; limit amount of a firm's stock a foreigner can own; and limit a citizen's ability to invest outside the country.
Capital control	Any policy intended to restrict the free movement of capital, especially financial capital, into or out of a country is referred to as capital control.
Political risk	Refers to the many different actions of people, subgroups, and whole countries that have the potential to affect the financial status of a firm is called political risk.
Contract	A contract is a "promise" or an "agreement" that is enforced or recognized by the law. In the civil law, a contract is considered to be part of the general law of obligations.

Chapter 4. International Parity Conditions

Chapter 4. International Parity Conditions

Gap	In December of 1995, Gap became the first major North American retailer to accept independent monitoring of the working conditions in a contract factory producing its garments. Gap is the largest specialty retailer in the United States.
Rate differential	The controversial practice of newspapers charging significantly higher rates to national advertisers as compared to local accounts is called rate differential.
Forward market	A market for exchange of currencies in the future is the forward market. Participants in a forward market enter into a contract to exchange currencies, not today, but at a specified date in the future, typically 30, 60, or 90 days from now, and at a price that is agreed upon.
Forward exchange rate	The exchange rates governing forward exchange transactions is called the forward exchange rate.
Expected value	A representative value from a probability distribution arrived at by multiplying each outcome by the associated probability and summing up the values is called the expected value.
Distribution	Distribution in economics, the manner in which total output and income is distributed among individuals or factors.
Frequency	Frequency refers to the speed of the up and down movements of a fluctuating economic variable; that is, the number of times per unit of time that the variable completes a cycle of up and down movement.
Perfect substitute	A good that is regarded by its demanders as identical to another good, so that the elasticity of substitution between them is infinite is referred to as perfect substitute.
Efficient market	Efficient market refers to a market in which, at a minimum, current price changes are independent of past price changes, or, more strongly, price reflects all available information.
Efficient market hypothesis	The application of the theory of rational expectations to financial markets is referred to as efficient market hypothesis.
Financial manager	Managers who make recommendations to top executives regarding strategies for improving the financial strength of a firm are referred to as a financial manager.
Insurance	Insurance refers to a system by which individuals can reduce their exposure to risk of large losses by spreading the risks among a large number of persons.
Variable	A variable is something measured by a number; it is used to analyze what happens to other things when the size of that number changes.
Honda	With more than 14 million internal combustion engines built each year, Honda is the largest engine-maker in the world. In 2004, the company began to produce diesel motors, which were both very quiet whilst not requiring particulate filters to pass pollution standards. It is arguable, however, that the foundation of their success is the motorcycle division.
Points	Loan origination fees that may be deductible as interest by a buyer of property. A seller of property who pays points reduces the selling price by the amount of the points paid for the buyer.
Dealer	People who link buyers with sellers by buying and selling securities at stated prices are referred to as a dealer.
Cost of living	The amount of money it takes to buy the goods and services that a typical family consumes is the cost of living.
Evaluation	The consumer's appraisal of the product or brand on important attributes is called

Chapter 4. International Parity Conditions

Chapter 4. International Parity Conditions

	evaluation.
Manufacturing	Production of goods primarily by the application of labor and capital to raw materials and other intermediate inputs, in contrast to agriculture, mining, forestry, fishing, and services a manufacturing.
Homogeneous	In the context of procurement/purchasing, homogeneous is used to describe goods that do not vary in their essential characteristic irrespective of the source of supply.
Assembly line	An assembly line is a manufacturing process in which interchangeable parts are added to a product in a sequential manner to create a finished product.
Forbes	David Churbuck founded online Forbes in 1996. The site drew attention when it uncovered Stephen Glass' journalistic fraud in The New Republic in 1998, a scoop that gave credibility to internet journalism.
Management	Management characterizes the process of leading and directing all or part of an organization, often a business, through the deployment and manipulation of resources. Early twentieth-century management writer Mary Parker Follett defined management as "the art of getting things done through people."
Credit sale	A credit sale occurs when a customer does not pay cash at the time of the sale but instead agrees to pay later. The sale occurs now, with payment from the customer to follow at a later time.
Credit	Credit refers to a recording as positive in the balance of payments, any transaction that gives rise to a payment into the country, such as an export, the sale of an asset, or borrowing from abroad.
Market share	That fraction of an industry's output accounted for by an individual firm or group of firms is called market share.
Operation	A standardized method or technique that is performed repetitively, often on different materials resulting in different finished goods is called an operation.
Financial crisis	A loss of confidence in a country's currency or other financial assets causing international investors to withdraw their funds from the country is referred to as a financial crisis.
Market position	Market position is a measure of the position of a company or product on a market.
General Motors	General Motors is the world's largest automaker. Founded in 1908, today it employs about 327,000 people around the world. With global headquarters in Detroit, it manufactures its cars and trucks in 33 countries.
Shares	Shares refer to an equity security, representing a shareholder's ownership of a corporation. Shares are one of a finite number of equal portions in the capital of a company, entitling the owner to a proportion of distributed, non-reinvested profits known as dividends and to a portion of the value of the company in case of liquidation.
Devaluation	Lowering the value of a nation's currency relative to other currencies is called devaluation.
Durable good	A durable good is a good which does not quickly wear out, or more specifically, it yields services or utility over time rather than being completely used up when used once.
Joint venture	Joint venture refers to an undertaking by two parties for a specific purpose and duration, taking any of several legal forms.
Utility	Utility refers to the want-satisfying power of a good or service; the satisfaction or pleasure a consumer obtains from the consumption of a good or service.
Marketing	Promoting and selling products or services to customers, or prospective customers, is referred to as marketing.

Chapter 4. International Parity Conditions

Chapter 4. International Parity Conditions

Closing	The finalization of a real estate sales transaction that passes title to the property from the seller to the buyer is referred to as a closing. Closing is a sales term which refers to the process of making a sale. It refers to reaching the final step, which may be an exchange of money or acquiring a signature.
Labor	People's physical and mental talents and efforts that are used to help produce goods and services are called labor.
Emerging markets	The term emerging markets is commonly used to describe business and market activity in industrializing or emerging regions of the world. It is sometimes loosely used as a replacement for emerging economies, but really signifies a business phenomenon that is not fully described by or constrained to geography or economic strength; such countries are considered to be in a transitional phase between developing and developed status.
Emerging market	The term emerging market is commonly used to describe business and market activity in industrializing or emerging regions of the world.

Chapter 5. Foreign Exchange Rate Determination

Complexity	The technical sophistication of the product and hence the amount of understanding required to use it is referred to as complexity. It is the opposite of simplicity.
Market	A market is, as defined in economics, a social arrangement that allows buyers and sellers to discover information and carry out a voluntary exchange of goods or services.
Economic infrastructure	Economic infrastructure refers to a country's communications, transportation, financial, and distribution systems.
Political economy	Early name for the discipline of economics. A field within economics encompassing several alternatives to neoclassical economics, including Marxist economics. Also called radical political economy.
Exchange rate	Exchange rate refers to the price at which one country's currency trades for another, typically on the exchange market.
Exchange	The trade of things of value between buyer and seller so that each is better off after the trade is called the exchange.
Economy	The income, expenditures, and resources that affect the cost of running a business and household are called an economy.
Gain	In finance, gain is a profit or an increase in value of an investment such as a stock or bond. Gain is calculated by fair market value or the proceeds from the sale of the investment minus the sum of the purchase price and all costs associated with it.
Interest rate	The rate of return on bonds, loans, or deposits. When one speaks of 'the' interest rate, it is usually in a model where there is only one.
Interest	In finance and economics, interest is the price paid by a borrower for the use of a lender's money. In other words, interest is the amount of paid to "rent" money for a period of time.
Supply	Supply is the aggregate amount of any material good that can be called into being at a certain price point; it comprises one half of the equation of supply and demand. In classical economic theory, a curve representing supply is one of the factors that produce price.
Asset	An item of property, such as land, capital, money, a share in ownership, or a claim on others for future payment, such as a bond or a bank deposit is an asset.
Exchange rate regime	Exchange rate regime refers to the rules under which a country's exchange rate is determined, especially the way the monetary or other government authorities do or do not intervene in the exchange market.
Foreign direct investment	Foreign direct investment refers to the buying of permanent property and businesses in foreign nations.
Portfolio investment	Portfolio investment refers to the acquisition of portfolio capital. Usually refers to such transactions across national borders and/or across currencies.
Direct investment	Direct investment refers to a domestic firm actually investing in and owning a foreign subsidiary or division.
Current account	Current account refers to a country's international transactions arising from current flows, as opposed to changes in stocks which are part of the capital account. Includes trade in goods and services plus inflows and outflows of transfers. A current account is a deposit account in the UK and countries with a UK banking heritage.
Emerging market	The term emerging market is commonly used to describe business and market activity in industrializing or emerging regions of the world.
Political risk	Refers to the many different actions of people, subgroups, and whole countries that have the potential to affect the financial status of a firm is called political risk.

Chapter 5. Foreign Exchange Rate Determination

Chapter 5. Foreign Exchange Rate Determination

Speculation	The purchase or sale of an asset in hopes that its price will rise or fall respectively, in order to make a profit is called speculation.
Investment	Investment refers to spending for the production and accumulation of capital and additions to inventories. In a financial sense, buying an asset with the expectation of making a return.
Portfolio	In finance, a portfolio is a collection of investments held by an institution or a private individual. Holding but not always a portfolio is part of an investment and risk-limiting strategy called diversification. By owning several assets, certain types of risk (in particular specific risk) can be reduced.
Liquidity	Liquidity refers to the capacity to turn assets into cash, or the amount of assets in a portfolio that have that capacity.
Balance	In banking and accountancy, the outstanding balance is the amount of money owned, (or due), that remains in a deposit account (or a loan account) at a given date, after all past remittances, payments and withdrawal have been accounted for. It can be positive (then, in the balance sheet of a firm, it is an asset) or negative (a liability).
Commodity	Could refer to any good, but in trade a commodity is usually a raw material or primary product that enters into international trade, such as metals or basic agricultural products.
Security	Security refers to a claim on the borrower future income that is sold by the borrower to the lender. A security is a type of transferable interest representing financial value.
Estate	An estate is the totality of the legal rights, interests, entitlements and obligations attaching to property. In the context of wills and probate, it refers to the totality of the property which the deceased owned or in which some interest was held.
Real interest rate	The real interest rate is the nominal interest rate minus the inflation rate. It is a better measure of the return that a lender receives (or the cost to the borrower) because it takes into account the fact that the value of money changes due to inflation over the course of the loan period.
Arbitrage	An arbitrage is a combination of nearly simultaneous transactions designed to profit from an existing discrepancy among prices, exchange rates, and/or interest rates on different markets without assuming risk.
Emerging markets	The term emerging markets is commonly used to describe business and market activity in industrializing or emerging regions of the world. It is sometimes loosely used as a replacement for emerging economies, but really signifies a business phenomenon that is not fully described by or constrained to geography or economic strength; such countries are considered to be in a transitional phase between developing and developed status.
Capital market	A financial market in which long-term debt and equity instruments are traded is referred to as a capital market. The capital market includes the stock market and the bond market.
Capital	Capital generally refers to financial wealth, especially that used to start or maintain a business. In classical economics, capital is one of four factors of production, the others being land and labor and entrepreneurship.
Transparency	Transparency refers to a concept that describes a company being so open to other companies working with it that the once-solid barriers between them become see-through and electronic information is shared as if the companies were one.
Public sector	Public sector refers to the part of the economy that contains all government entities; government.
Policy	Similar to a script in that a policy can be a less than completely rational decision-making method. Involves the use of a pre-existing set of decision steps for any problem that

Chapter 5. Foreign Exchange Rate Determination

Chapter 5. Foreign Exchange Rate Determination

	presents itself.
Asset market approach	An approach to determine asset prices using stocks of assets rather than flows is called asset market approach.
Consideration	Consideration in contract law, a basic requirement for an enforceable agreement under traditional contract principles, defined in this text as legal value, bargained for and given in exchange for an act or promise. In corporation law, cash or property contributed to a corporation in exchange for shares, or a promise to contribute such cash or property.
Balance of payments	Balance of payments refers to a list, or accounting, of all of a country's international transactions for a given time period, usually one year.
Foreign exchange	In finance, foreign exchange means currencies, such as U.S. Dollars and Euros. These are traded on foreign exchange markets.
Capital Outflow	Capital outflow is an economic term describing capital flowing out of (or leaving) a particular economy. Outflowing capital can be caused by any number of economic or political reasons but can often originate from instability in either sphere.
Capital inflow	Capital inflow refers to a net flow of capital, real and/or financial, into a country, in the form of increased purchases of domestic assets by foreigners and/or reduced holdings of foreign assets by domestic residents.
Service	Service refers to a "non tangible product" that is not embodied in a physical good and that typically effects some change in another product, person, or institution. Contrasts with good.
Export	In economics, an export is any good or commodity, shipped or otherwise transported out of a country, province, town to another part of the world in a legitimate fashion, typically for use in trade or sale.
Fixed exchange rate	A fixed exchange rate, sometimes is a type of exchange rate regime wherein a currency's value is matched to the value of another single currency or to a basket of other currencies, or to another measure of value, such as gold.
Foreign exchange reserves	Foreign exchange reserves are the foreign currency deposits held by national banks of different nations. These are assets of governments which are held in different reserve currencies such as the dollar, euro and yen.
Foreign exchange market	A market for converting the currency of one country into that of another country is called foreign exchange market. It is by far the largest market in the world, in terms of cash value traded, and includes trading between large banks, central banks, currency speculators, multinational corporations, governments, and other financial markets and institutions.
Exchange market	Exchange market refers to the market on which national currencies are bought and sold.
Capital account	The capital account is one of two primary components of the balance of payments. It tracks the movement of funds for investments and loans into and out of a country.
Domestic	From or in one's own country. A domestic producer is one that produces inside the home country. A domestic price is the price inside the home country. Opposite of 'foreign' or 'world.'.
Excess supply	Supply minus demand. Thus a country's supply of exports of a homogeneous good is its excess supply of that good.
Revaluation	Revaluation means a rise of a price of goods or products. This term is specially used as revaluation of a currency, where it means a rise of currency to the relation with a foreign currency in a fixed exchange rate.

Chapter 5. Foreign Exchange Rate Determination

Chapter 5. Foreign Exchange Rate Determination

Devaluation	Lowering the value of a nation's currency relative to other currencies is called devaluation.
Floating exchange rate	A system under which the exchange rate for converting one currency into another is continuously adjusted depending on the laws of supply and demand is referred to as a floating exchange rate.
Managed float	An exchange rate regime in which the rate is allowed to be determined in the exchange market without an announced par value as the goal of intervention, but the authorities do nonetheless intervene at their discretion to influence the rate is a managed float.
Economic growth	Economic growth refers to the increase over time in the capacity of an economy to produce goods and services and to improve the well-being of its citizens.
Current Account deficit	Current account deficit occurs when a country imports more goods and services than it exports.
Deficit	The deficit is the amount by which expenditure exceed revenue.
Stock market	An organized marketplace in which common stocks are traded. In the United States, the largest stock market is the New York Stock Exchange, on which are traded the stocks of the largest U.S. companies.
Stock	In financial terminology, stock is the capital raized by a corporation, through the issuance and sale of shares.
Financial market	In economics, a financial market is a mechanism which allows people to trade money for securities or commodities such as gold or other precious metals. In general, any commodity market might be considered to be a financial market, if the usual purpose of traders is not the immediate consumption of the commodity, but rather as a means of delaying or accelerating consumption over time.
Efficient financial market	A financial market displaying the characteristics of an efficient market is called efficient financial market.
Trade flow	The quantity or value of a country's bilateral trade with another country is called trade flow.
Variable	A variable is something measured by a number; it is used to analyze what happens to other things when the size of that number changes.
Technical analysis	Uses price and volume data to determine past trends, which are expected to continue into the future is called technical analysis.
Analyst	Analyst refers to a person or tool with a primary function of information analysis, generally with a more limited, practical and short term set of goals than a researcher.
Trend	Trend refers to the long-term movement of an economic variable, such as its average rate of increase or decrease over enough years to encompass several business cycles.
Equity	Equity is the name given to the set of legal principles, in countries following the English common law tradition, which supplement strict rules of law where their application would operate harshly, so as to achieve what is sometimes referred to as "natural justice."
Time horizon	A time horizon is a fixed point of time in the future at which point certain processes will be evaluated or assumed to end. It is necessary in an accounting, finance or risk management regime to assign such a fixed horizon time so that alternatives can be evaluated for performance over the same period of time.
Future value	Future value measures what money is worth at a specified time in the future assuming a certain interest rate. This is used in time value of money calculations.

Chapter 5. Foreign Exchange Rate Determination

Time series	In statistics and signal processing, a time series is a sequence of data points, measured typically at successive times, spaced at (often uniform) time intervals. Analysts throughout the economy will use these to aid in the management of their corresponding businesses.
Consultant	A professional that provides expert advice in a particular field or area in which customers occassionaly require this type of knowledge is a consultant.
Firm	An organization that employs resources to produce a good or service for profit and owns and operates one or more plants is referred to as a firm.
Econometric model	A model whose equations are estimated using statistical procedures is an econometric model. They are used by economists to find standard relationships among aspects of the macroeconomy and use those relationships to predict the effects of certain events (like government policies) on inflation, unemployment, growth, etc...
Inflation	An increase in the overall price level of an economy, usually as measured by the CPI or by the implicit price deflator is called inflation.
Dividend	Amount of corporate profits paid out for each share of stock is referred to as dividend.
Hedge	Hedge refers to a process of offsetting risk. In the foreign exchange market, hedgers use the forward market to cover a transaction or open position and thereby reduce exchange risk. The term applies most commonly to trade.
Volatility	Volatility refers to the extent to which an economic variable, such as a price or an exchange rate, moves up and down over time.
Random walk	The movements of a variable whose future changes cannot be predicted because the variable is just as likely to fall as to rise from today's value is called a random walk.
Short run	Short run refers to a period of time that permits an increase or decrease in current production volume with existing capacity, but one that is too short to permit enlargement of that capacity itself (eg, the building of new plants, training of additional workers, etc.).
Currency exchange rate	The rate between two currencies that specifies how much one country's currency is worth expressed in terms of the other country's currency is the currency exchange rate.
Financial manager	Managers who make recommendations to top executives regarding strategies for improving the financial strength of a firm are referred to as a financial manager.
Operating budget	An operating budget is the annual budget of an activity stated in terms of Budget Classification Code, functional/subfunctional categories and cost accounts. It contains estimates of the total value of resources required for the performance of the operation including reimbursable work or services for others.
Budget	Budget refers to an account, usually for a year, of the planned expenditures and the expected receipts of an entity. For a government, the receipts are tax revenues.
Cross rates	The exchange rate of two foreign currencies expressed in terms of a third currency, neither of which is the US Dollar are called cross rates.
Foreign subsidiary	A company owned in a foreign country by another company is referred to as foreign subsidiary.
Subsidiary	A company that is controlled by another company or corporation is a subsidiary.
Fundamental analysis	Fundamental analysis is a security or stock valuation method that uses financial and economic analysis to predict the movement of security prices such as Bond prices, but more commonly stock prices. The fundamental information that is analyzed can include a company's financial reports, and non-finanical information such as estimates of the growth of demand for competing products, industry comparisons, analysis of the effects of new regulations or

Chapter 5. Foreign Exchange Rate Determination

Chapter 5. Foreign Exchange Rate Determination

	demographic changes, and economy-wide changes.
Forward rate	Forward rate refers to the forward exchange rate, this is the exchange rate on a forward market transaction.
Intervention	Intervention refers to an activity in which a government buys or sells its currency in the foreign exchange market in order to affect its currency's exchange rate.
Management	Management characterizes the process of leading and directing all or part of an organization, often a business, through the deployment and manipulation of resources. Early twentieth-century management writer Mary Parker Follett defined management as "the art of getting things done through people."
Disequilibrium	Inequality or imbalance of supply and demand is referred to as disequilibrium.
Currency crisis	Occurs when a speculative attack on the exchange value of a currency results in a sharp depreciation in the value of the currency or forces authorities to expend large volumes of international currency reserves and sharply increase interest rates to defend the prevailing exchange rate are referred to as currency crisis.
Economics	The social science dealing with the use of scarce resources to obtain the maximum satisfaction of society's virtually unlimited economic wants is an economics.
Exporter	A firm that sells its product in another country is an exporter.
Pegged exchange rate	A pegged exchange rate, is a type of exchange rate regime wherein a currency's value is matched to the value of another single currency or to a basket of other currencies, or to another measure of value, such as gold.
Manufacturing	Production of goods primarily by the application of labor and capital to raw materials and other intermediate inputs, in contrast to agriculture, mining, forestry, fishing, and services a manufacturing.
Forming	The first stage of team development, where the team is formed and the objectives for the team are set is referred to as forming.
Profit	Profit refers to the return to the resource entrepreneurial ability; total revenue minus total cost.
Enterprise	Enterprise refers to another name for a business organization. Other similar terms are business firm, sometimes simply business, sometimes simply firm, as well as company, and entity.
Credit	Credit refers to a recording as positive in the balance of payments, any transaction that gives rise to a payment into the country, such as an export, the sale of an asset, or borrowing from abroad.
Capital flow	International capital movement is referred to as capital flow.
Margin	A deposit by a buyer in stocks with a seller or a stockbroker, as security to cover fluctuations in the market in reference to stocks that the buyer has purchased but for which he has not paid is a margin. Commodities are also traded on margin.
Central Bank	Central bank refers to the institution in a country that is normally responsible for managing the supply of the country's money and the value of its currency on the foreign exchange market.
Prime minister	The Prime Minister of the United Kingdom of Great Britain and Northern Ireland is the head of government and so exercises many of the executive functions nominally vested in the Sovereign, who is head of state. According to custom, the Prime Minister and the Cabinet (which he or she heads) are accountable for their actions to Parliament, of which they are

Go to **Cram101.com** for the Practice Tests for this Chapter.

Chapter 5. Foreign Exchange Rate Determination

Chapter 5. Foreign Exchange Rate Determination

	members by (modern) convention.
Hedge fund	Hedge fund refers to a special type of mutual fund that engages in 'market-neutral strategies'. They are primarily organized as limited partnerships, and previously were often simply called "limited partnerships" and were grouped with other similar partnerships such as those that invested in oil development.
Fund	Independent accounting entity with a self-balancing set of accounts segregated for the purposes of carrying on specific activities is referred to as a fund.
Expense	In accounting, an expense represents an event in which an asset is used up or a liability is incurred. In terms of the accounting equation, expenses reduce owners' equity.
Corporate governance	Corporate governance is the set of processes, customs, policies, laws and institutions affecting the way a corporation is directed, administered or controlled.
Socialism	An economic system under which the state owns the resources and makes the economic decisions is called socialism.
Free market	A free market is a market where price is determined by the unregulated interchange of supply and demand rather than set by artificial means.
Liability	A liability is a present obligation of the enterprise arizing from past events, the settlement of which is expected to result in an outflow from the enterprise of resources embodying economic benefits.
Bail	Bail refers to an amount of money the defendant pays to the court upon release from custody as security that he or she will return for trial.
Stockholder	A stockholder is an individual or company (including a corporation) that legally owns one or more shares of stock in a joined stock company. The shareholders are the owners of a corporation. Companies listed at the stock market strive to enhance shareholder value.
Creditor	A person to whom a debt or legal obligation is owed, and who has the right to enforce payment of that debt or obligation is referred to as creditor.
Bottom line	The bottom line is net income on the last line of a income statement.
Working capital	The dollar difference between total current assets and total current liabilities is called working capital.
Recession	A significant decline in economic activity. In the U.S., recession is approximately defined as two successive quarters of falling GDP, as judged by NBER.
Gross domestic product	Gross domestic product refers to the total value of new goods and services produced in a given year within the borders of a country, regardless of by whom.
Economic problem	Economic problem refers to how to determine the use of scarce resources among competing uses. Because resources are scarce, the economy must choose what products to produce; how these products are to be produced: and for whom.
External debt	The amount that a country owes to foreigners, including the debts of both the country's government and its private sector is an external debt.
Debt service	The payments made by a borrower on their debt, usually including both interest payments and partial repayment of principal, are called debt service.
Capital flight	Large financial capital outflows from a country prompted by fear of default or, especially, by fear of devaluation is called capital flight.
Foreign bonds	Bonds sold in a foreign country and denominated in that country's currency are foreign bonds. Many domestic markets are also open to foreign borrowers who, although domiciled outside the

Chapter 5. Foreign Exchange Rate Determination

Chapter 5. Foreign Exchange Rate Determination

	country, can issue bonds in the domestic currency for sale to local investors as long as they comply with the same local regulations as their domestic counterparts.
Bond	Bond refers to a debt instrument, issued by a borrower and promising a specified stream of payments to the purchaser, usually regular interest payments plus a final repayment of principal.
Aid	Assistance provided by countries and by international institutions such as the World Bank to developing countries in the form of monetary grants, loans at low interest rates, in kind, or a combination of these is called aid. Aid can also refer to assistance of any type rendered to benefit some group or individual.
Revenue	Revenue is a U.S. business term for the amount of money that a company receives from its activities, mostly from sales of products and/or services to customers.
Government debt	The total of government obligations in the form of bonds and shorter-term borrowings. Government debt held by the public excludes bonds held by quasi-governmental agencies such as the central bank.
Auction	A preexisting business model that operates successfully on the Internet by announcing an item for sale and permitting multiple purchasers to bid on them under specified rules and condition is an auction.
Press release	A written public news announcement normally distributed to major news services is referred to as press release.
Implicit cost	Implicit cost refers to the monetary income a firm sacrifices when it uses a resource it owns rather than supplying the resource in the market; equal to what the resource could have earned in the best-paying alternative employment.
Basis point	One one-hundredth of a percentage point is a basis point. Each one percent in interest is equal to 100 basis points.
Eurobonds	Eurobonds refer to bonds payable or denominated in the borrower's currency, but sold outside the country of the borrower, usually by an international syndicate. This market is dominated by bonds stated in U.S. dollars.
Eurobond	A bond that is issued outside of the jurisdiction of any single country, denominated in a eurocurrency is referred to as eurobond.
Points	Loan origination fees that may be deductible as interest by a buyer of property. A seller of property who pays points reduces the selling price by the amount of the points paid for the buyer.
Yield	The interest rate that equates a future value or an annuity to a given present value is a yield.
Remainder	A remainder in property law is a future interest created in a transferee that is capable of becoming possessory upon the natural termination of a prior estate created by the same instrument.
Bond market	The bond market refers to people and entities involved in buying and selling of bonds and the quantity and prices of those transactions over time.
Administration	Administration refers to the management and direction of the affairs of governments and institutions; a collective term for all policymaking officials of a government; the execution and implementation of public policy.
Default	In finance, default occurs when a debtor has not met its legal obligations according to the debt contract, e.g. it has not made a scheduled payment, or violated a covenant (condition) of the debt contract.

Chapter 5. Foreign Exchange Rate Determination

Chapter 5. Foreign Exchange Rate Determination

Inception	The date and time on which coverage under an insurance policy takes effect is inception. Also refers to the date at which a stock or mutual fund was first traded.
Closing	The finalization of a real estate sales transaction that passes title to the property from the seller to the buyer is referred to as a closing. Closing is a sales term which refers to the process of making a sale. It refers to reaching the final step, which may be an exchange of money or acquiring a signature.
Fixed exchange rate regime	A regime in which central banks buy and sell their own currencies to keep their exchange rates fixed at a certain level is referred to as fixed exchange rate regime.
Supply and demand	The partial equilibrium supply and demand economic model originally developed by Alfred Marshall attempts to describe, explain, and predict changes in the price and quantity of goods sold in competitive markets.
Purchasing power parity	purchasing power parity is a theory based on the law of one price which says that the long-run equilibrium exchange rate of two currencies is the rate that equalizes the currencies' purchasing power.
Purchasing power	The amount of goods that money will buy, usually measured by the CPI is referred to as purchasing power.
Inflation rate	The percentage increase in the price level per year is an inflation rate. Alternatively, the inflation rate is the rate of decrease in the purchasing power of money.
Purchasing	Purchasing refers to the function in a firm that searches for quality material resources, finds the best suppliers, and negotiates the best price for goods and services.
Property	Assets defined in the broadest legal sense. Property includes the unrealized receivables of a cash basis taxpayer, but not services rendered.
Financial account	This is the term used in the balance of payments statistics, since sometime in the 1990s, for what used to be called the 'capital account are referred to as financial account.
Differential rate	A difference in wage rate paid for the same work performed under differing conditions is a differential rate.
Spot exchange rate	The exchange rate at which a foreign exchange dealer will convert one currency into another that particular day is the spot exchange rate.
World Bank	The World Bank is a group of five international organizations responsible for providing finance and advice to countries for the purposes of economic development and poverty reduction, and for encouraging and safeguarding international investment.
Operation	A standardized method or technique that is performed repetitively, often on different materials resulting in different finished goods is called an operation.
License	A license in the sphere of Intellectual Property Rights (IPR) is a document, contract or agreement giving permission or the 'right' to a legally-definable entity to do something (such as manufacture a product or to use a service), or to apply something (such as a trademark), with the objective of achieving commercial gain.
Holder	A person in possession of a document of title or an instrument payable or indorsed to him, his order, or to bearer is a holder.
Business Week	Business Week is a business magazine published by McGraw-Hill. It was first published in 1929 under the direction of Malcolm Muir, who was serving as president of the McGraw-Hill Publishing company at the time. It is considered to be the standard both in industry and among students.
Government bond	A government bond is a bond issued by a national government denominated in the country's own

Go to **Cram101.com** for the Practice Tests for this Chapter.

Chapter 5. Foreign Exchange Rate Determination

	currency. Bonds issued by national governments in foreign currencies are normally referred to as sovereign bonds.
Industry	A group of firms that produce identical or similar products is an industry. It is also used specifically to refer to an area of economic production focused on manufacturing which involves large amounts of capital investment before any profit can be realized, also called "heavy industry".
Spot market	Spot market refers to a market in which commodities are bought and sold for cash and immediate delivery.
Conversion	Conversion refers to any distinct act of dominion wrongfully exerted over another's personal property in denial of or inconsistent with his rights therein. That tort committed by a person who deals with chattels not belonging to him in a manner that is inconsistent with the ownership of the lawful owner.
Budget deficit	A budget deficit occurs when an entity (often a government) spends more money than it takes
National debt	National debt refers to total of outstanding federal government bonds on which the federal government must pay interest.
Deficit spending	Deficit spending is the amount by which a government, private company, or individual's spending exceeds income over a particular period of time.
Disinflation	A condition where price increases are slowing is called disinflation.
Privatization	A process in which investment bankers take companies that were previously owned by the government to the public markets is referred to as privatization.
Controlling interest	A firm has a controlling interest in another business entity when it owns more than 50 percent of that entity's voting stock.
Controlling	A management function that involves determining whether or not an organization is progressing toward its goals and objectives, and taking corrective action if it is not is called controlling.
Union	A worker association that bargains with employers over wages and working conditions is called a union.
Stabilization program	An agreement between a borrower country and the International Monetary Fund in which the country agrees to revamp its economic policies to provide incentives for higher export earnings and lower imports is called stabilization program.
Credibility	The extent to which a source is perceived as having knowledge, skill, or experience relevant to a communication topic and can be trusted to give an unbiased opinion or present objective information on the issue is called credibility.
Corporate finance	Corporate finance is a specific area of finance dealing with the financial decisions corporations make and the tools as well as analyses used to make these decisions. The discipline as a whole may be divided among long-term and short-term decisions and techniques with the primary goal being the enhancing of corporate value by ensuring that return on capital exceeds cost of capital, without taking excessive financial risks.
Argument	The discussion by counsel for the respective parties of their contentions on the law and the facts of the case being tried in order to aid the jury in arriving at a correct and just conclusion is called argument.
Corruption	The unauthorized use of public office for private gain. The most common forms of corruption are bribery, extortion, and the misuse of inside information.

Chapter 5. Foreign Exchange Rate Determination

Chapter 6. The Foreign Exchange Market

Foreign exchange	In finance, foreign exchange means currencies, such as U.S. Dollars and Euros. These are traded on foreign exchange markets.
Exchange	The trade of things of value between buyer and seller so that each is better off after the trade is called the exchange.
Balance	In banking and accountancy, the outstanding balance is the amount of money owned, (or due), that remains in a deposit account (or a loan account) at a given date, after all past remittances, payments and withdrawal have been accounted for. It can be positive (then, in the balance sheet of a firm, it is an asset) or negative (a liability).
Draft	A signed, written order by which one party instructs another party to pay a specified sum to a third party, at sight or at a specific date is a draft.
Buyer	A buyer refers to a role in the buying center with formal authority and responsibility to select the supplier and negotiate the terms of the contract.
Market	A market is, as defined in economics, a social arrangement that allows buyers and sellers to discover information and carry out a voluntary exchange of goods or services.
Investment	Investment refers to spending for the production and accumulation of capital and additions to inventories. In a financial sense, buying an asset with the expectation of making a return.
Closing	The finalization of a real estate sales transaction that passes title to the property from the seller to the buyer is referred to as a closing. Closing is a sales term which refers to the process of making a sale. It refers to reaching the final step, which may be an exchange of money or acquiring a signature.
Exchange control	Rationing of foreign exchange, typically used when the exchange rate is fixed and the central bank is unable or unwilling to enforce the rate by exchange-market intervention is an exchange control.
Central Bank	Central bank refers to the institution in a country that is normally responsible for managing the supply of the country's money and the value of its currency on the foreign exchange market.
Export	In economics, an export is any good or commodity, shipped or otherwise transported out of a country, province, town to another part of the world in a legitimate fashion, typically for use in trade or sale.
Firm	An organization that employs resources to produce a good or service for profit and owns and operates one or more plants is referred to as a firm.
Exchange rate	Exchange rate refers to the price at which one country's currency trades for another, typically on the exchange market.
Broker	In commerce, a broker is a party that mediates between a buyer and a seller. A broker who also acts as a seller or as a buyer becomes a principal party to the deal.
Dealer	People who link buyers with sellers by buying and selling securities at stated prices are referred to as a dealer.
Reuters	Reuters is best known as a news service that provides reports from around the world to newspapers and broadcasters. Its main focus is on supplying the financial markets with information and trading products.
Matching	Matching refers to an accounting concept that establishes when expenses are recognized. Expenses are matched with the revenues they helped to generate and are recognized when those revenues are recognized.
International	The export of goods and services from a country and the import of goods and services into a

Chapter 6. The Foreign Exchange Market

Chapter 6. The Foreign Exchange Market

trade	country is referred to as the international trade.
Purchasing power	The amount of goods that money will buy, usually measured by the CPI is referred to as purchasing power.
Purchasing	Purchasing refers to the function in a firm that searches for quality material resources, finds the best suppliers, and negotiates the best price for goods and services.
Capital	Capital generally refers to financial wealth, especially that used to start or maintain a business. In classical economics, capital is one of four factors of production, the others being land and labor and entrepreneurship.
In transit	A state in which goods are in the possession of a bailee or carrier and not in the hands of the buyer, seller, lessee, or lessor is referred to as in transit.
Inventory	Tangible property held for sale in the normal course of business or used in producing goods or services for sale is an inventory.
Foreign exchange market	A market for converting the currency of one country into that of another country is called foreign exchange market. It is by far the largest market in the world, in terms of cash value traded, and includes trading between large banks, central banks, currency speculators, multinational corporations, governments, and other financial markets and institutions.
Exchange market	Exchange market refers to the market on which national currencies are bought and sold.
Credit	Credit refers to a recording as positive in the balance of payments, any transaction that gives rise to a payment into the country, such as an export, the sale of an asset, or borrowing from abroad.
Instrument	Instrument refers to an economic variable that is controlled by policy makers and can be used to influence other variables, called targets. Examples are monetary and fiscal policies used to achieve external and internal balance.
Securities market	The securities market is the market for securities, where companies and the government can raise long-term funds.
Security	Security refers to a claim on the borrower future income that is sold by the borrower to the lender. A security is a type of transferable interest representing financial value.
Bid	A bid price is a price offered by a buyer when he/she buys a good. In the context of stock trading on a stock exchange, the bid price is the highest price a buyer of a stock is willing to pay for a share of that given stock.
Market makers	Market makers refer to financial service companies that connect investors and borrowers, either directly or indirectly.
Incentive	An incentive is any factor (financial or non-financial) that provides a motive for a particular course of action, or counts as a reason for preferring one choice to the alternatives.
Profit center	Responsibility center where the manager is accountable for revenues and costs is referred to as a profit center.
Profit	Profit refers to the return to the resource entrepreneurial ability; total revenue minus total cost.
Investment banks	Investment banks, assist public and private corporations in raising funds in the capital markets (both equity and debt), as well as in providing strategic advisory services for mergers, acquisitions and other types of financial transactions. They also act as intermediaries in trading for clients. Investment banks differ from commercial banks, which take deposits and make commercial and retail loans.

Chapter 6. The Foreign Exchange Market

Net income	Net income is equal to the income that a firm has after subtracting costs and expenses from the total revenue. Expenses will typically include tax expense.
Portfolio	In finance, a portfolio is a collection of investments held by an institution or a private individual. Holding but not always a portfolio is part of an investment and risk-limiting strategy called diversification. By owning several assets, certain types of risk (in particular specific risk) can be reduced.
Exporter	A firm that sells its product in another country is an exporter.
Foreign exchange risk	Foreign exchange risk refers to a form of risk that refers to the possibility of experiencing a drop in revenue or an increase in cost in an international transaction due to a change in foreign exchange rates. Importers, exporters, investors, and multinational firms alike are exposed to this risk.
Hedge	Hedge refers to a process of offsetting risk. In the foreign exchange market, hedgers use the forward market to cover a transaction or open position and thereby reduce exchange risk. The term applies most commonly to trade.
Interest	In finance and economics, interest is the price paid by a borrower for the use of a lender's money. In other words, interest is the amount of paid to "rent" money for a period of time.
Speculation	The purchase or sale of an asset in hopes that its price will rise or fall respectively, in order to make a profit is called speculation.
Arbitrage	An arbitrage is a combination of nearly simultaneous transactions designed to profit from an existing discrepancy among prices, exchange rates, and/or interest rates on different markets without assuming risk.
Economy	The income, expenditures, and resources that affect the cost of running a business and household are called an economy.
Black market	Black market refers to an illegal market, in which something is bought and sold outside of official government-sanctioned channels. Black markets tend to arise when a government tries to fix a price without providing an alternative allocation method
Foreign exchange reserves	Foreign exchange reserves are the foreign currency deposits held by national banks of different nations. These are assets of governments which are held in different reserve currencies such as the dollar, euro and yen.
Wall Street Journal	Dow Jones & Company was founded in 1882 by reporters Charles Dow, Edward Jones and Charles Bergstresser. Jones converted the small Customers' Afternoon Letter into The Wall Street Journal, first published in 1889, and began delivery of the Dow Jones News Service via telegraph. The Journal featured the Jones 'Average', the first of several indexes of stock and bond prices on the New York Stock Exchange.
Journal	Book of original entry, in which transactions are recorded in a general ledger system, is referred to as a journal.
Principal	In agency law, one under whose direction an agent acts and for whose benefit that agent acts is a principal.
Agent	A person who makes economic decisions for another economic actor. A hired manager operates as an agent for a firm's owner.
Forward market	A market for exchange of currencies in the future is the forward market. Participants in a forward market enter into a contract to exchange currencies, not today, but at a specified date in the future, typically 30, 60, or 90 days from now, and at a price that is agreed upon.
Fraud	Tax fraud falls into two categories: civil and criminal. Under civil fraud, the IRS may

Chapter 6. The Foreign Exchange Market

Chapter 6. The Foreign Exchange Market

	impose as a penalty of an amount equal to as much as 75 percent of the underpayment.
Financial market	In economics, a financial market is a mechanism which allows people to trade money for securities or commodities such as gold or other precious metals. In general, any commodity market might be considered to be a financial market, if the usual purpose of traders is not the immediate consumption of the commodity, but rather as a means of delaying or accelerating consumption over time.
Commodity	Could refer to any good, but in trade a commodity is usually a raw material or primary product that enters into international trade, such as metals or basic agricultural products.
Futures	Futures refer to contracts for the sale and future delivery of stocks or commodities, wherein either party may waive delivery, and receive or pay, as the case may be, the difference in market price at the time set for delivery.
Option	A contract that gives the purchaser the option to buy or sell the underlying financial instrument at a specified price, called the exercise price or strike price, within a specific period of time.
Jurisdiction	The power of a court to hear and decide a case is called jurisdiction. It is the practical authority granted to a formally constituted body or to a person to deal with and make pronouncements on legal matters and, by implication, to administer justice within a defined area of responsibility.
Authority	Authority in agency law, refers to an agent's ability to affect his principal's legal relations with third parties. Also used to refer to an actor's legal power or ability to do something. In addition, sometimes used to refer to a statute, case, or other legal source that justifies a particular result.
Contract	A contract is a "promise" or an "agreement" that is enforced or recognized by the law. In the civil law, a contract is considered to be part of the general law of obligations.
Affiliates	Local television stations that are associated with a major network are called affiliates. Affiliates agree to preempt time during specified hours for programming provided by the network and carry the advertising contained in the program.
Complexity	The technical sophistication of the product and hence the amount of understanding required to use it is referred to as complexity. It is the opposite of simplicity.
Swap	In finance a swap is a derivative, where two counterparties exchange one stream of cash flows against another stream. These streams are called the legs of the swap. The cash flows are calculated over a notional principal amount. Swaps are often used to hedge certain risks, for instance interest rate risk. Another use is speculation.
Spot transaction	The predominant type of exchange rate transaction, involving the immediate exchange of bank deposits denominated in different currencies is a spot transaction.
Forward transaction	A transaction that involves the exchange of bank deposits denominated in different currencies at some specified future date is a forward transaction.
Futures contract	In finance, a futures contract is a standardized contract, traded on a futures exchange, to buy or sell a certain underlying instrument at a certain date in the future, at a pre-set price. The
Fund	Independent accounting entity with a self-balancing set of accounts segregated for the purposes of carrying on specific activities is referred to as a fund.
Financial risk	The risk related to the inability of the firm to meet its debt obligations as they come due is called financial risk.
Margin	A deposit by a buyer in stocks with a seller or a stockbroker, as security to cover

Chapter 6. The Foreign Exchange Market

Chapter 6. The Foreign Exchange Market

	fluctuations in the market in reference to stocks that the buyer has purchased but for which he has not paid is a margin. Commodities are also traded on margin.
Corporation	A legal entity chartered by a state or the Federal government that is distinct and separate from the individuals who own it is a corporation. This separation gives the corporation unique powers which other legal entities lack.
Payments system	The method of conducting transactions in the economy is referred to as the payments system. Collective term for mechanisms (both paper-backed and electronic) for moving funds, payments and money among financial institutions throughout the nation.
Federal Reserve	The Federal Reserve System was created via the Federal Reserve Act of December 23rd, 1913. All national banks were required to join the system and other banks could join. The Reserve Banks opened for business on November 16th, 1914. Federal Reserve Notes were created as part of the legislation, to provide an elastic supply of currency.
Clearing House Interbank Payments System	The Clearing House Interbank Payments System is the main privately held clearing house for large-value transactions in the United States, settling well over US$1 trillion a day in interbank payments. Together with Fedwire (which is operated by the Federal Reserve), it forms the primary U.S. network for large-value domestic and international payments.
Spot exchange rate	The exchange rate at which a foreign exchange dealer will convert one currency into another that particular day is the spot exchange rate.
Future value	Future value measures what money is worth at a specified time in the future assuming a certain interest rate. This is used in time value of money calculations.
Maturity	Maturity refers to the final payment date of a loan or other financial instrument, after which point no further interest or principal need be paid.
Forward exchange rate	The exchange rates governing forward exchange transactions is called the forward exchange rate.
Forward exchange	When two parties agree to exchange currency and execute a deal at some specific date in the future, we have forward exchange.
Euro	The common currency of a subset of the countries of the EU, adopted January 1, 1999 is called euro.
Counterparty	A counterparty is a legal and financial term. It means a party to a contract. Any legal entity can be a counterparty.
Spot market	Spot market refers to a market in which commodities are bought and sold for cash and immediate delivery.
Interest Rate Parity	The Interest Rate Parity is the basic identity that relates interest rates and exchange rates. The identity is theoretical, and usually follows from assumptions imposed in economics models.
Rate differential	The controversial practice of newspapers charging significantly higher rates to national advertisers as compared to local accounts is called rate differential.
Interest rate	The rate of return on bonds, loans, or deposits. When one speaks of 'the' interest rate, it is usually in a model where there is only one.
Derivative	A derivative is a generic term for specific types of investments from which payoffs over time are derived from the performance of assets (such as commodities, shares or bonds), interest rates, exchange rates, or indices (such as a stock market index, consumer price index (CPI) or an index of weather conditions).
Emerging market	The term emerging market is commonly used to describe business and market activity in

Chapter 6. The Foreign Exchange Market

Chapter 6. The Foreign Exchange Market

	industrializing or emerging regions of the world.
Eurocurrency	Eurocurrency is the term used to describe deposits residing in banks that are located outside the borders of the country that issues the currency the deposit is denominated in.
Money market	The money market, in macroeconomics and international finance, refers to the equilibration of demand for a country's domestic money to its money supply; market for short-term financial instruments.
Premium	Premium refers to the fee charged by an insurance company for an insurance policy. The rate of losses must be relatively predictable: In order to set the premium (prices) insurers must be able to estimate them accurately.
Turnover	Turnover in a financial context refers to the rate at which a provider of goods cycles through its average inventory. Turnover in a human resources context refers to the characteristic of a given company or industry, relative to rate at which an employer gains and loses staff.
Consolidation	The combination of two or more firms, generally of equal size and market power, to form an entirely new entity is a consolidation.
Shares	Shares refer to an equity security, representing a shareholder's ownership of a corporation. Shares are one of a finite number of equal portions in the capital of a company, entitling the owner to a proportion of distributed, non-reinvested profits known as dividends and to a portion of the value of the company in case of liquidation.
Financial capital	Common stock, preferred stock, bonds, and retained earnings are financial capital. Financial capital appears on the corporate balance sheet under long-term liabilities and equity.
Forward rate	Forward rate refers to the forward exchange rate, this is the exchange rate on a forward market transaction.
Swap rate	Swap rate is the difference between the spot and forward exchange rates.
Points	Loan origination fees that may be deductible as interest by a buyer of property. A seller of property who pays points reduces the selling price by the amount of the points paid for the buyer.
Spot rate	Spot rate refers to the rate at which the currency is traded for immediate delivery. It is the existing cash price.
Cross rates	The exchange rate of two foreign currencies expressed in terms of a third currency, neither of which is the US Dollar are called cross rates.
Standing	Standing refers to the legal requirement that anyone seeking to challenge a particular action in court must demonstrate that such action substantially affects his legitimate interests before he will be entitled to bring suit.
Ending rate	The spot exchange rate when budget and performance are being compared is referred to as the ending rate.
Holder	A person in possession of a document of title or an instrument payable or indorsed to him, his order, or to bearer is a holder.
Financial instrument	Formal or legal documents in writing, such as contracts, deeds, wills, bonds, leases, and mortgages is referred to as a financial instrument.
International Business	International business refers to any firm that engages in international trade or investment.
Yield	The interest rate that equates a future value or an annuity to a given present value is a yield.

Chapter 6. The Foreign Exchange Market

Forward premium	The difference between a forward exchange rate and the spot exchange rate, expressed as an annualized percentage return on buying foreign currency spot and selling it forward is a forward premium.
Discount	The difference between the face value of a bond and its selling price, when a bond is sold for less than its face value it's referred to as a discount.
Operation	A standardized method or technique that is performed repetitively, often on different materials resulting in different finished goods is called an operation.
Citibank	In April of 2006, Citibank struck a deal with 7-Eleven to put its ATMs in over 5,500 convenience stores in the U.S. In the same month, it also announced it would sell all of its Buffalo and Rochester New York branches and accounts to M&T Bank.
National bank	A National bank refers to federally chartered banks. They are an ordinary private bank which operates nationally (as opposed to regionally or locally or even internationally).
Chief executive officer	A chief executive officer is the highest-ranking corporate officer or executive officer of a corporation, or agency. In closely held corporations, it is general business culture that the office chief executive officer is also the chairman of the board.
Preparation	Preparation refers to usually the first stage in the creative process. It includes education and formal training.
Service	Service refers to a "non tangible product" that is not embodied in a physical good and that typically effects some change in another product, person, or institution. Contrasts with good.
Union	A worker association that bargains with employers over wages and working conditions is called a union.
Conversion	Conversion refers to any distinct act of dominion wrongfully exerted over another's personal property in denial of or inconsistent with his rights therein. That tort committed by a person who deals with chattels not belonging to him in a manner that is inconsistent with the ownership of the lawful owner.
Legal tender	Legal tender is payment that, by law, cannot be refused in settlement of a debt denominated in the same currency.
Tender	An unconditional offer of payment, consisting in the actual production in money or legal tender of a sum not less than the amount due.
Insurance	Insurance refers to a system by which individuals can reduce their exposure to risk of large losses by spreading the risks among a large number of persons.
Cost of goods sold	In accounting, the cost of goods sold describes the direct expenses incurred in producing a particular good for sale, including the actual cost of materials that comprise the good, and direct labor expense in putting the good in salable condition.
Dividend	Amount of corporate profits paid out for each share of stock is referred to as dividend.
Expense	In accounting, an expense represents an event in which an asset is used up or a liability is incurred. In terms of the accounting equation, expenses reduce owners' equity.
Translation exposure	The foreign-located assets and liabilities of a multinational corporation, which are denominated in foreign currency units, and are exposed to losses and gains due to changing exchange rates is called accounting or translation exposure.
Income statement	Income statement refers to a financial statement that presents the revenues and expenses and resulting net income or net loss of a company for a specific period of time.
Balance sheet	A statement of the assets, liabilities, and net worth of a firm or individual at some given

Chapter 6. The Foreign Exchange Market

time often at the end of its "fiscal year," is referred to as a balance sheet.

Sunk cost — Sunk cost refers to a cost that has been incurred and cannot be recovered to any significant degree.

Chapter 6. The Foreign Exchange Market

Chapter 7. Foreign Currency Derivatives

Financial derivatives	Instruments that have payoffs that are linked to previously issued securities, used as risk reduction tools are referred to as financial derivatives.
Financial manager	Managers who make recommendations to top executives regarding strategies for improving the financial strength of a firm are referred to as a financial manager.
Speculation	The purchase or sale of an asset in hopes that its price will rise or fall respectively, in order to make a profit is called speculation.
Derivative	A derivative is a generic term for specific types of investments from which payoffs over time are derived from the performance of assets (such as commodities, shares or bonds), interest rates, exchange rates, or indices (such as a stock market index, consumer price index (CPI) or an index of weather conditions).
Management	Management characterizes the process of leading and directing all or part of an organization, often a business, through the deployment and manipulation of resources. Early twentieth-century management writer Mary Parker Follett defined management as "the art of getting things done through people."
Instrument	Instrument refers to an economic variable that is controlled by policy makers and can be used to influence other variables, called targets. Examples are monetary and fiscal policies used to achieve external and internal balance.
Cash flow	In finance, cash flow refers to the amounts of cash being received and spent by a business during a defined period of time, sometimes tied to a specific project. Most of the time they are being used to determine gaps in the liquid position of a company.
Hedging	A technique for avoiding a risk by making a counteracting transaction is referred to as hedging.
Profit	Profit refers to the return to the resource entrepreneurial ability; total revenue minus total cost.
Financial instrument	Formal or legal documents in writing, such as contracts, deeds, wills, bonds, leases, and mortgages is referred to as a financial instrument.
Currency futures contract	A futures contract that may be used for hedging or speculation in foreign exchange is called a currency futures contract.
Futures contract	In finance, a futures contract is a standardized contract, traded on a futures exchange, to buy or sell a certain underlying instrument at a certain date in the future, at a pre-set price. The
Foreign exchange	In finance, foreign exchange means currencies, such as U.S. Dollars and Euros. These are traded on foreign exchange markets.
Contract	A contract is a "promise" or an "agreement" that is enforced or recognized by the law. In the civil law, a contract is considered to be part of the general law of obligations.
Exchange	The trade of things of value between buyer and seller so that each is better off after the trade is called the exchange.
Futures	Futures refer to contracts for the sale and future delivery of stocks or commodities, wherein either party may waive delivery, and receive or pay, as the case may be, the difference in market price at the time set for delivery.
Futures market	Futures market refers to a market for exchange in futures contracts. That is, participants contract to exchange currencies, not today, but at a specified calendar date in the future, and at a price that is agreed upon today.

Chapter 7. Foreign Currency Derivatives

Chapter 7. Foreign Currency Derivatives

Market	A market is, as defined in economics, a social arrangement that allows buyers and sellers to discover information and carry out a voluntary exchange of goods or services.
Chicago Mercantile Exchange	The Chicago Mercantile Exchange is the largest futures exchange in the United States. It has four major product areas: short term interest rates, stock market indexes, foreign exchange, and commodities. It has the largest options and futures contracts open interest (number of contracts outstanding) of any futures exchange in the world, which indicates a very high liquidity. This is vital to the success of any stock or futures exchange.
Notional principal	The amount on which interest is being paid in a swap arrangement is known as notional principal. In interest rate swaps the notional amounts are not exchanged, so any credit risk is limited to the net amount payable plus a potential future exposure factor.
Principal	In agency law, one under whose direction an agent acts and for whose benefit that agent acts is a principal.
Collateral	Property that is pledged to the lender to guarantee payment in the event that the borrower is unable to make debt payments is called collateral.
Margin	A deposit by a buyer in stocks with a seller or a stockbroker, as security to cover fluctuations in the market in reference to stocks that the buyer has purchased but for which he has not paid is a margin. Commodities are also traded on margin.
Marked to market	Repriced and settled in the margin account at the end of every trading day to reflect any change in the value of the futures contract is called marked to market.
Closing	The finalization of a real estate sales transaction that passes title to the property from the seller to the buyer is referred to as a closing. Closing is a sales term which refers to the process of making a sale. It refers to reaching the final step, which may be an exchange of money or acquiring a signature.
Buyer	A buyer refers to a role in the buying center with formal authority and responsibility to select the supplier and negotiate the terms of the contract.
Broker	In commerce, a broker is a party that mediates between a buyer and a seller. A broker who also acts as a seller or as a buyer becomes a principal party to the deal.
Open interest	The number of contracts outstanding is an open interest. That is, the total contracts for a specific strike price and expiration date, that have been traded, but have not yet expired or been terminated via early exercise.
Maturity	Maturity refers to the final payment date of a loan or other financial instrument, after which point no further interest or principal need be paid.
Interest	In finance and economics, interest is the price paid by a borrower for the use of a lender's money. In other words, interest is the amount of paid to "rent" money for a period of time.
Short position	In finance, a short position in a security, such as a stock or a Bond, means the holder of the position has sold a security that he does not own, with the intention to buy it back at a later time at a lower price.
Maturity date	The date on which the final payment on a bond is due from the bond issuer to the investor is a maturity date.
Spot market	Spot market refers to a market in which commodities are bought and sold for cash and immediate delivery.
Valuation	In finance, valuation is the process of estimating the market value of a financial asset or liability. They can be done on assets (for example, investments in marketable securities such as stocks, options, business enterprises, or intangible assets such as patents and trademarks) or on liabilities (e.g., Bonds issued by a company).

Chapter 7. Foreign Currency Derivatives

Spot exchange rate	The exchange rate at which a foreign exchange dealer will convert one currency into another that particular day is the spot exchange rate.
Exchange rate	Exchange rate refers to the price at which one country's currency trades for another, typically on the exchange market.
Long position	In finance, a long position in a security, such as a stock or a bond, means the holder of the position owns the security.
Service	Service refers to a "non tangible product" that is not embodied in a physical good and that typically effects some change in another product, person, or institution. Contrasts with good.
Fixed price	Fixed price is a phrase used to mean that no bargaining is allowed over the price of a good or, less commonly, a service.
Option	A contract that gives the purchaser the option to buy or sell the underlying financial instrument at a specified price, called the exercise price or strike price, within a specific period of time.
Grantor	A transferor of property. The creator of a trust is usually referred to as the grantor of the trust. In a franchise agreement, for example, the party selling the franchise is the grantor
Holder	A person in possession of a document of title or an instrument payable or indorsed to him, his order, or to bearer is a holder.
Strike price	The strike price is a key variable in a derivatives contract between two parties. Where the contract requires delivery of the underlying instrument, the trade will be at the strike price, regardless of the spot price of the underlying at that time.
Premium	Premium refers to the fee charged by an insurance company for an insurance policy. The rate of losses must be relatively predictable: In order to set the premium (prices) insurers must be able to estimate them accurately.
Strike	The withholding of labor services by an organized group of workers is referred to as a strike.
American option	A stock option that can be exercized at any time up to the expiration date of the contract is referred to as American option.
European option	An option that can be exercized only at the expiration date of the contract is referred to as european option.
Domestic	From or in one's own country. A domestic producer is one that produces inside the home country. A domestic price is the price inside the home country. Opposite of 'foreign' or 'world.'.
Exercise price	Exercise price refers to the price at which the purchaser of an option has the right to buy or sell the underlying financial instrument. Also known as the strike price.
Capital market	A financial market in which long-term debt and equity instruments are traded is referred to as a capital market. The capital market includes the stock market and the bond market.
Capital	Capital generally refers to financial wealth, especially that used to start or maintain a business. In classical economics, capital is one of four factors of production, the others being land and labor and entrepreneurship.
Stock exchange	A stock exchange is a corporation or mutual organization which provides facilities for stock brokers and traders, to trade company stocks and other securities.
Stock	In financial terminology, stock is the capital raized by a corporation, through the issuance and sale of shares.

Chapter 7. Foreign Currency Derivatives

Chapter 7. Foreign Currency Derivatives

Firm	An organization that employs resources to produce a good or service for profit and owns and operates one or more plants is referred to as a firm.
Euro	The common currency of a subset of the countries of the EU, adopted January 1, 1999 is called euro.
Financial institution	A financial institution acts as an agent that provides financial services for its clients. Financial institutions generally fall under financial regulation from a government authority.
Liquidity	Liquidity refers to the capacity to turn assets into cash, or the amount of assets in a portfolio that have that capacity.
Financial risk	The risk related to the inability of the firm to meet its debt obligations as they come due is called financial risk.
Counterparty	A counterparty is a legal and financial term. It means a party to a contract. Any legal entity can be a counterparty.
Swap	In finance a swap is a derivative, where two counterparties exchange one stream of cash flows against another stream. These streams are called the legs of the swap. The cash flows are calculated over a notional principal amount. Swaps are often used to hedge certain risks, for instance interest rate risk. Another use is speculation.
Chief financial officer	Chief financial officer refers to executive responsible for overseeing the financial operations of an organization.
Bid	A bid price is a price offered by a buyer when he/she buys a good. In the context of stock trading on a stock exchange, the bid price is the highest price a buyer of a stock is willing to pay for a share of that given stock.
Call option	Call option refers to an option contract that provides the right to buy a security at a specified price within a certain time period.
Market value	Market value refers to the price of an asset agreed on between a willing buyer and a willing seller; the price an asset could demand if it is sold on the open market.
Currency speculation	Involves short-term movement of funds from one currency to another in hopes of profiting from shifts in exchange rates are referred to as currency speculation.
Total cost	The sum of fixed cost and variable cost is referred to as total cost.
Foreign exchange market	A market for converting the currency of one country into that of another country is called foreign exchange market. It is by far the largest market in the world, in terms of cash value traded, and includes trading between large banks, central banks, currency speculators, multinational corporations, governments, and other financial markets and institutions.
Exchange market	Exchange market refers to the market on which national currencies are bought and sold.
Hedge	Hedge refers to a process of offsetting risk. In the foreign exchange market, hedgers use the forward market to cover a transaction or open position and thereby reduce exchange risk. The term applies most commonly to trade.
Insurance	Insurance refers to a system by which individuals can reduce their exposure to risk of large losses by spreading the risks among a large number of persons.
Securities and exchange commission	Securities and exchange commission refers to U.S. government agency that determines the financial statements that public companies must provide to stockholders and the measurement rules that they must use in producing those statements.
Security	Security refers to a claim on the borrower future income that is sold by the borrower to the lender. A security is a type of transferable interest representing financial value.

Chapter 7. Foreign Currency Derivatives

Chapter 7. Foreign Currency Derivatives

Audit	An examination of the financial reports to ensure that they represent what they claim and conform with generally accepted accounting principles is referred to as audit.
Forward rate	Forward rate refers to the forward exchange rate, this is the exchange rate on a forward market transaction.
Spot rate	Spot rate refers to the rate at which the currency is traded for immediate delivery. It is the existing cash price.
Time horizon	A time horizon is a fixed point of time in the future at which point certain processes will be evaluated or assumed to end. It is necessary in an accounting, finance or risk management regime to assign such a fixed horizon time so that alternatives can be evaluated for performance over the same period of time.
Opportunity cost	The cost of something in terms of opportunity foregone. The opportunity cost to a country of producing a unit more of a good, such as for export or to replace an import, is the quantity of some other good that could have been produced instead.
Interest income	Interest income refers to payments of income to those who supply the economy with capital.
Forward market	A market for exchange of currencies in the future is the forward market. Participants in a forward market enter into a contract to exchange currencies, not today, but at a specified date in the future, typically 30, 60, or 90 days from now, and at a price that is agreed upon.
Return on investment	Return on investment refers to the return a businessperson gets on the money he and other owners invest in the firm; for example, a business that earned $100 on a $1,000 investment would have a ROI of 10 percent: 100 divided by 1000.
Investment	Investment refers to spending for the production and accumulation of capital and additions to inventories. In a financial sense, buying an asset with the expectation of making a return.
Fund	Independent accounting entity with a self-balancing set of accounts segregated for the purposes of carrying on specific activities is referred to as a fund.
Gain	In finance, gain is a profit or an increase in value of an investment such as a stock or bond. Gain is calculated by fair market value or the proceeds from the sale of the investment minus the sum of the purchase price and all costs associated with it.
Money market	The money market, in macroeconomics and international finance, refers to the equilibration of demand for a country's domestic money to its money supply; market for short-term financial instruments.
Holding	The holding is a court's determination of a matter of law based on the issue presented in the particular case. In other words: under this law, with these facts, this result.
Operation	A standardized method or technique that is performed repetitively, often on different materials resulting in different finished goods is called an operation.
Accounting	A system that collects and processes financial information about an organization and reports that information to decision makers is referred to as accounting.
Gross profit	Net sales less cost of goods sold is called gross profit.
Put option	An option contract that provides the right to sell a security at a specified price within a specified period of time is a put option.
Intrinsic value	Intrinsic value refers to as applied to a warrant, this represents the market value of common stock minus the exercise price. The difference is then multiplied by the number of shares each warrant entitles the holder to purchase.
Standard	A measure of the spread or dispersion of a series of numbers around the expected value is the

Chapter 7. Foreign Currency Derivatives

deviation	standard deviation. The standard deviation tells us how well the expected value represents a series of values.
Interest rate	The rate of return on bonds, loans, or deposits. When one speaks of 'the' interest rate, it is usually in a model where there is only one.
Matching	Matching refers to an accounting concept that establishes when expenses are recognized. Expenses are matched with the revenues they helped to generate and are recognized when those revenues are recognized.
Volatility	Volatility refers to the extent to which an economic variable, such as a price or an exchange rate, moves up and down over time.
Market price	Market price is an economic concept with commonplace familiarity; it is the price that a good or service is offered at, or will fetch, in the marketplace; it is of interest mainly in the study of microeconomics.
Residual value	Residual value is one of the constituents of a leasing calculus or operation. It describes the future value of a good in terms of percentage of depreciation of its initial value.
Residual	Residual payments can refer to an ongoing stream of payments in respect of the completion of past achievements.
Short run	Short run refers to a period of time that permits an increase or decrease in current production volume with existing capacity, but one that is too short to permit enlargement of that capacity itself (eg, the building of new plants, training of additional workers, etc.).
Misuse	A defense that relieves a seller of product liability if the user abnormally misused the product is called misuse. Products must be designed to protect against foreseeable misuse.
Technology	The body of knowledge and techniques that can be used to combine economic resources to produce goods and services is called technology.
Risk aversion	Risk aversion is the reluctance of a person to accept a bargain with an uncertain payoff rather than another bargain with a more certain but possibly lower expected payoff.
Stock market	An organized marketplace in which common stocks are traded. In the United States, the largest stock market is the New York Stock Exchange, on which are traded the stocks of the largest U.S. companies.
Takeover	A takeover in business refers to one company (the acquirer) purchasing another (the target). Such events resemble mergers, but without the formation of a new company.
Utility	Utility refers to the want-satisfying power of a good or service; the satisfaction or pleasure a consumer obtains from the consumption of a good or service.
Consideration	Consideration in contract law, a basic requirement for an enforceable agreement under traditional contract principles, defined in this text as legal value, bargained for and given in exchange for an act or promise. In corporation law, cash or property contributed to a corporation in exchange for shares, or a promise to contribute such cash or property.
Variable	A variable is something measured by a number; it is used to analyze what happens to other things when the size of that number changes.
Bankers Trust	The Bankers Trust is a historic U.S. banking organization that was acquired by Deutsche Bank in 1998. It was originally set up when banks could not perform trust company services. A consortium of banks all invested in a new trust company, which was called Bankers Trust, so that they could refer clients to that company knowing that Bankers Trust would not try and poach their customer.
Trust	An arrangement in which shareholders of independent firms agree to give up their stock in

Go to Cram101.com for the Practice Tests for this Chapter.

Chapter 7. Foreign Currency Derivatives

Chapter 7. Foreign Currency Derivatives

	exchange for trust certificates that entitle them to a share of the trust's common profits.
Harvard Business Review	Harvard Business Review is a research-based magazine written for business practitioners, it claims a high ranking business readership and enjoys the reverence of academics, executives, and management consultants. It has been the frequent publishing home for well known scholars and management thinkers.
Wall Street Journal	Dow Jones & Company was founded in 1882 by reporters Charles Dow, Edward Jones and Charles Bergstresser. Jones converted the small Customers' Afternoon Letter into The Wall Street Journal, first published in 1889, and began delivery of the Dow Jones News Service via telegraph. The Journal featured the Jones 'Average', the first of several indexes of stock and bond prices on the New York Stock Exchange.
Journal	Book of original entry, in which transactions are recorded in a general ledger system, is referred to as a journal.
Contrarian	A contrarian is sometimes thought of as perma-bears—market participants who are permanently biased to a bear market view. However, the contrarian is not biased specifically towards a negative view of the price trend in a market, but rather takes a contrary position to the prevailing market trend, whether that trend is positive or negative.
Yield	The interest rate that equates a future value or an annuity to a given present value is a yield.
Expense	In accounting, an expense represents an event in which an asset is used up or a liability is incurred. In terms of the accounting equation, expenses reduce owners' equity.
Inputs	The inputs used by a firm or an economy are the labor, raw materials, electricity and other resources it uses to produce its outputs.
Federal Reserve	The Federal Reserve System was created via the Federal Reserve Act of December 23rd, 1913. All national banks were required to join the system and other banks could join. The Reserve Banks opened for business on November 16th, 1914. Federal Reserve Notes were created as part of the legislation, to provide an elastic supply of currency.
Underwriting	The process of selling securities and, at the same time, assuring the seller a specified price is underwriting. Underwriting is done by investment bankers and represents a form of risk taking.
Commodity	Could refer to any good, but in trade a commodity is usually a raw material or primary product that enters into international trade, such as metals or basic agricultural products.
Bond	Bond refers to a debt instrument, issued by a borrower and promising a specified stream of payments to the purchaser, usually regular interest payments plus a final repayment of principal.
Bank of England	The Bank of England is the central bank of the United Kingdom, sometimes known as "The Old Lady of Threadneedle Street" or "The Old Lady".
Supply	Supply is the aggregate amount of any material good that can be called into being at a certain price point; it comprises one half of the equation of supply and demand. In classical economic theory, a curve representing supply is one of the factors that produce price.
Bail	Bail refers to an amount of money the defendant pays to the court upon release from custody as security that he or she will return for trial.
Securities market	The securities market is the market for securities, where companies and the government can raise long-term funds.
Stockbroker	A registered representative who works as a market intermediary to buy and sell securities for clients is a stockbroker.

Chapter 7. Foreign Currency Derivatives

Chapter 7. Foreign Currency Derivatives

Specialist	A specialist is a trader who makes a market in one or several stocks and holds the limit order book for those stocks.
Bankruptcy	Bankruptcy is a legally declared inability or impairment of ability of an individual or organization to pay their creditors.
Back office	A back office is a part of most corporations where tasks dedicated to running the company itself take place.
Subsidiary	A company that is controlled by another company or corporation is a subsidiary.
License	A license in the sphere of Intellectual Property Rights (IPR) is a document, contract or agreement giving permission or the 'right' to a legally-definable entity to do something (such as manufacture a product or to use a service), or to apply something (such as a trademark), with the objective of achieving commercial gain.
Balance	In banking and accountancy, the outstanding balance is the amount of money owned, (or due), that remains in a deposit account (or a loan account) at a given date, after all past remittances, payments and withdrawal have been accounted for. It can be positive (then, in the balance sheet of a firm, it is an asset) or negative (a liability).
Purchasing	Purchasing refers to the function in a firm that searches for quality material resources, finds the best suppliers, and negotiates the best price for goods and services.
Asset	An item of property, such as land, capital, money, a share in ownership, or a claim on others for future payment, such as a bond or a bank deposit is an asset.
Government bond	A government bond is a bond issued by a national government denominated in the country's own currency. Bonds issued by national governments in foreign currencies are normally referred to as sovereign bonds.
Financial statement	Financial statement refers to a summary of all the transactions that have occurred over a particular period.
Proprietary	Proprietary indicates that a party, or proprietor, exercises private ownership, control or use over an item of property, usually to the exclusion of other parties. Where a party, holds or claims proprietary interests in relation to certain types of property (eg. a creative literary work, or software), that property may also be the subject of intellectual property law (eg. copyright or patents).
Balance sheet	A statement of the assets, liabilities, and net worth of a firm or individual at some given time often at the end of its "fiscal year," is referred to as a balance sheet.
Regulation	Regulation refers to restrictions state and federal laws place on business with regard to the conduct of its activities.
Eastman Kodak	Eastman Kodak Company is an American multinational public company producing photographic materials and equipment. Long known for its wide range of photographic film products, it has focused in recent years on three main businesses: digital photography, health imaging, and printing. This company remains the largest supplier of films in the world, both for the amateur and professional markets.
Internal audit	An internal audit is an independent appraisal of operations, conducted under the direction of management, to assess the effectiveness of internal administrative and accounting controls and help ensure conformance with managerial policies.
Front office	In Business, front office refers to Sales and Marketing divisions of a company. It may also refer to other divisions in a company that involves interactions with customers.
Merrill Lynch	Merrill Lynch through its subsidiaries and affiliates, provides capital markets services, investment banking and advisory services, wealth management, asset management, insurance,

Chapter 7. Foreign Currency Derivatives

Chapter 7. Foreign Currency Derivatives

	banking and related products and services on a global basis. It is best known for its Global Private Client services and its strong sales force.
Default	In finance, default occurs when a debtor has not met its legal obligations according to the debt contract, e.g. it has not made a scheduled payment, or violated a covenant (condition) of the debt contract.
Bail out	Bail out in economics and finance is a term used to describe a situation where a bankrupt or nearly bankrupt entity, such as a corporation or a bank, is given a fresh injection of liquidity.
Leadership	Management merely consists of leadership applied to business situations; or in other words: management forms a sub-set of the broader process of leadership.

Chapter 7. Foreign Currency Derivatives

Chapter 8. Transaction Exposure

Foreign exchange exposure	The risk that future changes in a country's exchange rate will hurt the firm is a foreign exchange exposure.
Financial manager	Managers who make recommendations to top executives regarding strategies for improving the financial strength of a firm are referred to as a financial manager.
Foreign exchange	In finance, foreign exchange means currencies, such as U.S. Dollars and Euros. These are traded on foreign exchange markets.
Market value	Market value refers to the price of an asset agreed on between a willing buyer and a willing seller; the price an asset could demand if it is sold on the open market.
Cash flow	In finance, cash flow refers to the amounts of cash being received and spent by a business during a defined period of time, sometimes tied to a specific project. Most of the time they are being used to determine gaps in the liquid position of a company.
Exchange	The trade of things of value between buyer and seller so that each is better off after the trade is called the exchange.
Market	A market is, as defined in economics, a social arrangement that allows buyers and sellers to discover information and carry out a voluntary exchange of goods or services.
Firm	An organization that employs resources to produce a good or service for profit and owns and operates one or more plants is referred to as a firm.
Exchange rate	Exchange rate refers to the price at which one country's currency trades for another, typically on the exchange market.
Transaction exposure	Transaction exposure refers to foreign exchange gains and losses resulting from actual international transactions. These may be hedged through the foreign exchange market, the money market, or the currency futures market.
Competitiveness	Competitiveness usually refers to characteristics that permit a firm to compete effectively with other firms due to low cost or superior technology, perhaps internationally.
Translation exposure	The foreign-located assets and liabilities of a multinational corporation, which are denominated in foreign currency units, and are exposed to losses and gains due to changing exchange rates is called accounting or translation exposure.
Financial statement	Financial statement refers to a summary of all the transactions that have occurred over a particular period.
Foreign subsidiary	A company owned in a foreign country by another company is referred to as foreign subsidiary.
Consolidated financial statement	A consolidated financial statement refers to a financial statement of a parent company and its subsidiaries that has been combined into a single set of financial statements as if the companies were one.
Accounting	A system that collects and processes financial information about an organization and reports that information to decision makers is referred to as accounting.
Subsidiary	A company that is controlled by another company or corporation is a subsidiary.
Equity	Equity is the name given to the set of legal principles, in countries following the English common law tradition, which supplement strict rules of law where their application would operate harshly, so as to achieve what is sometimes referred to as "natural justice."
Deductible	The dollar sum of costs that an insured individual must pay before the insurer begins to pay is called deductible.

Chapter 8. Transaction Exposure

Chapter 8. Transaction Exposure

Gain	In finance, gain is a profit or an increase in value of an investment such as a stock or bond. Gain is calculated by fair market value or the proceeds from the sale of the investment minus the sum of the purchase price and all costs associated with it.
Management	Management characterizes the process of leading and directing all or part of an organization, often a business, through the deployment and manipulation of resources. Early twentieth-century management writer Mary Parker Follett defined management as "the art of getting things done through people."
Policy	Similar to a script in that a policy can be a less than completely rational decision-making method. Involves the use of a pre-existing set of decision steps for any problem that presents itself.
Interest rate	The rate of return on bonds, loans, or deposits. When one speaks of 'the' interest rate, it is usually in a model where there is only one.
Commodity	Could refer to any good, but in trade a commodity is usually a raw material or primary product that enters into international trade, such as metals or basic agricultural products.
Interest	In finance and economics, interest is the price paid by a borrower for the use of a lender's money. In other words, interest is the amount of paid to "rent" money for a period of time.
Hedging	A technique for avoiding a risk by making a counteracting transaction is referred to as hedging.
Contract	A contract is a "promise" or an "agreement" that is enforced or recognized by the law. In the civil law, a contract is considered to be part of the general law of obligations.
Asset	An item of property, such as land, capital, money, a share in ownership, or a claim on others for future payment, such as a bond or a bank deposit is an asset.
Net present value	Net present value is a standard method in finance of capital budgeting – the planning of long-term investments. Using this method a potential investment project should be undertaken if the present value of all cash inflows minus the present value of all cash outflows (which equals the net present value) is greater than zero.
Present value	The value today of a stream of payments and/or receipts over time in the future and/or the past, converted to the present using an interest rate. If X t is the amount in period t and r the interest rate, then present value at time t=0 is V = ?T /t.
Variance	Variance refers to a measure of how much an economic or statistical variable varies across values or observations. Its calculation is the same as that of the covariance, being the covariance of the variable with itself.
Hedge	Hedge refers to a process of offsetting risk. In the foreign exchange market, hedgers use the forward market to cover a transaction or open position and thereby reduce exchange risk. The term applies most commonly to trade.
Currency risk	Currency risk is a form of risk that arises from the change in price of one currency against another. Whenever investors or companies have assets or business operations across national borders, they face currency risk if their positions are not hedged.
Distribution	Distribution in economics, the manner in which total output and income is distributed among individuals or factors.
Stockholder	A stockholder is an individual or company (including a corporation) that legally owns one or more shares of stock in a joined stock company. The shareholders are the owners of a corporation. Companies listed at the stock market strive to enhance shareholder value.
Preference	The act of a debtor in paying or securing one or more of his creditors in a manner more favorable to them than to other creditors or to the exclusion of such other creditors is a

Chapter 8. Transaction Exposure

Chapter 8. Transaction Exposure

preference. In the absence of statute, a preference is perfectly good, but to be legal it must be bona fide, and not a mere subterfuge of the debtor to secure a future benefit to himself or to prevent the application of his property to his debts.

Portfolio	In finance, a portfolio is a collection of investments held by an institution or a private individual. Holding but not always a portfolio is part of an investment and risk-limiting strategy called diversification. By owning several assets, certain types of risk (in particular specific risk) can be reduced.
Expense	In accounting, an expense represents an event in which an asset is used up or a liability is incurred. In terms of the accounting equation, expenses reduce owners' equity.
Agency theory	The analysis of how asymmetric information problems affect economic behavior is known as agency theory.
Shareholder	A shareholder is an individual or company (including a corporation) that legally owns one or more shares of stock in a joined stock company.
Income statement	Income statement refers to a financial statement that presents the revenues and expenses and resulting net income or net loss of a company for a specific period of time.
Interest expense	The cost a business incurs to borrow money. With respect to bonds payable, the interest expense is calculated by multiplying the market rate of interest by the carrying value of the bonds on the date of the payment.
Valuation	In finance, valuation is the process of estimating the market value of a financial asset or liability. They can be done on assets (for example, investments in marketable securities such as stocks, options, business enterprises, or intangible assets such as patents and trademarks) or on liabilities (e.g., Bonds issued by a company).
Forward market	A market for exchange of currencies in the future is the forward market. Participants in a forward market enter into a contract to exchange currencies, not today, but at a specified date in the future, typically 30, 60, or 90 days from now, and at a price that is agreed upon.
Dividend	Amount of corporate profits paid out for each share of stock is referred to as dividend.
Futures	Futures refer to contracts for the sale and future delivery of stocks or commodities, wherein either party may waive delivery, and receive or pay, as the case may be, the difference in market price at the time set for delivery.
Option	A contract that gives the purchaser the option to buy or sell the underlying financial instrument at a specified price, called the exercise price or strike price, within a specific period of time.
Derivative	A derivative is a generic term for specific types of investments from which payoffs over time are derived from the performance of assets (such as commodities, shares or bonds), interest rates, exchange rates, or indices (such as a stock market index, consumer price index (CPI) or an index of weather conditions).
Swap	In finance a swap is a derivative, where two counterparties exchange one stream of cash flows against another stream. These streams are called the legs of the swap. The cash flows are calculated over a notional principal amount. Swaps are often used to hedge certain risks, for instance interest rate risk. Another use is speculation.
Chief financial officer	Chief financial officer refers to executive responsible for overseeing the financial operations of an organization.
Investment interest	Payment for the use of funds used to acquire assets that produce investment income. The deduction for investment interest is limited to net investment income for the tax year.

Chapter 8. Transaction Exposure

Chapter 8. Transaction Exposure

Spot exchange rate	The exchange rate at which a foreign exchange dealer will convert one currency into another that particular day is the spot exchange rate.
Cost of capital	Cost of capital refers to the percentage cost of funds used for acquiring resources for an organization, typically a weighted average of the firms cost of equity and cost of debt.
Forward rate	Forward rate refers to the forward exchange rate, this is the exchange rate on a forward market transaction.
Strike price	The strike price is a key variable in a derivatives contract between two parties. Where the contract requires delivery of the underlying instrument, the trade will be at the strike price, regardless of the spot price of the underlying at that time.
Put option	An option contract that provides the right to sell a security at a specified price within a specified period of time is a put option.
Investment	Investment refers to spending for the production and accumulation of capital and additions to inventories. In a financial sense, buying an asset with the expectation of making a return.
Spot rate	Spot rate refers to the rate at which the currency is traded for immediate delivery. It is the existing cash price.
Discount	The difference between the face value of a bond and its selling price, when a bond is sold for less than its face value it's referred to as a discount.
Premium	Premium refers to the fee charged by an insurance company for an insurance policy. The rate of losses must be relatively predictable: In order to set the premium (prices) insurers must be able to estimate them accurately.
Service	Service refers to a "non tangible product" that is not embodied in a physical good and that typically effects some change in another product, person, or institution. Contrasts with good.
Capital	Capital generally refers to financial wealth, especially that used to start or maintain a business. In classical economics, capital is one of four factors of production, the others being land and labor and entrepreneurship.
Strike	The withholding of labor services by an organized group of workers is referred to as a strike.
Manufacturing	Production of goods primarily by the application of labor and capital to raw materials and other intermediate inputs, in contrast to agriculture, mining, forestry, fishing, and services a manufacturing.
Margin	A deposit by a buyer in stocks with a seller or a stockbroker, as security to cover fluctuations in the market in reference to stocks that the buyer has purchased but for which he has not paid is a margin. Commodities are also traded on margin.
Budget	Budget refers to an account, usually for a year, of the planned expenditures and the expected receipts of an entity. For a government, the receipts are tax revenues.
Fund	Independent accounting entity with a self-balancing set of accounts segregated for the purposes of carrying on specific activities is referred to as a fund.
Rate of exchange	Rate of exchange refers to the price paid in one's own money to acquire 1 unit of a foreign currency; the rate at which the money of one nation is exchanged for the money of another nation.
Foreign exchange risk	Foreign exchange risk refers to a form of risk that refers to the possibility of experiencing a drop in revenue or an increase in cost in an international transaction due to a change in foreign exchange rates. Importers, exporters, investors, and multinational firms alike are

Go to Cram101.com for the Practice Tests for this Chapter.

Chapter 8. Transaction Exposure

Chapter 8. Transaction Exposure

	exposed to this risk.
Operation	A standardized method or technique that is performed repetitively, often on different materials resulting in different finished goods is called an operation.
Residual	Residual payments can refer to an ongoing stream of payments in respect of the completion of past achievements.
Forward exchange	When two parties agree to exchange currency and execute a deal at some specific date in the future, we have forward exchange.
Spot market	Spot market refers to a market in which commodities are bought and sold for cash and immediate delivery.
Purchasing	Purchasing refers to the function in a firm that searches for quality material resources, finds the best suppliers, and negotiates the best price for goods and services.
Buyer	A buyer refers to a role in the buying center with formal authority and responsibility to select the supplier and negotiate the terms of the contract.
Money market	The money market, in macroeconomics and international finance, refers to the equilibration of demand for a country's domestic money to its money supply; market for short-term financial instruments.
Business operations	Business operations are those activities involved in the running of a business for the purpose of producing value for the stakeholders. The outcome of business operations is the harvesting of value from assets owned by a business.
Matching	Matching refers to an accounting concept that establishes when expenses are recognized. Expenses are matched with the revenues they helped to generate and are recognized when those revenues are recognized.
Cash inflow	Cash coming into the company as the result of a previous investment is a cash inflow.
Maturity	Maturity refers to the final payment date of a loan or other financial instrument, after which point no further interest or principal need be paid.
Interest Rate Parity	The Interest Rate Parity is the basic identity that relates interest rates and exchange rates. The identity is theoretical, and usually follows from assumptions imposed in economics models.
Efficient market	Efficient market refers to a market in which, at a minimum, current price changes are independent of past price changes, or, more strongly, price reflects all available information.
Liability	A liability is a present obligation of the enterprise arizing from past events, the settlement of which is expected to result in an outflow from the enterprise of resources embodying economic benefits.
Balance sheet	A statement of the assets, liabilities, and net worth of a firm or individual at some given time often at the end of its "fiscal year," is referred to as a balance sheet.
Net worth	Net worth is the total assets minus total liabilities of an individual or company
Principal	In agency law, one under whose direction an agent acts and for whose benefit that agent acts is a principal.
Balance	In banking and accountancy, the outstanding balance is the amount of money owned, (or due), that remains in a deposit account (or a loan account) at a given date, after all past remittances, payments and withdrawal have been accounted for. It can be positive (then, in the balance sheet of a firm, it is an asset) or negative (a liability).

Chapter 8. Transaction Exposure

Chapter 8. Transaction Exposure

Yield	The interest rate that equates a future value or an annuity to a given present value is a yield.
Depreciate	A nation's currency is said to depreciate when exchange rates change so that a unit of its currency can buy fewer units of foreign currency.
Exporter	A firm that sells its product in another country is an exporter.
Bid	A bid price is a price offered by a buyer when he/she buys a good. In the context of stock trading on a stock exchange, the bid price is the highest price a buyer of a stock is willing to pay for a share of that given stock.
Holding	The holding is a court's determination of a matter of law based on the issue presented in the particular case. In other words: under this law, with these facts, this result.
Future value	Future value measures what money is worth at a specified time in the future assuming a certain interest rate. This is used in time value of money calculations.
Call option	Call option refers to an option contract that provides the right to buy a security at a specified price within a certain time period.
Cost center	A cost center is a division that adds to the cost of the organization, but only indirectly adds to the profit of the company. Examples include Research and Development, Marketing and Customer service. A cost center is often identified with a speed type number.
Bottom line	The bottom line is net income on the last line of a income statement.
Profit	Profit refers to the return to the resource entrepreneurial ability; total revenue minus total cost.
Payables	Obligations to make future economic sacrifices, usually cash payments, are referred to as payables. Same as current liabilities.
Trend	Trend refers to the long-term movement of an economic variable, such as its average rate of increase or decrease over enough years to encompass several business cycles.
Revenue	Revenue is a U.S. business term for the amount of money that a company receives from its activities, mostly from sales of products and/or services to customers.
Internal Revenue Service	In 1862, during the Civil War, President Lincoln and Congress created the office of Commissioner of Internal Revenue and enacted an income tax to pay war expenses. The position of Commissioner still exists today. The Commissioner is the head of the Internal Revenue Service.
Parent company	Parent company refers to the entity that has a controlling influence over another company. It may have its own operations, or it may have been set up solely for the purpose of owning the Subject Company.
Consideration	Consideration in contract law, a basic requirement for an enforceable agreement under traditional contract principles, defined in this text as legal value, bargained for and given in exchange for an act or promise. In corporation law, cash or property contributed to a corporation in exchange for shares, or a promise to contribute such cash or property.
Speculation	The purchase or sale of an asset in hopes that its price will rise or fall respectively, in order to make a profit is called speculation.
Operating cash flows	Operating cash flows refers to the cash inflows and cash outflows from the general operating activities of the business; one of the three sections in the statement of cash flows.
Multinational enterprise	Multinational enterprise refers to a firm, usually a corporation, that operates in two or more countries.

Chapter 8. Transaction Exposure

Chapter 8. Transaction Exposure

Enterprise	Enterprise refers to another name for a business organization. Other similar terms are business firm, sometimes simply business, sometimes simply firm, as well as company, and entity.
Efficient market hypothesis	The application of the theory of rational expectations to financial markets is referred to as efficient market hypothesis.
Industry	A group of firms that produce identical or similar products is an industry. It is also used specifically to refer to an area of economic production focused on manufacturing which involves large amounts of capital investment before any profit can be realized, also called "heavy industry".
Weighted average	The weighted average unit cost of the goods available for sale for both cost of goods sold and ending inventory.
Weighted average cost of capital	Weighted average cost of capital refers to the computed cost of capital determined by multiplying the cost of each item in the optimal capital structure by its weighted representation in the overall capital structure and summing up the results.
Average cost	Average cost is equal to total cost divided by the number of goods produced (Quantity-Q). It is also equal to the sum of average variable costs (total variable costs divided by Q) plus average fixed costs (total fixed costs divided by Q).
Economy	The income, expenditures, and resources that affect the cost of running a business and household are called an economy.
Devaluation	Lowering the value of a nation's currency relative to other currencies is called devaluation.
Exercise price	Exercise price refers to the price at which the purchaser of an option has the right to buy or sell the underlying financial instrument. Also known as the strike price.
Butterfly	In option-trading, a butterfly is a combination trade resulting in the following net position: Long 1 call at (X - a) strike Short 2 calls at X strike Long 1 call at (X + a) strike all with the same expiration date.
Rate differential	The controversial practice of newspapers charging significantly higher rates to national advertisers as compared to local accounts is called rate differential.
Competitor	Other organizations in the same industry or type of business that provide a good or service to the same set of customers is referred to as a competitor.
Points	Loan origination fees that may be deductible as interest by a buyer of property. A seller of property who pays points reduces the selling price by the amount of the points paid for the buyer.
Export	In economics, an export is any good or commodity, shipped or otherwise transported out of a country, province, town to another part of the world in a legitimate fashion, typically for use in trade or sale.
Euro	The common currency of a subset of the countries of the EU, adopted January 1, 1999 is called euro.
Cost of equity	In finance, the cost of equity is the minimum rate of return a firm must offer shareholders to compensate for waiting for their returns, and for bearing some risk.
Equity capital	Equity capital refers to money raized from within the firm or through the sale of ownership in the firm.
Volatility	Volatility refers to the extent to which an economic variable, such as a price or an exchange rate, moves up and down over time.

Chapter 8. Transaction Exposure

Chapter 8. Transaction Exposure

Lufthansa	Lufthansa is a founding member of Star Alliance, the largest airline alliance in the world. The Lufthansa Group operates more than 400 aircraft and employs nearly 100,000 people worldwide.
Boeing	Boeing is the world's largest aircraft manufacturer by revenue. Headquartered in Chicago, Illinois, Boeing is the second-largest defense contractor in the world. In 2005, the company was the world's largest civil aircraft manufacturer in terms of value.
Analyst	Analyst refers to a person or tool with a primary function of information analysis, generally with a more limited, practical and short term set of goals than a researcher.
Total cost	The sum of fixed cost and variable cost is referred to as total cost.
Authority	Authority in agency law, refers to an agent's ability to affect his principal's legal relations with third parties. Also used to refer to an actor's legal power or ability to do something. In addition, sometimes used to refer to a statute, case, or other legal source that justifies a particular result.

Chapter 8. Transaction Exposure

Chapter 9. Operating Exposure

Operating cash flows	Operating cash flows refers to the cash inflows and cash outflows from the general operating activities of the business; one of the three sections in the statement of cash flows.
Economic exposure	The extent to which a firm's future international earning power is affected by changes in exchange rates is referred to as the economic exposure.
Present value	The value today of a stream of payments and/or receipts over time in the future and/or the past, converted to the present using an interest rate. If X t is the amount in period t and r the interest rate, then present value at time t=0 is V = ?T /t.
Exchange rate	Exchange rate refers to the price at which one country's currency trades for another, typically on the exchange market.
Cash flow	In finance, cash flow refers to the amounts of cash being received and spent by a business during a defined period of time, sometimes tied to a specific project. Most of the time they are being used to determine gaps in the liquid position of a company.
Exchange	The trade of things of value between buyer and seller so that each is better off after the trade is called the exchange.
Firm	An organization that employs resources to produce a good or service for profit and owns and operates one or more plants is referred to as a firm.
Operation	A standardized method or technique that is performed repetitively, often on different materials resulting in different finished goods is called an operation.
Transaction exposure	Transaction exposure refers to foreign exchange gains and losses resulting from actual international transactions. These may be hedged through the foreign exchange market, the money market, or the currency futures market.
Competitor	Other organizations in the same industry or type of business that provide a good or service to the same set of customers is referred to as a competitor.
Eastman Kodak	Eastman Kodak Company is an American multinational public company producing photographic materials and equipment. Long known for its wide range of photographic film products, it has focused in recent years on three main businesses: digital photography, health imaging, and printing. This company remains the largest supplier of films in the world, both for the amateur and professional markets.
Payables	Obligations to make future economic sacrifices, usually cash payments, are referred to as payables. Same as current liabilities.
Expense	In accounting, an expense represents an event in which an asset is used up or a liability is incurred. In terms of the accounting equation, expenses reduce owners' equity.
Market share	That fraction of an industry's output accounted for by an individual firm or group of firms is called market share.
Market	A market is, as defined in economics, a social arrangement that allows buyers and sellers to discover information and carry out a voluntary exchange of goods or services.
Domestic	From or in one's own country. A domestic producer is one that produces inside the home country. A domestic price is the price inside the home country. Opposite of 'foreign' or 'world.'.
Competitiveness	Competitiveness usually refers to characteristics that permit a firm to compete effectively with other firms due to low cost or superior technology, perhaps internationally.
Financing cash flows	One of the three sections in the statement of cash flows, showing cash inflows and cash outflows related to the firm's sources of capital, such as contributions from, and distributions to, the owners is a financing cash flows.

Go to **Cram101.com** for the Practice Tests for this Chapter.

Chapter 9. Operating Exposure

Chapter 9. Operating Exposure

Intellectual property	In law, intellectual property is an umbrella term for various legal entitlements which attach to certain types of information, ideas, or other intangibles in their expressed form. The holder of this legal entitlement is generally entitled to exercise various exclusive rights in relation to its subject matter.
Technology	The body of knowledge and techniques that can be used to combine economic resources to produce goods and services is called technology.
Management	Management characterizes the process of leading and directing all or part of an organization, often a business, through the deployment and manipulation of resources. Early twentieth-century management writer Mary Parker Follett defined management as "the art of getting things done through people."
Property	Assets defined in the broadest legal sense. Property includes the unrealized receivables of a cash basis taxpayer, but not services rendered.
License	A license in the sphere of Intellectual Property Rights (IPR) is a document, contract or agreement giving permission or the 'right' to a legally-definable entity to do something (such as manufacture a product or to use a service), or to apply something (such as a trademark), with the objective of achieving commercial gain.
Service	Service refers to a "non tangible product" that is not embodied in a physical good and that typically effects some change in another product, person, or institution. Contrasts with good.
Lease	A contract for the possession and use of land or other property, including goods, on one side, and a recompense of rent or other income on the other is the lease.
Purchasing	Purchasing refers to the function in a firm that searches for quality material resources, finds the best suppliers, and negotiates the best price for goods and services.
Production	The creation of finished goods and services using the factors of production: land, labor, capital, entrepreneurship, and knowledge.
Marketing	Promoting and selling products or services to customers, or prospective customers, is referred to as marketing.
Operating results	Operating results refers to measures that are important to monitoring and tracking the effectiveness of a company's operations.
Foreign exchange	In finance, foreign exchange means currencies, such as U.S. Dollars and Euros. These are traded on foreign exchange markets.
Market value	Market value refers to the price of an asset agreed on between a willing buyer and a willing seller; the price an asset could demand if it is sold on the open market.
Evaluation	The consumer's appraisal of the product or brand on important attributes is called evaluation.
Financial statement	Financial statement refers to a summary of all the transactions that have occurred over a particular period.
Budgeted financial statement	A set of planned financial statements showing what an organization's overall financial condition is expected to be at the end of the budget period if planned operations are carried out is referred to as a budgeted financial statement.
Operating budget	An operating budget is the annual budget of an activity stated in terms of Budget Classification Code, functional/subfunctional categories and cost accounts. It contains estimates of the total value of resources required for the performance of the operation including reimbursable work or services for others.

Go to **Cram101.com** for the Practice Tests for this Chapter.

Chapter 9. Operating Exposure

Chapter 9. Operating Exposure

Forward rate	Forward rate refers to the forward exchange rate, this is the exchange rate on a forward market transaction.
Spot rate	Spot rate refers to the rate at which the currency is traded for immediate delivery. It is the existing cash price.
Budget	Budget refers to an account, usually for a year, of the planned expenditures and the expected receipts of an entity. For a government, the receipts are tax revenues.
Fisher effect	Fisher effect refers to the outcome that when expected inflation occurs, interest rates will rise; named after economist Irving Fisher.
Amortize	To provide for the payment of a debt by creating a sinking fund or paying in installments is to amortize.
Principal	In agency law, one under whose direction an agent acts and for whose benefit that agent acts is a principal.
Interest	In finance and economics, interest is the price paid by a borrower for the use of a lender's money. In other words, interest is the amount of paid to "rent" money for a period of time.
Foreign exchange market	A market for converting the currency of one country into that of another country is called foreign exchange market. It is by far the largest market in the world, in terms of cash value traded, and includes trading between large banks, central banks, currency speculators, multinational corporations, governments, and other financial markets and institutions.
Exchange market	Exchange market refers to the market on which national currencies are bought and sold.
Inputs	The inputs used by a firm or an economy are the labor, raw materials, electricity and other resources it uses to produce its outputs.
Analyst	Analyst refers to a person or tool with a primary function of information analysis, generally with a more limited, practical and short term set of goals than a researcher.
Variable	A variable is something measured by a number; it is used to analyze what happens to other things when the size of that number changes.
Financial management	The job of managing a firm's resources so it can meet its goals and objectives is called financial management.
Euro	The common currency of a subset of the countries of the EU, adopted January 1, 1999 is called euro.
Earnings per share	Earnings per share refers to annual profit of the corporation divided by the number of shares outstanding.
Corporation	A legal entity chartered by a state or the Federal government that is distinct and separate from the individuals who own it is a corporation. This separation gives the corporation unique powers which other legal entities lack.
Subsidiary	A company that is controlled by another company or corporation is a subsidiary.
Profit	Profit refers to the return to the resource entrepreneurial ability; total revenue minus total cost.
Labor	People's physical and mental talents and efforts that are used to help produce goods and services are called labor.
Parent company	Parent company refers to the entity that has a controlling influence over another company. It may have its own operations, or it may have been set up solely for the purpose of owning the Subject Company.
Depreciation	Depreciation is an accounting and finance term for the method of attributing the cost of an

Chapter 9. Operating Exposure

Chapter 9. Operating Exposure

	asset across the useful life of the asset. Depreciation is a reduction in the value of a currency in floating exchange rate.
Direct cost	A direct cost is a cost that can be identified specifically with a particular sponsored project, an instructional activity, or any other institutional activity, or that can be directly assigned to such activities relatively easily with a high degree of accuracy.
Inventory	Tangible property held for sale in the normal course of business or used in producing goods or services for sale is an inventory.
Domestic price	The price of a good or service within a country, determined by domestic demand and supply is referred to as domestic price.
Devaluation	Lowering the value of a nation's currency relative to other currencies is called devaluation.
Price elasticity	The responsiveness of the market to change in price is called price elasticity. If price elasticity is low, a large change in price will lead to a small change in supply.
Price elasticity of demand	Price elasticity of demand refers to the ratio of the percentage change in quantity demanded of a product or resource to the percentage change in its price; a measure of the responsiveness of buyers to a change in the price of a product or resource.
Elasticity	In economics, elasticity is the ratio of the incremental percentage change in one variable with respect to an incremental percentage change in another variable. Elasticity is usually expressed as a positive number (i.e., an absolute value) when the sign is already clear from context.
Export	In economics, an export is any good or commodity, shipped or otherwise transported out of a country, province, town to another part of the world in a legitimate fashion, typically for use in trade or sale.
Raw material	Raw material refers to a good that has not been transformed by production; a primary product.
Inflation	An increase in the overall price level of an economy, usually as measured by the CPI or by the implicit price deflator is called inflation.
Wage	The payment for the service of a unit of labor, per unit time. In trade theory, it is the only payment to labor, usually unskilled labor. In empirical work, wage data may exclude other compenzation, which must be added to get the total cost of employment.
Accounts payable	A written record of all vendors to whom the business firm owes money is referred to as accounts payable.
Working capital	The dollar difference between total current assets and total current liabilities is called working capital.
Investment	Investment refers to spending for the production and accumulation of capital and additions to inventories. In a financial sense, buying an asset with the expectation of making a return.
Capital	Capital generally refers to financial wealth, especially that used to start or maintain a business. In classical economics, capital is one of four factors of production, the others being land and labor and entrepreneurship.
Accounts receivable	Accounts receivable is one of a series of accounting transactions dealing with the billing of customers which owe money to a person, company or organization for goods and services that have been provided to the customer. This is typically done in a one person organization by writing an invoice and mailing or delivering it to each customer.
Current asset	A current asset is an asset on the balance sheet which is expected to be sold or otherwise used up in the near future, usually within one year.
Cash outflow	Cash flowing out of the business from all sources over a period of time is cash outflow.

Chapter 9. Operating Exposure

Chapter 9. Operating Exposure

Asset	An item of property, such as land, capital, money, a share in ownership, or a claim on others for future payment, such as a bond or a bank deposit is an asset.
Gain	In finance, gain is a profit or an increase in value of an investment such as a stock or bond. Gain is calculated by fair market value or the proceeds from the sale of the investment minus the sum of the purchase price and all costs associated with it.
Price level	The overall level of prices in a country, as usually measured empirically by a price index, but often captured in theoretical models by a single variable is a price level.
Operating leverage	Effects that fixed costs have on changes in operating income as changes occur in units sold and hence in contribution margin are called operating leverage.
Leverage	Leverage is using given resources in such a way that the potential positive or negative outcome is magnified. In finance, this generally refers to borrowing.
Revenue	Revenue is a U.S. business term for the amount of money that a company receives from its activities, mostly from sales of products and/or services to customers.
Foreign exchange exposure	The risk that future changes in a country's exchange rate will hurt the firm is a foreign exchange exposure.
Strategic management	A philosophy of management that links strategic planning with dayto-day decision making. Strategic management seeks a fit between an organization's external and internal environments.
Policy	Similar to a script in that a policy can be a less than completely rational decision-making method. Involves the use of a pre-existing set of decision steps for any problem that presents itself.
Disequilibrium	Inequality or imbalance of supply and demand is referred to as disequilibrium.
Capital market	A financial market in which long-term debt and equity instruments are traded is referred to as a capital market. The capital market includes the stock market and the bond market.
Fund	Independent accounting entity with a self-balancing set of accounts segregated for the purposes of carrying on specific activities is referred to as a fund.
Diversification strategy	Diversification strategy is a corporate strategy that takes the organization away from both its current markets and products, as opposed to either market or product development.
Diversification	Investing in a collection of assets whose returns do not always move together, with the result that overall risk is lower than for individual assets is referred to as diversification.
Preference	The act of a debtor in paying or securing one or more of his creditors in a manner more favorable to them than to other creditors or to the exclusion of such other creditors is a preference. In the absence of statute, a preference is perfectly good, but to be legal it must be bona fide, and not a mere subterfuge of the debtor to secure a future benefit to himself or to prevent the application of his property to his debts.
Income elasticity	Normally the income elasticity of demand; that is, the elasticity of demand with respect to income. Measured as the percentage change in demand relative to the percentage change in income.
Profit margin	Profit margin is a measure of profitability. It is calculated using a formula and written as a percentage or a number. Profit margin = Net income before tax and interest / Revenue.
Margin	A deposit by a buyer in stocks with a seller or a stockbroker, as security to cover fluctuations in the market in reference to stocks that the buyer has purchased but for which

Go to **Cram101.com** for the Practice Tests for this Chapter.

Chapter 9. Operating Exposure

Chapter 9. Operating Exposure

	he has not paid is a margin. Commodities are also traded on margin.
Portfolio effect	Portfolio effect refers to the impact of a given investment on the overall risk-return composition of the firm. A firm must consider not only the individual investment characteristics of a project but also how the project relates to the entire portfolio of undertakings.
Portfolio	In finance, a portfolio is a collection of investments held by an institution or a private individual. Holding but not always a portfolio is part of an investment and risk-limiting strategy called diversification. By owning several assets, certain types of risk (in particular specific risk) can be reduced.
International diversification	Achieving diversification through many different foreign investments that are influenced by a variety of factors is referred to as international diversification. By diversifying across nations whose economic cycles are not perfectly correlated, investors can typically reduce the variability of their returns.
Goodyear	Goodyear was founded in 1898 by German immigrants Charles and Frank Seiberling. Today it is the third largest tire and rubber company in the world.
Warehouse	Warehouse refers to a location, often decentralized, that a firm uses to store, consolidate, age, or mix stock; house product-recall programs; or ease tax burdens.
Buyer	A buyer refers to a role in the buying center with formal authority and responsibility to select the supplier and negotiate the terms of the contract.
Supply	Supply is the aggregate amount of any material good that can be called into being at a certain price point; it comprises one half of the equation of supply and demand. In classical economic theory, a curve representing supply is one of the factors that produce price.
Exporter	A firm that sells its product in another country is an exporter.
Option	A contract that gives the purchaser the option to buy or sell the underlying financial instrument at a specified price, called the exercise price or strike price, within a specific period of time.
Rate differential	The controversial practice of newspapers charging significantly higher rates to national advertisers as compared to local accounts is called rate differential.
Cost of capital	Cost of capital refers to the percentage cost of funds used for acquiring resources for an organization, typically a weighted average of the firms cost of equity and cost of debt.
Interest rate	The rate of return on bonds, loans, or deposits. When one speaks of 'the' interest rate, it is usually in a model where there is only one.
Foreign exchange risk	Foreign exchange risk refers to a form of risk that refers to the possibility of experiencing a drop in revenue or an increase in cost in an international transaction due to a change in foreign exchange rates. Importers, exporters, investors, and multinational firms alike are exposed to this risk.
Political risk	Refers to the many different actions of people, subgroups, and whole countries that have the potential to affect the financial status of a firm is called political risk.
Expropriation	Expropriation is the act of removing from control the owner of an item of property. The term is used to both refer to acts by a government or by any group of people.
Industry	A group of firms that produce identical or similar products is an industry. It is also used specifically to refer to an area of economic production focused on manufacturing which involves large amounts of capital investment before any profit can be realized, also called "heavy industry".

Chapter 9. Operating Exposure

Chapter 9. Operating Exposure

Proactive	To be proactive is to act before a situation becomes a source of confrontation or crisis. It is the opposite of "retroactive," which refers to actions taken after an event.
Parallel loan	Parallel loan refers to a U.S. firm that wishes to lend funds to a foreign affiliate locates a foreign parent firm that wishes to loan money to a U.S. affiliate. Avoiding the foreign exchange markets entirely, the U.S. parent lends dollars to the Dutch affiliate in the United States, while the Dutch parent lends guilders to the American affiliate in the Netherlands. At maturity, the two loans would each be repaid to the original lender. Notice that neither loan carries any foreign exchange risk in this arrangement.
Currency swap	Currency swap refers to the exchange of a set of payments in one currency for a set of payments in another currency.
Matching	Matching refers to an accounting concept that establishes when expenses are recognized. Expenses are matched with the revenues they helped to generate and are recognized when those revenues are recognized.
Swap	In finance a swap is a derivative, where two counterparties exchange one stream of cash flows against another stream. These streams are called the legs of the swap. The cash flows are calculated over a notional principal amount. Swaps are often used to hedge certain risks, for instance interest rate risk. Another use is speculation.
Interest payment	The payment to holders of bonds payable, calculated by multiplying the stated rate on the face of the bond by the par, or face, value of the bond. If bonds are issued at a discount or premium, the interest payment does not equal the interest expense.
Cash inflow	Cash coming into the company as the result of a previous investment is a cash inflow.
Financial instrument	Formal or legal documents in writing, such as contracts, deeds, wills, bonds, leases, and mortgages is referred to as a financial instrument.
Instrument	Instrument refers to an economic variable that is controlled by policy makers and can be used to influence other variables, called targets. Examples are monetary and fiscal policies used to achieve external and internal balance.
Contract	A contract is a "promise" or an "agreement" that is enforced or recognized by the law. In the civil law, a contract is considered to be part of the general law of obligations.
Hedge	Hedge refers to a process of offsetting risk. In the foreign exchange market, hedgers use the forward market to cover a transaction or open position and thereby reduce exchange risk. The term applies most commonly to trade.
Currency risk	Currency risk is a form of risk that arises from the change in price of one currency against another. Whenever investors or companies have assets or business operations across national borders, they face currency risk if their positions are not hedged.
Cooperative	A business owned and controlled by the people who use it, producers, consumers, or workers with similar needs who pool their resources for mutual gain is called cooperative.
Ford	Ford is an American company that manufactures and sells automobiles worldwide. Ford introduced methods for large-scale manufacturing of cars, and large-scale management of an industrial workforce, especially elaborately engineered manufacturing sequences typified by the moving assembly lines.
Stockholder	A stockholder is an individual or company (including a corporation) that legally owns one or more shares of stock in a joined stock company. The shareholders are the owners of a corporation. Companies listed at the stock market strive to enhance shareholder value.
Invoice	The itemized bill for a transaction, stating the nature of the transaction and its cost. In international trade, the invoice price is often the preferred basis for levying an ad valorem

Chapter 9. Operating Exposure

Chapter 9. Operating Exposure

	tariff.
Credit	Credit refers to a recording as positive in the balance of payments, any transaction that gives rise to a payment into the country, such as an export, the sale of an asset, or borrowing from abroad.
Maturity	Maturity refers to the final payment date of a loan or other financial instrument, after which point no further interest or principal need be paid.
Lender	Suppliers and financial institutions that lend money to companies is referred to as a lender.
Default	In finance, default occurs when a debtor has not met its legal obligations according to the debt contract, e.g. it has not made a scheduled payment, or violated a covenant (condition) of the debt contract.
Collateral	Property that is pledged to the lender to guarantee payment in the event that the borrower is unable to make debt payments is called collateral.
Balance sheet	A statement of the assets, liabilities, and net worth of a firm or individual at some given time often at the end of its "fiscal year," is referred to as a balance sheet.
Balance	In banking and accountancy, the outstanding balance is the amount of money owned, (or due), that remains in a deposit account (or a loan account) at a given date, after all past remittances, payments and withdrawal have been accounted for. It can be positive (then, in the balance sheet of a firm, it is an asset) or negative (a liability).
Dealer	People who link buyers with sellers by buying and selling securities at stated prices are referred to as a dealer.
Exporting	Selling products to another country is called exporting.
Financial market	In economics, a financial market is a mechanism which allows people to trade money for securities or commodities such as gold or other precious metals. In general, any commodity market might be considered to be a financial market, if the usual purpose of traders is not the immediate consumption of the commodity, but rather as a means of delaying or accelerating consumption over time.
Counterparty	A counterparty is a legal and financial term. It means a party to a contract. Any legal entity can be a counterparty.
Forward exchange	When two parties agree to exchange currency and execute a deal at some specific date in the future, we have forward exchange.
Derivative	A derivative is a generic term for specific types of investments from which payoffs over time are derived from the performance of assets (such as commodities, shares or bonds), interest rates, exchange rates, or indices (such as a stock market index, consumer price index (CPI) or an index of weather conditions).
Hedging	A technique for avoiding a risk by making a counteracting transaction is referred to as hedging.
Put option	An option contract that provides the right to sell a security at a specified price within a specified period of time is a put option.
Insurance	Insurance refers to a system by which individuals can reduce their exposure to risk of large losses by spreading the risks among a large number of persons.
Niche	In industry, a niche is a situation or an activity perfectly suited to a person. A niche can imply a working position or an area suited to a person who occupies it. Basically, a job where a person is able to succeed and thrive.
Leadership	Management merely consists of leadership applied to business situations; or in other words:

Chapter 9. Operating Exposure

Chapter 9. Operating Exposure

	management forms a sub-set of the broader process of leadership.
Premium	Premium refers to the fee charged by an insurance company for an insurance policy. The rate of losses must be relatively predictable: In order to set the premium (prices) insurers must be able to estimate them accurately.
Long run	In economic models, the long run time frame assumes no fixed factors of production. Firms can enter or leave the marketplace, and the cost (and availability) of land, labor, raw materials, and capital goods can be assumed to vary.
Translation exposure	The foreign-located assets and liabilities of a multinational corporation, which are denominated in foreign currency units, and are exposed to losses and gains due to changing exchange rates is called accounting or translation exposure.
Foreign subsidiary	A company owned in a foreign country by another company is referred to as foreign subsidiary.
Debt financing	Obtaining financing by borrowing money is debt financing.
Patent	The legal right to the proceeds from and control over the use of an invented product or process, granted for a fixed period of time, usually 20 years. Patent is one form of intellectual property that is subject of the TRIPS agreement.
Currency appreciation	Currency appreciation is when currency rises in value relative to another currency; it buys more foreign exchange.
Appreciation	Appreciation refers to a rise in the value of a country's currency on the exchange market, relative either to a particular other currency or to a weighted average of other currencies. The currency is said to appreciate. Opposite of 'depreciation.' Appreciation can also refer to the increase in value of any asset.
Aid	Assistance provided by countries and by international institutions such as the World Bank to developing countries in the form of monetary grants, loans at low interest rates, in kind, or a combination of these is called aid. Aid can also refer to assistance of any type rendered to benefit some group or individual.
Journal	Book of original entry, in which transactions are recorded in a general ledger system, is referred to as a journal.
Annual report	An annual report is prepared by corporate management that presents financial information including financial statements, footnotes, and the management discussion and analysis.
Toyota	Toyota is a Japanese multinational corporation that manufactures automobiles, trucks and buses. Toyota is the world's second largest automaker by sales. Toyota also provides financial services through its subsidiary, Toyota Financial Services, and participates in other lines of business.
Manufacturing	Production of goods primarily by the application of labor and capital to raw materials and other intermediate inputs, in contrast to agriculture, mining, forestry, fishing, and services a manufacturing.
Economies of scale	In economics, returns to scale and economies of scale are related terms that describe what happens as the scale of production increases. They are different terms and not to be used interchangeably.
Consolidation	The combination of two or more firms, generally of equal size and market power, to form an entirely new entity is a consolidation.
Economy	The income, expenditures, and resources that affect the cost of running a business and household are called an economy.

Go to Cram101.com for the Practice Tests for this Chapter.

Chapter 9. Operating Exposure

Chapter 9. Operating Exposure

Scope Scope of a project is the sum total of all projects products and their requirements or features.

Procurement Procurement is the acquisition of goods or services at the best possible total cost of ownership, in the right quantity, at the right time, in the right place for the direct benefit or use of the governments, corporations, or individuals generally via, but not limited to a contract.

Chapter 9. Operating Exposure

Chapter 10. Translation Exposure

Foreign subsidiary	A company owned in a foreign country by another company is referred to as foreign subsidiary.
Income statement	Income statement refers to a financial statement that presents the revenues and expenses and resulting net income or net loss of a company for a specific period of time.
Balance sheet	A statement of the assets, liabilities, and net worth of a firm or individual at some given time often at the end of its "fiscal year," is referred to as a balance sheet.
Subsidiary	A company that is controlled by another company or corporation is a subsidiary.
Balance	In banking and accountancy, the outstanding balance is the amount of money owned, (or due), that remains in a deposit account (or a loan account) at a given date, after all past remittances, payments and withdrawal have been accounted for. It can be positive (then, in the balance sheet of a firm, it is an asset) or negative (a liability).
Euro	The common currency of a subset of the countries of the EU, adopted January 1, 1999 is called euro.
Translation exposure	The foreign-located assets and liabilities of a multinational corporation, which are denominated in foreign currency units, and are exposed to losses and gains due to changing exchange rates is called accounting or translation exposure.
Exchange rate	Exchange rate refers to the price at which one country's currency trades for another, typically on the exchange market.
Net income	Net income is equal to the income that a firm has after subtracting costs and expenses from the total revenue. Expenses will typically include tax expense.
Net worth	Net worth is the total assets minus total liabilities of an individual or company
Exchange	The trade of things of value between buyer and seller so that each is better off after the trade is called the exchange.
Management	Management characterizes the process of leading and directing all or part of an organization, often a business, through the deployment and manipulation of resources. Early twentieth-century management writer Mary Parker Follett defined management as "the art of getting things done through people."
Restatement	Restatement refers to collections of legal rules produced by the American Law Institute, covering certain subject matter areas. Although restatements are often persuasive to courts, they are not legally binding unless adopted by the highest court of a particular state.
Assessment	Collecting information and providing feedback to employees about their behavior, communication style, or skills is an assessment.
Financial statement	Financial statement refers to a summary of all the transactions that have occurred over a particular period.
Parent company	Parent company refers to the entity that has a controlling influence over another company. It may have its own operations, or it may have been set up solely for the purpose of owning the Subject Company.
Consolidation	The combination of two or more firms, generally of equal size and market power, to form an entirely new entity is a consolidation.
Compromise	Compromise occurs when the interaction is moderately important to meeting goals and the goals are neither completely compatible nor completely incompatible.
Valuation	In finance, valuation is the process of estimating the market value of a financial asset or liability. They can be done on assets (for example, investments in marketable securities such as stocks, options, business enterprises, or intangible assets such as patents and

Chapter 10. Translation Exposure

Chapter 10. Translation Exposure

	trademarks) or on liabilities (e.g., Bonds issued by a company).
Market	A market is, as defined in economics, a social arrangement that allows buyers and sellers to discover information and carry out a voluntary exchange of goods or services.
Current liability	Current liability refers to a debt that can reasonably be expected to be paid from existing current assets or through the creation of other current liabilities, within one year or the operating cycle, whichever is longer.
Current asset	A current asset is an asset on the balance sheet which is expected to be sold or otherwise used up in the near future, usually within one year.
Fixed asset	Fixed asset, also known as property, plant, and equipment (PP&E), is a term used in accountancy for assets and property which cannot easily be converted into cash. This can be compared with current assets such as cash or bank accounts, which are described as liquid assets. In most cases, only tangible assets are referred to as fixed.
Inventory	Tangible property held for sale in the normal course of business or used in producing goods or services for sale is an inventory.
Liability	A liability is a present obligation of the enterprise arizing from past events, the settlement of which is expected to result in an outflow from the enterprise of resources embodying economic benefits.
Expense	In accounting, an expense represents an event in which an asset is used up or a liability is incurred. In terms of the accounting equation, expenses reduce owners' equity.
Equity	Equity is the name given to the set of legal principles, in countries following the English common law tradition, which supplement strict rules of law where their application would operate harshly, so as to achieve what is sometimes referred to as "natural justice."
Asset	An item of property, such as land, capital, money, a share in ownership, or a claim on others for future payment, such as a bond or a bank deposit is an asset.
Firm	An organization that employs resources to produce a good or service for profit and owns and operates one or more plants is referred to as a firm.
Business operations	Business operations are those activities involved in the running of a business for the purpose of producing value for the stakeholders. The outcome of business operations is the harvesting of value from assets owned by a business.
Operation	A standardized method or technique that is performed repetitively, often on different materials resulting in different finished goods is called an operation.
Extension	Extension refers to an out-of-court settlement in which creditors agree to allow the firm more time to meet its financial obligations. A new repayment schedule will be developed, subject to the acceptance of creditors.
Cash flow	In finance, cash flow refers to the amounts of cash being received and spent by a business during a defined period of time, sometimes tied to a specific project. Most of the time they are being used to determine gaps in the liquid position of a company.
Economic environment	The economic environment represents the external conditions under which people are engaged in, and benefit from, economic activity. It includes aspects of economic status, paid employment, and finances.
Marketing	Promoting and selling products or services to customers, or prospective customers, is referred to as marketing.
Functional currency	Functional currency refers to the currency of the economic environment in which the taxpayer carries on most of its activities, and in which the taxpayer transacts most of its business.

Go to **Cram101.com** for the Practice Tests for this Chapter.

Chapter 10. Translation Exposure

Financial accounting	Financial accounting is the branch of accountancy concerned with the preparation of financial statements for external decision makers, such as stockholders, suppliers, banks and government agencies. The fundamental need for financial accounting is to reduce principal-agent problem by measuring and monitoring agents' performance.
Financial accounting standards board	Financial accounting standards board refers to the private sector body given the primary responsibility to work out the detailed rules that become generally accepted accounting principles.
Financial accounting Standards	Financial Accounting Standards refers to a set of standards that dictate accounting rules concerning financial reporting; establish generally accepted accounting principles.
Accounting Standards Board	The role of the Accounting Standards Board is to issue accounting standards in the United Kingdom. It is recognized for that purpose under the Companies Act 1985. It took over the task of setting accounting standards from the Accounting Standards Committee (ASC) in 1990.
Accounting	A system that collects and processes financial information about an organization and reports that information to decision makers is referred to as accounting.
Current rate method	Using the exchange rate at the balance sheet date to translate the financial statements of a foreign subsidiary into the home currency is referred to as current rate method.
Temporal method	Temporal method refers to translating assets valued in a foreign currency into the home currency using the exchange rate that existed when the assets were originally purchased.
Contract	A contract is a "promise" or an "agreement" that is enforced or recognized by the law. In the civil law, a contract is considered to be part of the general law of obligations.
Service	Service refers to a "non tangible product" that is not embodied in a physical good and that typically effects some change in another product, person, or institution. Contrasts with good.
Fund	Independent accounting entity with a self-balancing set of accounts segregated for the purposes of carrying on specific activities is referred to as a fund.
Holder	A person in possession of a document of title or an instrument payable or indorsed to him, his order, or to bearer is a holder.
Spot exchange rate	The exchange rate at which a foreign exchange dealer will convert one currency into another that particular day is the spot exchange rate.
Arthur Andersen	Arthur Andersen was once one of the Big Five accounting firms, performing auditing, tax, and consulting services for large corporations. In 2002 the firm voluntarily surrendered its licenses to practice as Certified Public Accountants in the U.S. pending the result of prosecution by the U.S. Department of Justice over the firm's handling of the auditing of Enron.
Retained earnings	Cumulative earnings of a company that are not distributed to the owners and are reinvested in the business are called retained earnings.
Capital stock	The total amount of physical capital that has been accumulated, usually in a country is capital stock. Also refers to the total issued capital of a firm, including ordinary and preferred shares.
Capital	Capital generally refers to financial wealth, especially that used to start or maintain a business. In classical economics, capital is one of four factors of production, the others being land and labor and entrepreneurship.
Stock	In financial terminology, stock is the capital raized by a corporation, through the issuance and sale of shares.

Chapter 10. Translation Exposure

Chapter 10. Translation Exposure

Depreciation	Depreciation is an accounting and finance term for the method of attributing the cost of an asset across the useful life of the asset. Depreciation is a reduction in the value of a currency in floating exchange rate.
Appreciation	Appreciation refers to a rise in the value of a country's currency on the exchange market, relative either to a particular other currency or to a weighted average of other currencies. The currency is said to appreciate. Opposite of 'depreciation.' Appreciation can also refer to the increase in value of any asset.
Context	The effect of the background under which a message often takes on more and richer meaning is a context. Context is especially important in cross-cultural interactions because some cultures are said to be high context or low context.
Gain	In finance, gain is a profit or an increase in value of an investment such as a stock or bond. Gain is calculated by fair market value or the proceeds from the sale of the investment minus the sum of the purchase price and all costs associated with it.
Depreciate	A nation's currency is said to depreciate when exchange rates change so that a unit of its currency can buy fewer units of foreign currency.
Accounting method	Accounting method refers to the method under which income and expenses are determined for tax purposes. Important accounting methods include the cash basis and the accrual basis.
Investment	Investment refers to spending for the production and accumulation of capital and additions to inventories. In a financial sense, buying an asset with the expectation of making a return.
Profit	Profit refers to the return to the resource entrepreneurial ability; total revenue minus total cost.
Forward market	A market for exchange of currencies in the future is the forward market. Participants in a forward market enter into a contract to exchange currencies, not today, but at a specified date in the future, typically 30, 60, or 90 days from now, and at a price that is agreed upon.
Hedge	Hedge refers to a process of offsetting risk. In the foreign exchange market, hedgers use the forward market to cover a transaction or open position and thereby reduce exchange risk. The term applies most commonly to trade.
Spot rate	Spot rate refers to the rate at which the currency is traded for immediate delivery. It is the existing cash price.
Speculation	The purchase or sale of an asset in hopes that its price will rise or fall respectively, in order to make a profit is called speculation.
Foreign exchange risk	Foreign exchange risk refers to a form of risk that refers to the possibility of experiencing a drop in revenue or an increase in cost in an international transaction due to a change in foreign exchange rates. Importers, exporters, investors, and multinational firms alike are exposed to this risk.
Foreign exchange	In finance, foreign exchange means currencies, such as U.S. Dollars and Euros. These are traded on foreign exchange markets.
Corporation	A legal entity chartered by a state or the Federal government that is distinct and separate from the individuals who own it is a corporation. This separation gives the corporation unique powers which other legal entities lack.
Dividend	Amount of corporate profits paid out for each share of stock is referred to as dividend.
Authority	Authority in agency law, refers to an agent's ability to affect his principal's legal relations with third parties. Also used to refer to an actor's legal power or ability to do something. In addition, sometimes used to refer to a statute, case, or other legal source

Chapter 10. Translation Exposure

Chapter 10. Translation Exposure

	that justifies a particular result.
Covenant	A covenant is a signed written agreement between two or more parties. Also referred to as a contract.
Hedging	A technique for avoiding a risk by making a counteracting transaction is referred to as hedging.
Bond	Bond refers to a debt instrument, issued by a borrower and promising a specified stream of payments to the purchaser, usually regular interest payments plus a final repayment of principal.
Transaction exposure	Transaction exposure refers to foreign exchange gains and losses resulting from actual international transactions. These may be hedged through the foreign exchange market, the money market, or the currency futures market.
Export	In economics, an export is any good or commodity, shipped or otherwise transported out of a country, province, town to another part of the world in a legitimate fashion, typically for use in trade or sale.
Consolidated financial statement	A consolidated financial statement refers to a financial statement of a parent company and its subsidiaries that has been combined into a single set of financial statements as if the companies were one.
Deductible	The dollar sum of costs that an insured individual must pay before the insurer begins to pay is called deductible.
Hyperinflation	Hyperinflation refers to a very rapid rise in the price level; an extremely high rate of inflation.
Policy	Similar to a script in that a policy can be a less than completely rational decision-making method. Involves the use of a pre-existing set of decision steps for any problem that presents itself.
Manufacturing	Production of goods primarily by the application of labor and capital to raw materials and other intermediate inputs, in contrast to agriculture, mining, forestry, fishing, and services a manufacturing.
Contribution	In business organization law, the cash or property contributed to a business by its owners is referred to as contribution.
Devaluation	Lowering the value of a nation's currency relative to other currencies is called devaluation.
Financial derivatives	Instruments that have payoffs that are linked to previously issued securities, used as risk reduction tools are referred to as financial derivatives.
Derivative	A derivative is a generic term for specific types of investments from which payoffs over time are derived from the performance of assets (such as commodities, shares or bonds), interest rates, exchange rates, or indices (such as a stock market index, consumer price index (CPI) or an index of weather conditions).
Interest	In finance and economics, interest is the price paid by a borrower for the use of a lender's money. In other words, interest is the amount of paid to "rent" money for a period of time.
Press release	A written public news announcement normally distributed to major news services is referred to as press release.
Nestle	Nestle is the world's biggest food and beverage company. In the 1860s, a pharmacist, developed a food for babies who were unable to be breastfed. His first success was a premature infant who could not tolerate his own mother's milk nor any of the usual substitutes. The value of the new product was quickly recognized when his new formula saved

Chapter 10. Translation Exposure

Chapter 10. Translation Exposure

	the child's life.
Business Week	Business Week is a business magazine published by McGraw-Hill. It was first published in 1929 under the direction of Malcolm Muir, who was serving as president of the McGraw-Hill Publishing company at the time. It is considered to be the standard both in industry and among students.
Swap	In finance a swap is a derivative, where two counterparties exchange one stream of cash flows against another stream. These streams are called the legs of the swap. The cash flows are calculated over a notional principal amount. Swaps are often used to hedge certain risks, for instance interest rate risk. Another use is speculation.
Aid	Assistance provided by countries and by international institutions such as the World Bank to developing countries in the form of monetary grants, loans at low interest rates, in kind, or a combination of these is called aid. Aid can also refer to assistance of any type rendered to benefit some group or individual.
Credit risk	The risk of loss due to a counterparty defaulting on a contract, or more generally the risk of loss due to some "credit event" is called credit risk.
Credit	Credit refers to a recording as positive in the balance of payments, any transaction that gives rise to a payment into the country, such as an export, the sale of an asset, or borrowing from abroad.

Chapter 10. Translation Exposure

Chapter 11. Global Cost and Availability of Capital

Capital market	A financial market in which long-term debt and equity instruments are traded is referred to as a capital market. The capital market includes the stock market and the bond market.
Integration	Economic integration refers to reducing barriers among countries to transactions and to movements of goods, capital, and labor, including harmonization of laws, regulations, and standards. Integrated markets theoretically function as a unified market.
Capital	Capital generally refers to financial wealth, especially that used to start or maintain a business. In classical economics, capital is one of four factors of production, the others being land and labor and entrepreneurship.
Market	A market is, as defined in economics, a social arrangement that allows buyers and sellers to discover information and carry out a voluntary exchange of goods or services.
Fund	Independent accounting entity with a self-balancing set of accounts segregated for the purposes of carrying on specific activities is referred to as a fund.
Firm	An organization that employs resources to produce a good or service for profit and owns and operates one or more plants is referred to as a firm.
Securities market	The securities market is the market for securities, where companies and the government can raise long-term funds.
Competitiveness	Competitiveness usually refers to characteristics that permit a firm to compete effectively with other firms due to low cost or superior technology, perhaps internationally.
Cost of capital	Cost of capital refers to the percentage cost of funds used for acquiring resources for an organization, typically a weighted average of the firms cost of equity and cost of debt.
Domestic	From or in one's own country. A domestic producer is one that produces inside the home country. A domestic price is the price inside the home country. Opposite of 'foreign' or 'world.'.
Security	Security refers to a claim on the borrower future income that is sold by the borrower to the lender. A security is a type of transferable interest representing financial value.
Equity	Equity is the name given to the set of legal principles, in countries following the English common law tradition, which supplement strict rules of law where their application would operate harshly, so as to achieve what is sometimes referred to as "natural justice."
Devise	In a will, a gift of real property is called a devise.
Transparency	Transparency refers to a concept that describes a company being so open to other companies working with it that the once-solid barriers between them become see-through and electronic information is shared as if the companies were one.
Foreign exchange risk	Foreign exchange risk refers to a form of risk that refers to the possibility of experiencing a drop in revenue or an increase in cost in an international transaction due to a change in foreign exchange rates. Importers, exporters, investors, and multinational firms alike are exposed to this risk.
Foreign exchange	In finance, foreign exchange means currencies, such as U.S. Dollars and Euros. These are traded on foreign exchange markets.
Insider trading	Insider trading is the trading of a corporation's stock or other securities (e.g. Bonds or stock options) by corporate insiders such as officers, directors, or holders of more than ten percent of the firm's shares.
Political risk	Refers to the many different actions of people, subgroups, and whole countries that have the potential to affect the financial status of a firm is called political risk.
Exchange	The trade of things of value between buyer and seller so that each is better off after the

Chapter 11. Global Cost and Availability of Capital

Chapter 11. Global Cost and Availability of Capital

	trade is called the exchange.
Liquidity	Liquidity refers to the capacity to turn assets into cash, or the amount of assets in a portfolio that have that capacity.
Weighted average	The weighted average unit cost of the goods available for sale for both cost of goods sold and ending inventory.
Weighted average cost of capital	Weighted average cost of capital refers to the computed cost of capital determined by multiplying the cost of each item in the optimal capital structure by its weighted representation in the overall capital structure and summing up the results.
Average cost	Average cost is equal to total cost divided by the number of goods produced (Quantity-Q). It is also equal to the sum of average variable costs (total variable costs divided by Q) plus average fixed costs (total fixed costs divided by Q).
Cost of equity	In finance, the cost of equity is the minimum rate of return a firm must offer shareholders to compensate for waiting for their returns, and for bearing some risk.
Cost of debt	The cost of debt is the cost of borrowing money (usually denoted by Kd). It is derived by dividing debt's interest payments on the total market value of the debts.
Systematic risk	Movements in a stock portfolio's value that are attributable to macroeconomic forces affecting all firms in an economy, rather than factors specific to an individual firm are referred to as systematic risk.
Expected return	Expected return refers to the return on an asset expected over the next period.
Stock	In financial terminology, stock is the capital raized by a corporation, through the issuance and sale of shares.
Standard deviation	A measure of the spread or dispersion of a series of numbers around the expected value is the standard deviation. The standard deviation tells us how well the expected value represents a series of values.
Correlation	A correlation is the measure of the extent to which two economic or statistical variables move together, normalized so that its values range from -1 to +1. It is defined as the covariance of the two variables divided by the square root of the product of their variances.
Holding	The holding is a court's determination of a matter of law based on the issue presented in the particular case. In other words: under this law, with these facts, this result.
Corporate income tax	A tax levied on the net income of corporations is called the corporate income tax.
Interest rate	The rate of return on bonds, loans, or deposits. When one speaks of 'the' interest rate, it is usually in a model where there is only one.
Interest	In finance and economics, interest is the price paid by a borrower for the use of a lender's money. In other words, interest is the amount of paid to "rent" money for a period of time.
Discount rate	Discount rate refers to the rate, per year, at which future values are diminished to make them comparable to values in the present. Can be either subjective or objective.
Discount	The difference between the face value of a bond and its selling price, when a bond is sold for less than its face value it's referred to as a discount.
Industry	A group of firms that produce identical or similar products is an industry. It is also used specifically to refer to an area of economic production focused on manufacturing which involves large amounts of capital investment before any profit can be realized, also called "heavy industry".

Go to **Cram101.com** for the Practice Tests for this Chapter.

Chapter 11. Global Cost and Availability of Capital

Inputs	The inputs used by a firm or an economy are the labor, raw materials, electricity and other resources it uses to produce its outputs.
Bond	Bond refers to a debt instrument, issued by a borrower and promising a specified stream of payments to the purchaser, usually regular interest payments plus a final repayment of principal.
Expected rate of return	Expected rate of return refers to the increase in profit a firm anticipates it will obtain by purchasing capital ; expressed as a percentage of the total cost of the investment activity.
Rate of return	A rate of return is a comparison of the money earned (or lost) on an investment to the amount of money invested.
Portfolio	In finance, a portfolio is a collection of investments held by an institution or a private individual. Holding but not always a portfolio is part of an investment and risk-limiting strategy called diversification. By owning several assets, certain types of risk (in particular specific risk) can be reduced.
Diversified portfolio	Diversified portfolio refers to a portfolio that includes a variety of assets whose prices are not likely all to change together. In international economics, this usually means holding assets denominated in different currencies.
Risk premium	In finance, the risk premium can be the expected rate of return above the risk-free interest rate.
Premium	Premium refers to the fee charged by an insurance company for an insurance policy. The rate of losses must be relatively predictable: In order to set the premium (prices) insurers must be able to estimate them accurately.
Capital asset pricing model	The capital asset pricing model is used in finance to determine a theoretically appropriate required rate of return (and thus the price if expected cash flows can be estimated) of an asset, if that asset is to be added to an already well-diversified portfolio, given that asset's non-diversifiable risk.
Capital asset	In accounting, a capital asset is an asset that is recorded as property that creates more property, e.g. a factory that creates shoes, or a forest that yields a quantity of wood.
Asset	An item of property, such as land, capital, money, a share in ownership, or a claim on others for future payment, such as a bond or a bank deposit is an asset.
Investment	Investment refers to spending for the production and accumulation of capital and additions to inventories. In a financial sense, buying an asset with the expectation of making a return.
Appreciation	Appreciation refers to a rise in the value of a country's currency on the exchange market, relative either to a particular other currency or to a weighted average of other currencies. The currency is said to appreciate. Opposite of 'depreciation.' Appreciation can also refer to the increase in value of any asset.
Distribution	Distribution in economics, the manner in which total output and income is distributed among individuals or factors.
Dividend	Amount of corporate profits paid out for each share of stock is referred to as dividend.
Volatility	Volatility refers to the extent to which an economic variable, such as a price or an exchange rate, moves up and down over time.
Corporation	A legal entity chartered by a state or the Federal government that is distinct and separate from the individuals who own it is a corporation. This separation gives the corporation unique powers which other legal entities lack.
Net present	Net present value is a standard method in finance of capital budgeting – the planning of long-

Chapter 11. Global Cost and Availability of Capital

value	term investments. Using this method a potential investment project should be undertaken if the present value of all cash inflows minus the present value of all cash outflows (which equals the net present value) is greater than zero.
Present value	The value today of a stream of payments and/or receipts over time in the future and/or the past, converted to the present using an interest rate. If X t is the amount in period t and r the interest rate, then present value at time t=0 is V = ?T /t.
Cash flow	In finance, cash flow refers to the amounts of cash being received and spent by a business during a defined period of time, sometimes tied to a specific project. Most of the time they are being used to determine gaps in the liquid position of a company.
Deregulation	The lessening or complete removal of government regulations on an industry, especially concerning the price that firms are allowed to charge and leaving price to be determined by market forces a deregulation.
Competitor	Other organizations in the same industry or type of business that provide a good or service to the same set of customers is referred to as a competitor.
Valuation	In finance, valuation is the process of estimating the market value of a financial asset or liability. They can be done on assets (for example, investments in marketable securities such as stocks, options, business enterprises, or intangible assets such as patents and trademarks) or on liabilities (e.g., Bonds issued by a company).
Portfolio investment	Portfolio investment refers to the acquisition of portfolio capital. Usually refers to such transactions across national borders and/or across currencies.
Shares	Shares refer to an equity security, representing a shareholder's ownership of a corporation. Shares are one of a finite number of equal portions in the capital of a company, entitling the owner to a proportion of distributed, non-reinvested profits known as dividends and to a portion of the value of the company in case of liquidation.
Portfolio theory	Portfolio theory refers to an economic theory that describes how rational investors allocate their wealth among different financial assets-that is, how they put their wealth into a 'portfolio.'
Currency risk	Currency risk is a form of risk that arises from the change in price of one currency against another. Whenever investors or companies have assets or business operations across national borders, they face currency risk if their positions are not hedged.
Asset allocation	Asset Allocation is a concept of determining and maintaining a plan of investment in terms of a chosen mix of investments in different assets. A large part of financial planning is finding an asset allocation that is appropriate for a given person in terms of their appetite for and ability to shoulder risk.
Foreign ownership	Foreign ownership refers to the complete or majority ownership/control of businesses or resources in a country, by individuals who are not citizens of that country, or by companies whose headquarters are not in that country.
Diversification	Investing in a collection of assets whose returns do not always move together, with the result that overall risk is lower than for individual assets is referred to as diversification.
Required rate of return	Required rate of return refers to the rate of return that investors demand from an investment to compensate them for the amount of risk involved.
Capital budget	A long-term budget that shows planned acquisition and disposal of capital assets, such as land, building, and equipment is a capital budget. Also a separate budget used by state governments for items such as new construction, major renovations, and acquisition of physical property.

Chapter 11. Global Cost and Availability of Capital

Chapter 11. Global Cost and Availability of Capital

Debt capital	Debt capital refers to funds raized through various forms of borrowing to finance a company that must be repaid.
Budget	Budget refers to an account, usually for a year, of the planned expenditures and the expected receipts of an entity. For a government, the receipts are tax revenues.
Market price	Market price is an economic concept with commonplace familiarity; it is the price that a good or service is offered at, or will fetch, in the marketplace; it is of interest mainly in the study of microeconomics.
Supply and demand	The partial equilibrium supply and demand economic model originally developed by Alfred Marshall attempts to describe, explain, and predict changes in the price and quantity of goods sold in competitive markets.
Supply	Supply is the aggregate amount of any material good that can be called into being at a certain price point; it comprises one half of the equation of supply and demand. In classical economic theory, a curve representing supply is one of the factors that produce price.
Marginal cost of capital	Marginal cost of capital refers to the cost of the last dollar of funds raized. It is assumed that each dollar is financed in proportion to the firm's optimum capital structure.
Marginal cost	Marginal cost refers to the increase in cost that accompanies a unit increase in output; the partial derivative of the cost function with respect to output.
Long run	In economic models, the long run time frame assumes no fixed factors of production. Firms can enter or leave the marketplace, and the cost (and availability) of land, labor, raw materials, and capital goods can be assumed to vary.
Foreign subsidiary	A company owned in a foreign country by another company is referred to as foreign subsidiary.
Subsidiary	A company that is controlled by another company or corporation is a subsidiary.
Market segmentation	The process of dividing the total market into several groups whose members have similar characteristics is market segmentation.
Financial market	In economics, a financial market is a mechanism which allows people to trade money for securities or commodities such as gold or other precious metals. In general, any commodity market might be considered to be a financial market, if the usual purpose of traders is not the immediate consumption of the commodity, but rather as a means of delaying or accelerating consumption over time.
Corporate governance	Corporate governance is the set of processes, customs, policies, laws and institutions affecting the way a corporation is directed, administered or controlled.
Asymmetric information	Asymmetric information refers to the failure of two parties to a transaction to have the same relevant information. Examples are buyers who know less about product quality than sellers, and lenders who know less about likely default than borrowers.
Transaction cost	A transaction cost is a cost incurred in making an economic exchange. For example, most people, when buying or selling a stock, must pay a commission to their broker; that commission is a transaction cost of doing the stock deal.
Context	The effect of the background under which a message often takes on more and richer meaning is a context. Context is especially important in cross-cultural interactions because some cultures are said to be high context or low context.
Users	Users refer to people in the organization who actually use the product or service purchased by the buying center.
Financial risk	The risk related to the inability of the firm to meet its debt obligations as they come due

Go to Cram101.com for the Practice Tests for this Chapter.

Chapter 11. Global Cost and Availability of Capital

Chapter 11. Global Cost and Availability of Capital

	is called financial risk.
Debt ratio	Debt ratio refers to the calculation of the total liabilities divided by the total liabilities plus capital. This results in the measurment of the debt level of the business (leverage).
Short run	Short run refers to a period of time that permits an increase or decrease in current production volume with existing capacity, but one that is too short to permit enlargement of that capacity itself (eg, the building of new plants, training of additional workers, etc.).
Issuer	The company that borrows money from investors by issuing bonds is referred to as issuer. They are legally responsible for the obligations of the issue and for reporting financial conditions, material developments and any other operational activities as required by the regulations of their jurisdictions.
Gain	In finance, gain is a profit or an increase in value of an investment such as a stock or bond. Gain is calculated by fair market value or the proceeds from the sale of the investment minus the sum of the purchase price and all costs associated with it.
Arbitrage	An arbitrage is a combination of nearly simultaneous transactions designed to profit from an existing discrepancy among prices, exchange rates, and/or interest rates on different markets without assuming risk.
Case study	A case study is a particular method of qualitative research. Rather than using large samples and following a rigid protocol to examine a limited number of variables, case study methods involve an in-depth, longitudinal examination of a single instance or event: a case. They provide a systematic way of looking at events, collecting data, analyzing information, and reporting the results.
Stock market	An organized marketplace in which common stocks are traded. In the United States, the largest stock market is the New York Stock Exchange, on which are traded the stocks of the largest U.S. companies.
Technology	The body of knowledge and techniques that can be used to combine economic resources to produce goods and services is called technology.
Policy	Similar to a script in that a policy can be a less than completely rational decision-making method. Involves the use of a pre-existing set of decision steps for any problem that presents itself.
Equity securities	Equity securities refer to representation of ownership rights to the corporation.
Regulation	Regulation refers to restrictions state and federal laws place on business with regard to the conduct of its activities.
Personnel	A collective term for all of the employees of an organization. Personnel is also commonly used to refer to the personnel management function or the organizational unit responsible for administering personnel programs.
Analyst	Analyst refers to a person or tool with a primary function of information analysis, generally with a more limited, practical and short term set of goals than a researcher.
Service	Service refers to a "non tangible product" that is not embodied in a physical good and that typically effects some change in another product, person, or institution. Contrasts with good.
Institutional investors	Institutional investors refers to large organizations such as pension funds, mutual funds, insurance companies, and banks that invest their own funds or the funds of others.
Accounting	A system that collects and processes financial information about an organization and reports

Chapter 11. Global Cost and Availability of Capital

Chapter 11. Global Cost and Availability of Capital

	that information to decision makers is referred to as accounting.
Common stock	Common stock refers to the basic, normal, voting stock issued by a corporation; called residual equity because it ranks after preferred stock for dividend and liquidation distributions.
Capital gain	Capital gain refers to the gain in value that the owner of an asset experiences when the price of the asset rises, including when the currency in which the asset is denominated appreciates.
Prohibition	Prohibition refers to denial of the right to import or export, applying to particular products and/or particular countries. Includes embargo.
Government bond	A government bond is a bond issued by a national government denominated in the country's own currency. Bonds issued by national governments in foreign currencies are normally referred to as sovereign bonds.
Mortgage bond	Type of secured bond that conditionally transfers title of a designated piece of property to the bondholder until the bond is paid is referred to as mortgage bond.
Mortgage	Mortgage refers to a note payable issued for property, such as a house, usually repaid in equal installments consisting of part principle and part interest, over a specified period.
Real rate of return	The adjusted after-inflation return on an investment, calculated by subtracting the current rate of inflation from the rate of return is called the real rate of return.
Inflation	An increase in the overall price level of an economy, usually as measured by the CPI or by the implicit price deflator is called inflation.
Yield	The interest rate that equates a future value or an annuity to a given present value is a yield.
Financial leverage	A measure of the amount of debt used in the capital structure of the firm is the financial leverage.
Leverage	Leverage is using given resources in such a way that the potential positive or negative outcome is magnified. In finance, this generally refers to borrowing.
Variable interest rate	Interest rate that fluctuates from period to period over the life of the loan is the variable interest rate. These rates are most often tied to the prime rate of a particular lending institution, the Consumer Price Index, Federal Funds rates or other money market measurements.
Variable	A variable is something measured by a number; it is used to analyze what happens to other things when the size of that number changes.
Management	Management characterizes the process of leading and directing all or part of an organization, often a business, through the deployment and manipulation of resources. Early twentieth-century management writer Mary Parker Follett defined management as "the art of getting things done through people."
Operation	A standardized method or technique that is performed repetitively, often on different materials resulting in different finished goods is called an operation.
Globalization	The increasing world-wide integration of markets for goods, services and capital that attracted special attention in the late 1990s is called globalization.
Stock exchange	A stock exchange is a corporation or mutual organization which provides facilities for stock brokers and traders, to trade company stocks and other securities.
Foundation	A Foundation is a type of philanthropic organization set up by either individuals or institutions as a legal entity (either as a corporation or trust) with the purpose of

Chapter 11. Global Cost and Availability of Capital

Chapter 11. Global Cost and Availability of Capital

	distributing grants to support causes in line with the goals of the foundation.
A share	In finance the term A share has two distinct meanings, both relating to securities. The first is a designation for a 'class' of common or preferred stock. A share of common or preferred stock typically has enhanced voting rights or other benefits compared to the other forms of shares that may have been created. The equity structure, or how many types of shares are offered, is determined by the corporate charter.
Disclosure	Disclosure means the giving out of information, either voluntarily or to be in compliance with legal regulations or workplace rules.
Disparity	Disparity refers to the regional and economic differences in a country, province, state, or continent
Conversion	Conversion refers to any distinct act of dominion wrongfully exerted over another's personal property in denial of or inconsistent with his rights therein. That tort committed by a person who deals with chattels not belonging to him in a manner that is inconsistent with the ownership of the lawful owner.
Eurobond	A bond that is issued outside of the jurisdiction of any single country, denominated in a eurocurrency is referred to as eurobond.
Gap	In December of 1995, Gap became the first major North American retailer to accept independent monitoring of the working conditions in a contract factory producing its garments. Gap is the largest specialty retailer in the United States.
Financial statement	Financial statement refers to a summary of all the transactions that have occurred over a particular period.
Preemptive right	Preemptive right refers to a shareholder's option to purchase new issuances of shares in proportion to the shareholder's current ownership of the corporation.
Market value	Market value refers to the price of an asset agreed on between a willing buyer and a willing seller; the price an asset could demand if it is sold on the open market.
Issued stock	The actual number of shares of stock currently classified as issued-comprises all the shares given in return for ownership in the corporation less any shares that have been retired is called issued stock.
Par value	The central value of a pegged exchange rate, around which the actual rate is permitted to fluctuate within set bounds is a par value.
At par	At equality refers to at par. Two currencies are said to be 'at par' if they are trading one-for-one.
Points	Loan origination fees that may be deductible as interest by a buyer of property. A seller of property who pays points reduces the selling price by the amount of the points paid for the buyer.
Earnings per share	Earnings per share refers to annual profit of the corporation divided by the number of shares outstanding.
Functional currency	Functional currency refers to the currency of the economic environment in which the taxpayer carries on most of its activities, and in which the taxpayer transacts most of its business.
Hurdle rate	The minimum acceptable rate of return in a capital budgeting decision is the hurdle rate. The hurdle rate should reflect the riskiness of the investment, typically measured by volatility of cash flows, and must take into account the financing mix.
Working capital	The dollar difference between total current assets and total current liabilities is called working capital.

Chapter 11. Global Cost and Availability of Capital

Chapter 11. Global Cost and Availability of Capital

Emerging market	The term emerging market is commonly used to describe business and market activity in industrializing or emerging regions of the world.
Dollarization	Dollarization refers to the official adoption by a country other than the United States of the U.S. dollar as its local currency.
Market niche	A market niche or niche market is a focused, targetable portion of a market. By definition, then, a business that focuses on a niche market is addressing a need for a product or service that is not being addressed by mainstream providers.
Niche	In industry, a niche is a situation or an activity perfectly suited to a person. A niche can imply a working position or an area suited to a person who occupies it. Basically, a job where a person is able to succeed and thrive.
Organization for economic cooperation and development	Organization for economic cooperation and development refers to Paris-based intergovernmental organization of 'wealthy' nations whose purpose is to provide its 29 member states with a forum in which governments can compare their experiences, discuss the problems they share, and seek solutions that can then be applied within their own national contexts.
Union	A worker association that bargains with employers over wages and working conditions is called a union.
Privatization	A process in which investment bankers take companies that were previously owned by the government to the public markets is referred to as privatization.
Relative cost	Relative cost refers to the relationship between the price paid for advertising time or space and the size of the audience delivered; it is used to compare the prices of various media vehicles.
Foreign exchange market	A market for converting the currency of one country into that of another country is called foreign exchange market. It is by far the largest market in the world, in terms of cash value traded, and includes trading between large banks, central banks, currency speculators, multinational corporations, governments, and other financial markets and institutions.
Exchange market	Exchange market refers to the market on which national currencies are bought and sold.
Cash inflow	Cash coming into the company as the result of a previous investment is a cash inflow.
Multinational corporation	An organization that manufactures and markets products in many different countries and has multinational stock ownership and multinational management is referred to as multinational corporation.
International diversification	Achieving diversification through many different foreign investments that are influenced by a variety of factors is referred to as international diversification. By diversifying across nations whose economic cycles are not perfectly correlated, investors can typically reduce the variability of their returns.
Multinational corporations	Firms that own production facilities in two or more countries and produce and sell their products globally are referred to as multinational corporations.
International Business	International business refers to any firm that engages in international trade or investment.
Domestic corporation	A corporation in the state in which it was formed is a domestic corporation.
Capital structure	Capital Structure refers to the way a corporation finances itself through some combination of equity sales, equity options, bonds, and loans. Optimal capital structure refers to the particular combination that minimizes the cost of capital while maximizing the stock price.
Journal	Book of original entry, in which transactions are recorded in a general ledger system, is

Chapter 11. Global Cost and Availability of Capital

	referred to as a journal.
Bankruptcy	Bankruptcy is a legally declared inability or impairment of ability of an individual or organization to pay their creditors.
Yield curve	In finance, the yield curve is the relation between the interest rate (or cost of borrowing) and the maturity of the debt for a given borrower in a given currency.
Internationa-ization	Internationalization refers to another term for fragmentation. Used by Grossman and Helpman.
Economy	The income, expenditures, and resources that affect the cost of running a business and household are called an economy.
Agency cost	An agency cost is the cost incurred by an organization that is associated with problems such as divergent management-shareholder objectives and information asymmetry.
Multinational enterprise	Multinational enterprise refers to a firm, usually a corporation, that operates in two or more countries.
Demand schedule	Demand schedule refers to a list of prices and corresponding quantities consumers are willing to buy, or the graph of that information. Thus a demand curve.
Enterprise	Enterprise refers to another name for a business organization. Other similar terms are business firm, sometimes simply business, sometimes simply firm, as well as company, and entity.
Empirical finding	Something that is observed from real-world observation or data, in contrast to something that is deduced from theory is an empirical finding.
Emerging markets	The term emerging markets is commonly used to describe business and market activity in industrializing or emerging regions of the world. It is sometimes loosely used as a replacement for emerging economies, but really signifies a business phenomenon that is not fully described by or constrained to geography or economic strength; such countries are considered to be in a transitional phase between developing and developed status.
Acer	Acer is one of the world's top five branded PC vendors. It owns the largest computer retail chain in Taiwan. Acer's product offering includes desktop and mobile PCs, servers and storage, displays, peripherals, and e-business solutions for business, government, education, and home users.
Mutual fund	A mutual fund is a form of collective investment that pools money from many investors and invests the money in stocks, bonds, short-term money market instruments, and/or other securities. In a mutual fund, the fund manager trades the fund's underlying securities, realizing capital gains or loss, and collects the dividend or interest income.
Composition	An out-of-court settlement in which creditors agree to accept a fractional settlement on their original claim is referred to as composition.
Eli Lilly	Eli Lilly is a global pharmaceutical company and one of the world's largest corporations. Eli Lilly was the first distributor of methadone, an analgesic used frequently in the treatment of heroin, opium and other opioid and narcotic drug addictions.
Strategic alliance	Strategic alliance refers to a long-term partnership between two or more companies established to help each company build competitive market advantages.
Synergy	Corporate synergy occurs when corporations interact congruently. A corporate synergy refers to a financial benefit that a corporation expects to realize when it merges with or acquires another corporation.
Tradeoff	The sacrifice of some or all of one economic goal, good, or service to achieve some other

goal, good, or service is a tradeoff.

Chapter 12. Sourcing Equity Globally

Restructuring	Restructuring is the corporate management term for the act of partially dismantling and reorganizing a company for the purpose of making it more efficient and therefore more profitable.
Accounting	A system that collects and processes financial information about an organization and reports that information to decision makers is referred to as accounting.
Disclosure	Disclosure means the giving out of information, either voluntarily or to be in compliance with legal regulations or workplace rules.
Firm	An organization that employs resources to produce a good or service for profit and owns and operates one or more plants is referred to as a firm.
Domestic	From or in one's own country. A domestic producer is one that produces inside the home country. A domestic price is the price inside the home country. Opposite of 'foreign' or 'world.'.
Market	A market is, as defined in economics, a social arrangement that allows buyers and sellers to discover information and carry out a voluntary exchange of goods or services.
Capital	Capital generally refers to financial wealth, especially that used to start or maintain a business. In classical economics, capital is one of four factors of production, the others being land and labor and entrepreneurship.
Equity	Equity is the name given to the set of legal principles, in countries following the English common law tradition, which supplement strict rules of law where their application would operate harshly, so as to achieve what is sometimes referred to as "natural justice."
Instrument	Instrument refers to an economic variable that is controlled by policy makers and can be used to influence other variables, called targets. Examples are monetary and fiscal policies used to achieve external and internal balance.
Management	Management characterizes the process of leading and directing all or part of an organization, often a business, through the deployment and manipulation of resources. Early twentieth-century management writer Mary Parker Follett defined management as "the art of getting things done through people."
Investment	Investment refers to spending for the production and accumulation of capital and additions to inventories. In a financial sense, buying an asset with the expectation of making a return.
Investment banker	Investment banker refers to a financial organization that specializes in selling primary offerings of securities. Investment bankers can also perform other financial functions, such as advising clients, negotiating mergers and takeovers, and selling secondary offerings.
Stock exchange	A stock exchange is a corporation or mutual organization which provides facilities for stock brokers and traders, to trade company stocks and other securities.
Exchange	The trade of things of value between buyer and seller so that each is better off after the trade is called the exchange.
Shares	Shares refer to an equity security, representing a shareholder's ownership of a corporation. Shares are one of a finite number of equal portions in the capital of a company, entitling the owner to a proportion of distributed, non-reinvested profits known as dividends and to a portion of the value of the company in case of liquidation.
NASDAQ	NASDAQ is an American electronic stock exchange. It was founded in 1971 by the National Association of Securities Dealers who divested it in a series of sales in 2000 and 2001.
Stock	In financial terminology, stock is the capital raised by a corporation, through the issuance and sale of shares.

Go to **Cram101.com** for the Practice Tests for this Chapter.

Chapter 12. Sourcing Equity Globally

Chapter 12. Sourcing Equity Globally

Negotiable	A negotiable instrument is one that can be bought and sold after being issued - in other words, it is a tradable instrument.
Custodian	Custodian as a financial term, refers to a bank (Custodian bank), agent, or other organization responsible for safeguarding a firm's or individual's financial assets.
Trust	An arrangement in which shareholders of independent firms agree to give up their stock in exchange for trust certificates that entitle them to a share of the trust's common profits.
American Depositary Receipt	An American Depositary Receipt is how the stock of most foreign companies trades in United States stock markets. Each is issued by U.S. depositary banks and represents one or more shares of a foreign stock or a fraction of a share.
Shareholder	A shareholder is an individual or company (including a corporation) that legally owns one or more shares of stock in a joined stock company.
Dividend	Amount of corporate profits paid out for each share of stock is referred to as dividend.
Holder	A person in possession of a document of title or an instrument payable or indorsed to him, his order, or to bearer is a holder.
Bearer	A person in possession of a negotiable instrument that is payable to him, his order, or to whoever is in possession of the instrument is referred to as bearer.
Securities and exchange commission	Securities and exchange commission refers to U.S. government agency that determines the financial statements that public companies must provide to stockholders and the measurement rules that they must use in producing those statements.
Security	Security refers to a claim on the borrower future income that is sold by the borrower to the lender. A security is a type of transferable interest representing financial value.
Liquidity	Liquidity refers to the capacity to turn assets into cash, or the amount of assets in a portfolio that have that capacity.
Supply	Supply is the aggregate amount of any material good that can be called into being at a certain price point; it comprises one half of the equation of supply and demand. In classical economic theory, a curve representing supply is one of the factors that produce price.
Prospectus	Prospectus refers to a report detailing a future stock offering containing a set of financial statements; required by the SEC from a company that wishes to make an initial public offering of its stock.
Capital market	A financial market in which long-term debt and equity instruments are traded is referred to as a capital market. The capital market includes the stock market and the bond market.
Creditor	A person to whom a debt or legal obligation is owed, and who has the right to enforce payment of that debt or obligation is referred to as creditor.
Financial economics	That branch of economics which analyzes how rational investors should invest their funds to attain their objectives in the best possible manner is called financial economics.
Economics	The social science dealing with the use of scarce resources to obtain the maximum satisfaction of society's virtually unlimited economic wants is an economics.
Journal	Book of original entry, in which transactions are recorded in a general ledger system, is referred to as a journal.
Secondary market	Secondary market refers to the market for securities that have already been issued. It is a market in which investors trade back and forth with each other.
Channel	Channel, in communications (sometimes called communications channel), refers to the medium used to convey information from a sender (or transmitter) to a receiver.

Chapter 12. Sourcing Equity Globally

Chapter 12. Sourcing Equity Globally

Fund	Independent accounting entity with a self-balancing set of accounts segregated for the purposes of carrying on specific activities is referred to as a fund.
Market capitalization	Market capitalization is a business term that refers to the aggregate value of a firm's outstanding common shares. In essence, market capitalization reflects the total value of a firm's equity currently available on the market. This measure differs from equity value to the extent that a firm has outstanding stock options or other securities convertible to common shares. The size and growth of a firm's market capitalization is often one of the critical measurements of a public company's success or failure.
Turnover	Turnover in a financial context refers to the rate at which a provider of goods cycles through its average inventory. Turnover in a human resources context refers to the characteristic of a given company or industry, relative to rate at which an employer gains and loses staff.
Market concentration	Market concentration is a function of the number of firms and their respective shares of the total production (alternatively, total capacity or total reserves) in a market which reflects the degree of competition in the market.
Market value	Market value refers to the price of an asset agreed on between a willing buyer and a willing seller; the price an asset could demand if it is sold on the open market.
Gain	In finance, gain is a profit or an increase in value of an investment such as a stock or bond. Gain is calculated by fair market value or the proceeds from the sale of the investment minus the sum of the purchase price and all costs associated with it.
Transaction cost	A transaction cost is a cost incurred in making an economic exchange. For example, most people, when buying or selling a stock, must pay a commission to their broker; that commission is a transaction cost of doing the stock deal.
Dealer	People who link buyers with sellers by buying and selling securities at stated prices are referred to as a dealer.
Crisis management	Crisis management involves identifying a crisis, planning a response to the crisis and confronting and resolving the crisis.
Specialist	A specialist is a trader who makes a market in one or several stocks and holds the limit order book for those stocks.
Equity capital	Equity capital refers to money raized from within the firm or through the sale of ownership in the firm.
Market makers	Market makers refer to financial service companies that connect investors and borrowers, either directly or indirectly.
Industry	A group of firms that produce identical or similar products is an industry. It is also used specifically to refer to an area of economic production focused on manufacturing which involves large amounts of capital investment before any profit can be realized, also called "heavy industry".
Emerging markets	The term emerging markets is commonly used to describe business and market activity in industrializing or emerging regions of the world. It is sometimes loosely used as a replacement for emerging economies, but really signifies a business phenomenon that is not fully described by or constrained to geography or economic strength; such countries are considered to be in a transitional phase between developing and developed status.
Emerging market	The term emerging market is commonly used to describe business and market activity in industrializing or emerging regions of the world.
Abnormal returns	Abnormal returns is a term used by stock market traders to describe the difference between a

Chapter 12. Sourcing Equity Globally

Chapter 12. Sourcing Equity Globally

	single stock or portfolio's performance in regard to the average market performance (usually a broad index s.a. the S&P 500 and EURO STOXX 50 or a national index like the Nikkei) over a set period of time.
Capital flow	International capital movement is referred to as capital flow.
Underwriters	Investment banks that guarantee prices on securities to corporations and then sell the securities to the public are underwriters.
Marketing	Promoting and selling products or services to customers, or prospective customers, is referred to as marketing.
Working capital	The dollar difference between total current assets and total current liabilities is called working capital.
Corporate image	A corporate image refers to how a corporation is perceived. It is a generally accepted image of what a company "stands for".
Trademark	A distinctive word, name, symbol, device, or combination thereof, which enables consumers to identify favored products or services and which may find protection under state or federal law is a trademark.
Joint venture	Joint venture refers to an undertaking by two parties for a specific purpose and duration, taking any of several legal forms.
International Business	International business refers to any firm that engages in international trade or investment.
Valuation	In finance, valuation is the process of estimating the market value of a financial asset or liability. They can be done on assets (for example, investments in marketable securities such as stocks, options, business enterprises, or intangible assets such as patents and trademarks) or on liabilities (e.g., Bonds issued by a company).
Host country	The country in which the parent-country organization seeks to locate or has already located a facility is a host country.
Acquisition	A company's purchase of the property and obligations of another company is an acquisition.
Swap	In finance a swap is a derivative, where two counterparties exchange one stream of cash flows against another stream. These streams are called the legs of the swap. The cash flows are calculated over a notional principal amount. Swaps are often used to hedge certain risks, for instance interest rate risk. Another use is speculation.
A share	In finance the term A share has two distinct meanings, both relating to securities. The first is a designation for a 'class' of common or preferred stock. A share of common or preferred stock typically has enhanced voting rights or other benefits compared to the other forms of shares that may have been created. The equity structure, or how many types of shares are offered, is determined by the corporate charter.
Stock option	A stock option is a specific type of option that uses the stock itself as an underlying instrument to determine the option's pay-off and therefore its value.
Option	A contract that gives the purchaser the option to buy or sell the underlying financial instrument at a specified price, called the exercise price or strike price, within a specific period of time.
Foreign exchange	In finance, foreign exchange means currencies, such as U.S. Dollars and Euros. These are traded on foreign exchange markets.
Beneficiary	The person for whose benefit an insurance policy, trust, will, or contract is established is a beneficiary. In the case of a contract, the beneficiary is called a third-party

Go to **Cram101.com** for the Practice Tests for this Chapter.

Chapter 12. Sourcing Equity Globally

Chapter 12. Sourcing Equity Globally

	beneficiary.
Operating results	Operating results refers to measures that are important to monitoring and tracking the effectiveness of a company's operations.
Balance sheet	A statement of the assets, liabilities, and net worth of a firm or individual at some given time often at the end of its "fiscal year," is referred to as a balance sheet.
Balance	In banking and accountancy, the outstanding balance is the amount of money owned, (or due), that remains in a deposit account (or a loan account) at a given date, after all past remittances, payments and withdrawal have been accounted for. It can be positive (then, in the balance sheet of a firm, it is an asset) or negative (a liability).
Financial disclosure	Presentation of financial information to the investment community is a financial disclosure. It is a requirement to obtain a loan by providing information on assets and income in the form of tax returns when a person is self-employed.
Cost of equity	In finance, the cost of equity is the minimum rate of return a firm must offer shareholders to compensate for waiting for their returns, and for bearing some risk.
Trend	Trend refers to the long-term movement of an economic variable, such as its average rate of increase or decrease over enough years to encompass several business cycles.
Probability distribution	A specification of the probabilities for each possible value of a random variable is called probability distribution.
Expected return	Expected return refers to the return on an asset expected over the next period.
Distribution	Distribution in economics, the manner in which total output and income is distributed among individuals or factors.
Cost of capital	Cost of capital refers to the percentage cost of funds used for acquiring resources for an organization, typically a weighted average of the firms cost of equity and cost of debt.
Corporation	A legal entity chartered by a state or the Federal government that is distinct and separate from the individuals who own it is a corporation. This separation gives the corporation unique powers which other legal entities lack.
Chrysler	The Chrysler Corporation was an American automobile manufacturer that existed independently from 1925–1998. The company was formed by Walter Percy Chrysler on June 6, 1925, with the remaining assets of Maxwell Motor Company.
Strategic alliance	Strategic alliance refers to a long-term partnership between two or more companies established to help each company build competitive market advantages.
Private placement	Private placement refers to the sale of securities directly to a financial institution by a corporation. This eliminates the middleman and reduces the cost of issue to the corporation.
Target market	One or more specific groups of potential consumers toward which an organization directs its marketing program are a target market.
Market niche	A market niche or niche market is a focused, targetable portion of a market. By definition, then, a business that focuses on a niche market is addressing a need for a product or service that is not being addressed by mainstream providers.
Technology	The body of knowledge and techniques that can be used to combine economic resources to produce goods and services is called technology.
Personnel	A collective term for all of the employees of an organization. Personnel is also commonly used to refer to the personnel management function or the organizational unit responsible for administering personnel programs.

Go to Cram101.com for the Practice Tests for this Chapter.

Chapter 12. Sourcing Equity Globally

Chapter 12. Sourcing Equity Globally

Leverage	Leverage is using given resources in such a way that the potential positive or negative outcome is magnified. In finance, this generally refers to borrowing.
Niche	In industry, a niche is a situation or an activity perfectly suited to a person. A niche can imply a working position or an area suited to a person who occupies it. Basically, a job where a person is able to succeed and thrive.
Marginal cost of capital	Marginal cost of capital refers to the cost of the last dollar of funds raized. It is assumed that each dollar is financed in proportion to the firm's optimum capital structure.
Marginal cost	Marginal cost refers to the increase in cost that accompanies a unit increase in output; the partial derivative of the cost function with respect to output.
Integration	Economic integration refers to reducing barriers among countries to transactions and to movements of goods, capital, and labor, including harmonization of laws, regulations, and standards. Integrated markets theoretically function as a unified market.
Issuer	The company that borrows money from investors by issuing bonds is referred to as issuer. They are legally responsible for the obligations of the issue and for reporting financial conditions, material developments and any other operational activities as required by the regulations of their jurisdictions.
Euro	The common currency of a subset of the countries of the EU, adopted January 1, 1999 is called euro.
Privatization	A process in which investment bankers take companies that were previously owned by the government to the public markets is referred to as privatization.
Enterprise	Enterprise refers to another name for a business organization. Other similar terms are business firm, sometimes simply business, sometimes simply firm, as well as company, and entity.
Tranche	In structured finance the word tranche refers to one of several related securitized bonds offered as part of the same deal. They are called tranches since each bond is a slice of the deal's risk. The legal documents usually refer to the tranches as "classes" of notes identified by letter (e.g. the Class A, Class B, Class C securities).
Profit	Profit refers to the return to the resource entrepreneurial ability; total revenue minus total cost.
Underwriting syndicate	Underwriting syndicate refers to a group of investment bankers that is formed to share the risk of a security offering and also to facilitate the distribution of the securities.
Investment banks	Investment banks, assist public and private corporations in raising funds in the capital markets (both equity and debt), as well as in providing strategic advisory services for mergers, acquisitions and other types of financial transactions. They also act as intermediaries in trading for clients. Investment banks differ from commercial banks, which take deposits and make commercial and retail loans.
Underwriting	The process of selling securities and, at the same time, assuring the seller a specified price is underwriting. Underwriting is done by investment bankers and represents a form of risk taking.
Performance improvement	Performance improvement is the concept of measuring the output of a particular process or procedure then modifying the process or procedure in order to increase the output, increase efficiency, or increase the effectiveness of the process or procedure.
Buyer	A buyer refers to a role in the buying center with formal authority and responsibility to select the supplier and negotiate the terms of the contract.
Insurance	Insurance refers to a system by which individuals can reduce their exposure to risk of large

Chapter 12. Sourcing Equity Globally

	losses by spreading the risks among a large number of persons.
Buy and hold	Buy and hold is a long term investment strategy based on the concept that in the long run financial markets give a good rate of return despite periods of volatility or decline. This viewpoint also holds that market timing, i.e. the concept that one can enter the market on the lows and sell on the highs, does not work or does not work for small investors so it is better to simply buy and hold.
Policy	Similar to a script in that a policy can be a less than completely rational decision-making method. Involves the use of a pre-existing set of decision steps for any problem that presents itself.
Net worth	Net worth is the total assets minus total liabilities of an individual or company
Pension fund	Amounts of money put aside by corporations, nonprofit organizations, or unions to cover part of the financial needs of members when they retire is a pension fund.
Pension	A pension is a steady income given to a person (usually after retirement). Pensions are typically payments made in the form of a guaranteed annuity to a retired or disabled employee.
Regulation	Regulation refers to restrictions state and federal laws place on business with regard to the conduct of its activities.
Debt security	Type of security acquired by loaning assets is called a debt security.
Globalization	The increasing world-wide integration of markets for goods, services and capital that attracted special attention in the late 1990s is called globalization.
Limited partnership	A partnership in which some of the partners are limited partners. At least one of the partners in a limited partnership must be a general partner.
Partnership	In the common law, a partnership is a type of business entity in which partners share with each other the profits or losses of the business undertaking in which they have all invested.
Venture capital	Venture capital is capital provided by outside investors for financing of new, growing or struggling businesses. Venture capital investments generally are high risk investments but offer the potential for above average returns.
Developed country	A developed country is one that enjoys a relatively high standard of living derived through an industrialized, diversified economy. Countries with a very high Human Development Index are generally considered developed countries.
Buyout	A buyout is an investment transaction by which the entire or a controlling part of the stock of a company is sold. A firm buysout the stake of the company to strengthen its influence on the company's decision making body. A buyout can take the forms of a leveraged buyout or a management buyout.
Divestment	In finance and economics, divestment or divestiture is the reduction of some kind of asset, for either financial or social goals. A divestment is the opposite of an investment.
Operation	A standardized method or technique that is performed repetitively, often on different materials resulting in different finished goods is called an operation.
Stock market	An organized marketplace in which common stocks are traded. In the United States, the largest stock market is the New York Stock Exchange, on which are traded the stocks of the largest U.S. companies.
Principal	In agency law, one under whose direction an agent acts and for whose benefit that agent acts is a principal.
Siemens	Siemens is the world's largest conglomerate company. Worldwide, Siemens and its subsidiaries

Chapter 12. Sourcing Equity Globally

Chapter 12. Sourcing Equity Globally

	employs 461,000 people (2005) in 190 countries and reported global sales of €75.4 billion in fiscal year 2005.
Toyota	Toyota is a Japanese multinational corporation that manufactures automobiles, trucks and buses. Toyota is the world's second largest automaker by sales. Toyota also provides financial services through its subsidiary, Toyota Financial Services, and participates in other lines of business.
Nokia	Nokia Corporation is the world's largest manufacturer of mobile telephones (as of June 2006), with a global market share of approximately 34% in Q2 of 2006. It produces mobile phones for every major market and protocol, including GSM, CDMA, and W-CDMA (UMTS).
Foreign corporation	Foreign corporation refers to a corporation incorporated in one state doing business in another state. A corporation doing business in a jurisdiction in which it was not formed.
Analyst	Analyst refers to a person or tool with a primary function of information analysis, generally with a more limited, practical and short term set of goals than a researcher.
Innovation	Innovation refers to the first commercially successful introduction of a new product, the use of a new method of production, or the creation of a new form of business organization.
Deutsche Bank	Deutsche Bank was founded in Germany on January 22, 1870 as a specialist bank for foreign trade. Major projects in its first decades included the Northern Pacific Railroad in the United States (1883) and the Baghdad Railway (1888). It also financed bond offerings of the steel concern Krupp (1885) and introduced the chemical company Bayer on the Berlin stock market.
Stockholder	A stockholder is an individual or company (including a corporation) that legally owns one or more shares of stock in a joined stock company. The shareholders are the owners of a corporation. Companies listed at the stock market strive to enhance shareholder value.
Service	Service refers to a "non tangible product" that is not embodied in a physical good and that typically effects some change in another product, person, or institution. Contrasts with good.
Subsidiary	A company that is controlled by another company or corporation is a subsidiary.
DaimlerChrysler	In 2002, the merged company, DaimlerChrysler, appeared to run two independent product lines, with few signs of corporate integration. In 2003, however, it was alleged by the Detroit News that the "merger of equals" was, in fact, a takeover.
Novartis	Novartis was created in 1996 from the merger of Ciba-Geigy and Sandoz Laboratories, both Swiss companies with long individual histories. At the time of the merger, it was the largest corporate merger in history.
Merger	Merger refers to the combination of two firms into a single firm.
BASF	BASF produces a wide range of chemicals, for example solvents, amines, resins, glues, electronic-grade chemicals, industrial gases, basic petrochemicals and inorganic chemicals. The most important customers for this segment are the pharmaceutical, construction, textile and automotive industries.

Go to **Cram101.com** for the Practice Tests for this Chapter.

Chapter 13. Financial Structure and International Debt

Firm	An organization that employs resources to produce a good or service for profit and owns and operates one or more plants is referred to as a firm.
Compromise	Compromise occurs when the interaction is moderately important to meeting goals and the goals are neither completely compatible nor completely incompatible.
Cost of capital	Cost of capital refers to the percentage cost of funds used for acquiring resources for an organization, typically a weighted average of the firms cost of equity and cost of debt.
Business risk	The risk related to the inability of the firm to hold its competitive position and maintain stability and growth in earnings is business risk.
Bankruptcy	Bankruptcy is a legally declared inability or impairment of ability of an individual or organization to pay their creditors.
Capital	Capital generally refers to financial wealth, especially that used to start or maintain a business. In classical economics, capital is one of four factors of production, the others being land and labor and entrepreneurship.
Equity	Equity is the name given to the set of legal principles, in countries following the English common law tradition, which supplement strict rules of law where their application would operate harshly, so as to achieve what is sometimes referred to as "natural justice."
Financial risk	The risk related to the inability of the firm to meet its debt obligations as they come due is called financial risk.
Foreign exchange risk	Foreign exchange risk refers to a form of risk that refers to the possibility of experiencing a drop in revenue or an increase in cost in an international transaction due to a change in foreign exchange rates. Importers, exporters, investors, and multinational firms alike are exposed to this risk.
Foreign exchange	In finance, foreign exchange means currencies, such as U.S. Dollars and Euros. These are traded on foreign exchange markets.
Diversification	Investing in a collection of assets whose returns do not always move together, with the result that overall risk is lower than for individual assets is referred to as diversification.
Portfolio	In finance, a portfolio is a collection of investments held by an institution or a private individual. Holding but not always a portfolio is part of an investment and risk-limiting strategy called diversification. By owning several assets, certain types of risk (in particular specific risk) can be reduced.
Cash flow	In finance, cash flow refers to the amounts of cash being received and spent by a business during a defined period of time, sometimes tied to a specific project. Most of the time they are being used to determine gaps in the liquid position of a company.
Exchange	The trade of things of value between buyer and seller so that each is better off after the trade is called the exchange.
Domestic	From or in one's own country. A domestic producer is one that produces inside the home country. A domestic price is the price inside the home country. Opposite of 'foreign' or 'world.'.
Variable	A variable is something measured by a number; it is used to analyze what happens to other things when the size of that number changes.
Cost of equity	In finance, the cost of equity is the minimum rate of return a firm must offer shareholders to compensate for waiting for their returns, and for bearing some risk.
Market	A market is, as defined in economics, a social arrangement that allows buyers and sellers to

Go to **Cram101.com** for the Practice Tests for this Chapter.

Chapter 13. Financial Structure and International Debt

Chapter 13. Financial Structure and International Debt

	discover information and carry out a voluntary exchange of goods or services.
Debt ratio	Debt ratio refers to the calculation of the total liabilities divided by the total liabilities plus capital. This results in the measurment of the debt level of the business (leverage).
Fund	Independent accounting entity with a self-balancing set of accounts segregated for the purposes of carrying on specific activities is referred to as a fund.
Capital market	A financial market in which long-term debt and equity instruments are traded is referred to as a capital market. The capital market includes the stock market and the bond market.
Foreign exchange market	A market for converting the currency of one country into that of another country is called foreign exchange market. It is by far the largest market in the world, in terms of cash value traded, and includes trading between large banks, central banks, currency speculators, multinational corporations, governments, and other financial markets and institutions.
Exchange market	Exchange market refers to the market on which national currencies are bought and sold.
Security	Security refers to a claim on the borrower future income that is sold by the borrower to the lender. A security is a type of transferable interest representing financial value.
Holding	The holding is a court's determination of a matter of law based on the issue presented in the particular case. In other words: under this law, with these facts, this result.
International diversification	Achieving diversification through many different foreign investments that are influenced by a variety of factors is referred to as international diversification. By diversifying across nations whose economic cycles are not perfectly correlated, investors can typically reduce the variability of their returns.
Cash inflow	Cash coming into the company as the result of a previous investment is a cash inflow.
Operation	A standardized method or technique that is performed repetitively, often on different materials resulting in different finished goods is called an operation.
Argument	The discussion by counsel for the respective parties of their contentions on the law and the facts of the case being tried in order to aid the jury in arriving at a correct and just conclusion is called argument.
Asymmetric information	Asymmetric information refers to the failure of two parties to a transaction to have the same relevant information. Examples are buyers who know less about product quality than sellers, and lenders who know less about likely default than borrowers.
Political risk	Refers to the many different actions of people, subgroups, and whole countries that have the potential to affect the financial status of a firm is called political risk.
Agency cost	An agency cost is the cost incurred by an organization that is associated with problems such as divergent management-shareholder objectives and information asymmetry.
Cost of debt	The cost of debt is the cost of borrowing money (usually denoted by Kd). It is derived by dividing debt's interest payments on the total market value of the debts.
Principal	In agency law, one under whose direction an agent acts and for whose benefit that agent acts is a principal.
Interest	In finance and economics, interest is the price paid by a borrower for the use of a lender's money. In other words, interest is the amount of paid to "rent" money for a period of time.
Appreciation	Appreciation refers to a rise in the value of a country's currency on the exchange market, relative either to a particular other currency or to a weighted average of other currencies. The currency is said to appreciate. Opposite of 'depreciation.' Appreciation can also refer to the increase in value of any asset.

Chapter 13. Financial Structure and International Debt

Spot rate	Spot rate refers to the rate at which the currency is traded for immediate delivery. It is the existing cash price.
Bond	Bond refers to a debt instrument, issued by a borrower and promising a specified stream of payments to the purchaser, usually regular interest payments plus a final repayment of principal.
Gain	In finance, gain is a profit or an increase in value of an investment such as a stock or bond. Gain is calculated by fair market value or the proceeds from the sale of the investment minus the sum of the purchase price and all costs associated with it.
Export credit	Export credit refers to a loan to the buyer of an export, extended by the exporting firm when shipping the good prior to payment, or by a facility of the exporting country's government.
Credit	Credit refers to a recording as positive in the balance of payments, any transaction that gives rise to a payment into the country, such as an export, the sale of an asset, or borrowing from abroad.
Export	In economics, an export is any good or commodity, shipped or otherwise transported out of a country, province, town to another part of the world in a legitimate fashion, typically for use in trade or sale.
Eurobond	A bond that is issued outside of the jurisdiction of any single country, denominated in a eurocurrency is referred to as eurobond.
Maturity	Maturity refers to the final payment date of a loan or other financial instrument, after which point no further interest or principal need be paid.
Coupon	In finance, a coupon is "attached" to a bond, either physically (as with old bonds) or electronically. Each coupon represents a predetermined payment promized to the bond-holder in return for his or her loan of money to the bond-issuer. .
Exchange rate	Exchange rate refers to the price at which one country's currency trades for another, typically on the exchange market.
Corporate governance	Corporate governance is the set of processes, customs, policies, laws and institutions affecting the way a corporation is directed, administered or controlled.
Corporate bond	A Corporate bond is a bond issued by a corporation, as the name suggests. The term is usually applied to longer term debt instruments, generally with a maturity date falling at least 12 months after their issue date (the term "commercial paper" being sometimes used for instruments with a shorter maturity).
Bond market	The bond market refers to people and entities involved in buying and selling of bonds and the quantity and prices of those transactions over time.
Regulation	Regulation refers to restrictions state and federal laws place on business with regard to the conduct of its activities.
Trend	Trend refers to the long-term movement of an economic variable, such as its average rate of increase or decrease over enough years to encompass several business cycles.
Foreign subsidiary	A company owned in a foreign country by another company is referred to as foreign subsidiary.
Equity investment	Equity investment generally refers to the buying and holding of shares of stock on a stock market by individuals and funds in anticipation of income from dividends and capital gain as the value of the stock rises.
Host country	The country in which the parent-country organization seeks to locate or has already located a facility is a host country.

Chapter 13. Financial Structure and International Debt

Chapter 13. Financial Structure and International Debt

Subsidiary	A company that is controlled by another company or corporation is a subsidiary.
Investment	Investment refers to spending for the production and accumulation of capital and additions to inventories. In a financial sense, buying an asset with the expectation of making a return.
Monetary policy	The use of the money supply and/or the interest rate to influence the level of economic activity and other policy objectives including the balance of payments or the exchange rate is called monetary policy.
Policy	Similar to a script in that a policy can be a less than completely rational decision-making method. Involves the use of a pre-existing set of decision steps for any problem that presents itself.
Return on equity	Net profit after taxes per dollar of equity capital is referred to as return on equity.
Competitor	Other organizations in the same industry or type of business that provide a good or service to the same set of customers is referred to as a competitor.
Management	Management characterizes the process of leading and directing all or part of an organization, often a business, through the deployment and manipulation of resources. Early twentieth-century management writer Mary Parker Follett defined management as "the art of getting things done through people."
Industry	A group of firms that produce identical or similar products is an industry. It is also used specifically to refer to an area of economic production focused on manufacturing which involves large amounts of capital investment before any profit can be realized, also called "heavy industry".
Return on Assets	The Return on Assets percentage shows how profitable a company's assets are in generating revenue.
Full employment	Full employment refers to the unemployment rate at which there is no cyclical unemployment of the labor force; equal to between 4 and 5 percent in the United States because some frictional and structural unemployment is unavoidable.
Interest rate	The rate of return on bonds, loans, or deposits. When one speaks of 'the' interest rate, it is usually in a model where there is only one.
Scarcity	Scarcity is defined as not having sufficient resources to produce enough to fulfill unlimited subjective wants. Alternatively, scarcity implies that not all of society's goals can be attained at the same time, so that trade-offs one good against others are made.
Leverage	Leverage is using given resources in such a way that the potential positive or negative outcome is magnified. In finance, this generally refers to borrowing.
Economy	The income, expenditures, and resources that affect the cost of running a business and household are called an economy.
Labor	People's physical and mental talents and efforts that are used to help produce goods and services are called labor.
Asset	An item of property, such as land, capital, money, a share in ownership, or a claim on others for future payment, such as a bond or a bank deposit is an asset.
Comparative advantage	The ability to produce a good at lower cost, relative to other goods, compared to another country is a comparative advantage.
Balance sheet	A statement of the assets, liabilities, and net worth of a firm or individual at some given time often at the end of its "fiscal year," is referred to as a balance sheet.
Balance	In banking and accountancy, the outstanding balance is the amount of money owned, (or due), that remains in a deposit account (or a loan account) at a given date, after all past

Chapter 13. Financial Structure and International Debt

	remittances, payments and withdrawal have been accounted for. It can be positive (then, in the balance sheet of a firm, it is an asset) or negative (a liability).
Money market	The money market, in macroeconomics and international finance, refers to the equilibration of demand for a country's domestic money to its money supply; market for short-term financial instruments.
Time deposit	The technical name for a savings account is a time deposit; the bank can require prior notice before the owner withdraws money from a time deposit.
Certificates of deposit	Certificates of deposit refer to a certificate offered by banks, savings and loans, and other financial institutions for the deposit of funds at a given interest rate over a specified time period.
Fractional reserve	A reserve requirement that is less than 100 percent of the checkable-deposit liabilities of a commercial bank or thrift institution is a fractional reserve.
Demand deposit	Demand deposit refers to a bank deposit that can be withdrawn 'on demand.' The term usually refers only to checking accounts, even though depositors in many other kinds of accounts may be able to write checks and regard their deposits as readily available.
Analogy	Analogy is either the cognitive process of transferring information from a particular subject to another particular subject (the target), or a linguistic expression corresponding to such a process. In a narrower sense, analogy is an inference or an argument from a particular to another particular, as opposed to deduction, induction, and abduction, where at least one of the premises or the conclusion is general.
Convertible currency	Convertible currency refers to a currency that can legally be exchanged for another or for gold.
Euro	The common currency of a subset of the countries of the EU, adopted January 1, 1999 is called euro.
Eurodollars	Eurodollars refers to u.S. dollars that are deposited in foreign banks outside the United States or in foreign branches of U.S. banks.
Eurocurrency	Eurocurrency is the term used to describe deposits residing in banks that are located outside the borders of the country that issues the currency the deposit is denominated in.
Eurocurrencies	A variant of the Eurobond, which are foreign currencies deposited in banks outside the home country is an eurocurrencies.
Financial intermediary	Financial intermediary refers to a financial institution, such as a bank or a life insurance company, which directs other people's money into such investments as government and corporate securities.
Bid	A bid price is a price offered by a buyer when he/she buys a good. In the context of stock trading on a stock exchange, the bid price is the highest price a buyer of a stock is willing to pay for a share of that given stock.
World Bank	The World Bank is a group of five international organizations responsible for providing finance and advice to countries for the purposes of economic development and poverty reduction, and for encouraging and safeguarding international investment.
Holder	A person in possession of a document of title or an instrument payable or indorsed to him, his order, or to bearer is a holder.
Union	A worker association that bargains with employers over wages and working conditions is called a union.
Central Bank	Central bank refers to the institution in a country that is normally responsible for managing

Go to **Cram101.com** for the Practice Tests for this Chapter.

Chapter 13. Financial Structure and International Debt

Chapter 13. Financial Structure and International Debt

	the supply of the country's money and the value of its currency on the foreign exchange market.
Yield	The interest rate that equates a future value or an annuity to a given present value is a yield.
Commercial bank	A firm that engages in the business of banking is a commercial bank.
Insurance	Insurance refers to a system by which individuals can reduce their exposure to risk of large losses by spreading the risks among a large number of persons.
Economic efficiency	Economic efficiency refers to the use of the minimum necessary resources to obtain the socially optimal amounts of goods and services; entails both productive efficiency and allocative efficiency.
Authority	Authority in agency law, refers to an agent's ability to affect his principal's legal relations with third parties. Also used to refer to an actor's legal power or ability to do something. In addition, sometimes used to refer to a statute, case, or other legal source that justifies a particular result.
Bank of England	The Bank of England is the central bank of the United Kingdom, sometimes known as "The Old Lady of Threadneedle Street" or "The Old Lady".
Balance of payments	Balance of payments refers to a list, or accounting, of all of a country's international transactions for a given time period, usually one year.
Instrument	Instrument refers to an economic variable that is controlled by policy makers and can be used to influence other variables, called targets. Examples are monetary and fiscal policies used to achieve external and internal balance.
Interest rate spread	Difference between the interest rates that banks pay their depositors and the interest rates they receive on their loans and investments is referred to as interest rate spread.
Eurodollar loans	Eurodollar loans refer to loans made by foreign banks denominated in U.S. dollars.
Interest expense	The cost a business incurs to borrow money. With respect to bonds payable, the interest expense is calculated by multiplying the market rate of interest by the carrying value of the bonds on the date of the payment.
Basis point	One one-hundredth of a percentage point is a basis point. Each one percent in interest is equal to 100 basis points.
Expense	In accounting, an expense represents an event in which an asset is used up or a liability is incurred. In terms of the accounting equation, expenses reduce owners' equity.
Points	Loan origination fees that may be deductible as interest by a buyer of property. A seller of property who pays points reduces the selling price by the amount of the points paid for the buyer.
Risk premium	In finance, the risk premium can be the expected rate of return above the risk-free interest rate.
Premium	Premium refers to the fee charged by an insurance company for an insurance policy. The rate of losses must be relatively predictable: In order to set the premium (prices) insurers must be able to estimate them accurately.
Syndicated loan	A syndicated loan (or "syndicated bank facility") is a large loan in which a group of banks work together to provide funds for a borrower. There is usually one lead bank (the "Arranger") that takes a small percentage of the loan and syndicates the rest to other banks. A syndicated loan is the opposite of a bilateral loan, which only involves one borrower and one lender (often a bank or financial institution.)

Chapter 13. Financial Structure and International Debt

Chapter 13. Financial Structure and International Debt

Underwriters	Investment banks that guarantee prices on securities to corporations and then sell the securities to the public are underwriters.
Citibank	In April of 2006, Citibank struck a deal with 7-Eleven to put its ATMs in over 5,500 convenience stores in the U.S. In the same month, it also announced it would sell all of its Buffalo and Rochester New York branches and accounts to M&T Bank.
Channel	Channel, in communications (sometimes called communications channel), refers to the medium used to convey information from a sender (or transmitter) to a receiver.
Airbus	In 2003, for the first time in its 33-year history, Airbus delivered more jet-powered airliners than Boeing. Boeing states that the Boeing 777 has outsold its Airbus counterparts, which include the A340 family as well as the A330-300. The smaller A330-200 competes with the 767, outselling its Boeing counterpart.
Margin	A deposit by a buyer in stocks with a seller or a stockbroker, as security to cover fluctuations in the market in reference to stocks that the buyer has purchased but for which he has not paid is a margin. Commodities are also traded on margin.
Underwriting	The process of selling securities and, at the same time, assuring the seller a specified price is underwriting. Underwriting is done by investment bankers and represents a form of risk taking.
Aid	Assistance provided by countries and by international institutions such as the World Bank to developing countries in the form of monetary grants, loans at low interest rates, in kind, or a combination of these is called aid. Aid can also refer to assistance of any type rendered to benefit some group or individual.
Debt service	The payments made by a borrower on their debt, usually including both interest payments and partial repayment of principal, are called debt service.
Service	Service refers to a "non tangible product" that is not embodied in a physical good and that typically effects some change in another product, person, or institution. Contrasts with good.
Distribution	Distribution in economics, the manner in which total output and income is distributed among individuals or factors.
Negotiable	A negotiable instrument is one that can be bought and sold after being issued - in other words, it is a tradable instrument.
Secondary market	Secondary market refers to the market for securities that have already been issued. It is a market in which investors trade back and forth with each other.
Commercial paper	Commercial paper is a money market security issued by large banks and corporations. It is generally not used to finance long-term investments but rather for purchases of inventory or to manage working capital. It is commonly bought by money funds (the issuing amounts are often too high for individual investors), and is generally regarded as a very safe investment.
Corporation	A legal entity chartered by a state or the Federal government that is distinct and separate from the individuals who own it is a corporation. This separation gives the corporation unique powers which other legal entities lack.
Gap	In December of 1995, Gap became the first major North American retailer to accept independent monitoring of the working conditions in a contract factory producing its garments. Gap is the largest specialty retailer in the United States.
Shelf registration	Shelf registration is an arrangement with the U.S. Securities and Exchange Commission that allows a single registration document to be filed that permits the issuance of multiple

Chapter 13. Financial Structure and International Debt

Chapter 13. Financial Structure and International Debt

	securities.
Securities and exchange commission	Securities and exchange commission refers to U.S. government agency that determines the financial statements that public companies must provide to stockholders and the measurement rules that they must use in producing those statements.
Coupon rate	In bonds, notes or other fixed income securities, the stated percentage rate of interest, usually paid twice a year is the coupon rate.
Foreign bonds	Bonds sold in a foreign country and denominated in that country's currency are foreign bonds. Many domestic markets are also open to foreign borrowers who, although domiciled outside the country, can issue bonds in the domestic currency for sale to local investors as long as they comply with the same local regulations as their domestic counterparts.
Eurobonds	Eurobonds refer to bonds payable or denominated in the borrower's currency, but sold outside the country of the borrower, usually by an international syndicate. This market is dominated by bonds stated in U.S. dollars.
Multinational corporation	An organization that manufactures and markets products in many different countries and has multinational stock ownership and multinational management is referred to as multinational corporation.
Domestic corporation	A corporation in the state in which it was formed is a domestic corporation.
Multinational corporations	Firms that own production facilities in two or more countries and produce and sell their products globally are referred to as multinational corporations.
Enterprise	Enterprise refers to another name for a business organization. Other similar terms are business firm, sometimes simply business, sometimes simply firm, as well as company, and entity.
Call provision	Call provision refers to bonds and some preferred stock, in which a call allows the corporation to retire securities before maturity by forcing the bondholders to sell bonds back to it at a set price. The call provisions are included in the bond indenture.
Sinking fund	A sinking fund is a method by which an organization sets aside money over time to retire its indebtedness. More specifically, it is a fund into which money can be deposited, so that over time its preferred stock, debentures or stocks can be retired.
Bearer	A person in possession of a negotiable instrument that is payable to him, his order, or to whoever is in possession of the instrument is referred to as bearer.
Merchant	Under the Uniform Commercial Code, one who regularly deals in goods of the kind sold in the contract at issue, or holds himself out as having special knowledge or skill relevant to such goods, or who makes the sale through an agent who regularly deals in such goods or claims such knowledge or skill is referred to as merchant.
Maturity date	The date on which the final payment on a bond is due from the bond issuer to the investor is a maturity date.
Bearer bond	A bearer bond is a legal certificate that usually represents a bond obligation of, or stock in, a corporation or some other intangible property.
Perpetuity	A perpetuity is an annuity in which the periodic payments begin on a fixed date and continue indefinitely. Fixed coupon payments on permanently invested (irredeemable) sums of money are prime examples of perpetuities. Scholarships paid perpetually from an endowment fit the definition of perpetuity.
Shares	Shares refer to an equity security, representing a shareholder's ownership of a corporation. Shares are one of a finite number of equal portions in the capital of a company, entitling

Chapter 13. Financial Structure and International Debt

Chapter 13. Financial Structure and International Debt

	the owner to a proportion of distributed, non-reinvested profits known as dividends and to a portion of the value of the company in case of liquidation.
Stock	In financial terminology, stock is the capital raized by a corporation, through the issuance and sale of shares.
Issuer	The company that borrows money from investors by issuing bonds is referred to as issuer. They are legally responsible for the obligations of the issue and for reporting financial conditions, material developments and any other operational activities as required by the regulations of their jurisdictions.
Investment banker	Investment banker refers to a financial organization that specializes in selling primary offerings of securities. Investment bankers can also perform other financial functions, such as advising clients, negotiating mergers and takeovers, and selling secondary offerings.
Samurai bond	A Samurai bond is a Japanese Yen-denominated bond that is issued in Japan by a foreign institution or government.
Yankee bond	A Yankee bond is a US Dollar-denominated bond that is issued in the United States by a foreign institution or government.
Disclosure	Disclosure means the giving out of information, either voluntarily or to be in compliance with legal regulations or workplace rules.
Private placement	Private placement refers to the sale of securities directly to a financial institution by a corporation. This eliminates the middleman and reduces the cost of issue to the corporation.
Agent	A person who makes economic decisions for another economic actor. A hired manager operates as an agent for a firm's owner.
Registered bond	A registered bond refers to a bond for which the issuing company keeps a record of the name and address of the bondholder and pays interest and principal payments directly to the registered owner.
Tax avoidance	The minimization of one's tax liability by taking advantage of legally available tax planning opportunities. Tax avoidance can be contrasted with tax evasion, which entails the reduction of tax liability by illegal means.
Financial statement	Financial statement refers to a summary of all the transactions that have occurred over a particular period.
Creditworthiness	Creditworthiness indicates whether a borrower has in the past made loan payments when due.
Evaluation	The consumer's appraisal of the product or brand on important attributes is called evaluation.
Assessment	Collecting information and providing feedback to employees about their behavior, communication style, or skills is an assessment.
Bond ratings	Bond ratings refers to rating of bonds according to risk by Standard & Poor's and Moody's Investor Service. A bond that is rated A by Moody's has the lowest risk, while a bond with a C rating has the highest risk. Coupon rates are greatly influenced by a corporation's bond rating.
Economic risk	The likelihood that events, including economic mismanagement, will cause drastic changes in a country's business environment that adversely affects the profit and other goals of a particular business enterprise is referred to as economic risk.
Liquidity	Liquidity refers to the capacity to turn assets into cash, or the amount of assets in a portfolio that have that capacity.
Shareholder	A shareholder is an individual or company (including a corporation) that legally owns one or

Chapter 13. Financial Structure and International Debt

Chapter 13. Financial Structure and International Debt

	more shares of stock in a joined stock company.
Emerging markets	The term emerging markets is commonly used to describe business and market activity in industrializing or emerging regions of the world. It is sometimes loosely used as a replacement for emerging economies, but really signifies a business phenomenon that is not fully described by or constrained to geography or economic strength; such countries are considered to be in a transitional phase between developing and developed status.
Emerging market	The term emerging market is commonly used to describe business and market activity in industrializing or emerging regions of the world.
Production	The creation of finished goods and services using the factors of production: land, labor, capital, entrepreneurship, and knowledge.
Entrepreneur	The owner/operator. The person who organizes, manages, and assumes the risks of a firm, taking a new idea or a new product and turning it into a successful business is an entrepreneur.
Lender	Suppliers and financial institutions that lend money to companies is referred to as a lender.
Property	Assets defined in the broadest legal sense. Property includes the unrealized receivables of a cash basis taxpayer, but not services rendered.
Legal entity	A legal entity is a legal construct through which the law allows a group of natural persons to act as if it were an individual for certain purposes. The most common purposes are lawsuits, property ownership, and contracts.
Inception	The date and time on which coverage under an insurance policy takes effect is inception. Also refers to the date at which a stock or mutual fund was first traded.
Homogeneous	In the context of procurement/purchasing, homogeneous is used to describe goods that do not vary in their essential characteristic irrespective of the source of supply.
Commodity	Could refer to any good, but in trade a commodity is usually a raw material or primary product that enters into international trade, such as metals or basic agricultural products.
Inflation	An increase in the overall price level of an economy, usually as measured by the CPI or by the implicit price deflator is called inflation.
Contract	A contract is a "promise" or an "agreement" that is enforced or recognized by the law. In the civil law, a contract is considered to be part of the general law of obligations.
Financial distress	Financial distress is a term in Corporate Finance used to indicate a condition when promises to creditors of a company are broken or honored with difficulty. Sometimes financial distress can lead to bankruptcy. Financial distress is usually associated with some costs to the company and these are known as Costs of Financial Distress. A common example of a cost of financial distress is bankrupty costs.
Revenue	Revenue is a U.S. business term for the amount of money that a company receives from its activities, mostly from sales of products and/or services to customers.
British Petroleum	British Petroleum, is a British energy company with headquarters in London, one of four vertically integrated private sector oil, natural gas, and petrol (gasoline) "supermajors" in the world, along with Royal Dutch Shell, ExxonMobil and Total.
Joint venture	Joint venture refers to an undertaking by two parties for a specific purpose and duration, taking any of several legal forms.
Mobil	Mobil is a major oil company which merged with the Exxon Corporation in 1999. Today Mobil continues as a major brand name within the combined company.
Exxon	Exxon formally replaced the Esso, Enco, and Humble brands on January 1, 1973, in the USA. The

Chapter 13. Financial Structure and International Debt

Chapter 13. Financial Structure and International Debt

	name Esso, pronounced S-O, attracted protests from other Standard Oil spinoffs because of its similarity to the name of the parent company, Standard Oil.
Marginal cost of capital	Marginal cost of capital refers to the cost of the last dollar of funds raized. It is assumed that each dollar is financed in proportion to the firm's optimum capital structure.
Capital budget	A long-term budget that shows planned acquisition and disposal of capital assets, such as land, building, and equipment is a capital budget. Also a separate budget used by state governments for items such as new construction, major renovations, and acquisition of physical property.
Marginal cost	Marginal cost refers to the increase in cost that accompanies a unit increase in output; the partial derivative of the cost function with respect to output.
Budget	Budget refers to an account, usually for a year, of the planned expenditures and the expected receipts of an entity. For a government, the receipts are tax revenues.
Localization	As an element of wireless marketing strategy, transmitting messages that are relevant to the user's current geographical location are referred to as localization.
Context	The effect of the background under which a message often takes on more and richer meaning is a context. Context is especially important in cross-cultural interactions because some cultures are said to be high context or low context.
Weighted average	The weighted average unit cost of the goods available for sale for both cost of goods sold and ending inventory.
Weighted average cost of capital	Weighted average cost of capital refers to the computed cost of capital determined by multiplying the cost of each item in the optimal capital structure by its weighted representation in the overall capital structure and summing up the results.
Average cost	Average cost is equal to total cost divided by the number of goods produced (Quantity-Q). It is also equal to the sum of average variable costs (total variable costs divided by Q) plus average fixed costs (total fixed costs divided by Q).
Creditor	A person to whom a debt or legal obligation is owed, and who has the right to enforce payment of that debt or obligation is referred to as creditor.
Manufacturing	Production of goods primarily by the application of labor and capital to raw materials and other intermediate inputs, in contrast to agriculture, mining, forestry, fishing, and services a manufacturing.
Appeal	Appeal refers to the act of asking an appellate court to overturn a decision after the trial court's final judgment has been entered.
Depreciate	A nation's currency is said to depreciate when exchange rates change so that a unit of its currency can buy fewer units of foreign currency.
At par	At equality refers to at par. Two currencies are said to be 'at par' if they are trading one-for-one.
Credit risk	The risk of loss due to a counterparty defaulting on a contract, or more generally the risk of loss due to some "credit event" is called credit risk.
Working capital	The dollar difference between total current assets and total current liabilities is called working capital.
Currency risk	Currency risk is a form of risk that arises from the change in price of one currency against another. Whenever investors or companies have assets or business operations across national borders, they face currency risk if their positions are not hedged.
Default risk	The chance that the issuer of a debt instrument will be unable to make interest payments or

Chapter 13. Financial Structure and International Debt

Chapter 13. Financial Structure and International Debt

	pay off the face value when the instrument matures is called default risk.
Default	In finance, default occurs when a debtor has not met its legal obligations according to the debt contract, e.g. it has not made a scheduled payment, or violated a covenant (condition) of the debt contract.
Brady Bonds	Brady bonds are dollar-denominated bonds, issued mostly by Latin American countries in the 1980s. Brady bonds were created in March 1989 in order to convert bonds issued by mostly Latin American countries into a variety or "menu" of new bonds after many of those countries defaulted on their debt in the 1980's. At that time, the market for sovereign debt was small and illiquid, and the standardization of emerging-market debt facilitated risk-spreading and trading. In exchange for commercial bank loans, the countries issued new bonds for the principal and, in some cases, unpaid interest.
Financial crisis	A loss of confidence in a country's currency or other financial assets causing international investors to withdraw their funds from the country is referred to as a financial crisis.
Financial institution	A financial institution acts as an agent that provides financial services for its clients. Financial institutions generally fall under financial regulation from a government authority.
Shell	One of the original Seven Sisters, Royal Dutch/Shell is the world's third-largest oil company by revenue, and a major player in the petrochemical industry and the solar energy business. Shell has six core businesses: Exploration and Production, Gas and Power, Downstream, Chemicals, Renewables, and Trading/Shipping, and operates in more than 140 countries.
DuPont	DuPont was the inventor of CFCs (along with General Motors) and the largest producer of these ozone depleting chemicals (used primarily in aerosol sprays and refrigerants) in the world, with a 25% market share in the late 1980s.
Technology	The body of knowledge and techniques that can be used to combine economic resources to produce goods and services is called technology.
Total cost	The sum of fixed cost and variable cost is referred to as total cost.
Cost overrun	Cost overrun is defined as excess of actual cost over budget. Cost overrun is typically calculated in one of two ways. Either as a percentage, namely actual cost minus budgeted cost, in percent of budgeted cost. Or as a ratio, viz. actual cost divided by budgeted cost.
Market price	Market price is an economic concept with commonplace familiarity; it is the price that a good or service is offered at, or will fetch, in the marketplace; it is of interest mainly in the study of microeconomics.
Debt financing	Obtaining financing by borrowing money is debt financing.
Treasury bills	Short-term obligations of the federal government are treasury bills. They are like zero coupon bonds in that they do not pay interest prior to maturity; instead they are sold at a discount of the par value to create a positive yield to maturity.

Chapter 13. Financial Structure and International Debt

Chapter 14. Interest Rate and Currency Swaps

Financial management	The job of managing a firm's resources so it can meet its goals and objectives is called financial management.
Financial risk	The risk related to the inability of the firm to meet its debt obligations as they come due is called financial risk.
Interest rate	The rate of return on bonds, loans, or deposits. When one speaks of 'the' interest rate, it is usually in a model where there is only one.
Management	Management characterizes the process of leading and directing all or part of an organization, often a business, through the deployment and manipulation of resources. Early twentieth-century management writer Mary Parker Follett defined management as "the art of getting things done through people."
Commodity	Could refer to any good, but in trade a commodity is usually a raw material or primary product that enters into international trade, such as metals or basic agricultural products.
Interest	In finance and economics, interest is the price paid by a borrower for the use of a lender's money. In other words, interest is the amount of paid to "rent" money for a period of time.
Cash flow	In finance, cash flow refers to the amounts of cash being received and spent by a business during a defined period of time, sometimes tied to a specific project. Most of the time they are being used to determine gaps in the liquid position of a company.
Firm	An organization that employs resources to produce a good or service for profit and owns and operates one or more plants is referred to as a firm.
Foreign exchange risk	Foreign exchange risk refers to a form of risk that refers to the possibility of experiencing a drop in revenue or an increase in cost in an international transaction due to a change in foreign exchange rates. Importers, exporters, investors, and multinational firms alike are exposed to this risk.
Interest rate risk	Interest rate risk is the risk that the relative value of a security, especially a bond, will worsen due to an interest rate increase. This risk is commonly measured by the bond's duration.
Foreign exchange	In finance, foreign exchange means currencies, such as U.S. Dollars and Euros. These are traded on foreign exchange markets.
Exchange	The trade of things of value between buyer and seller so that each is better off after the trade is called the exchange.
Debt service	The payments made by a borrower on their debt, usually including both interest payments and partial repayment of principal, are called debt service.
Service	Service refers to a "non tangible product" that is not embodied in a physical good and that typically effects some change in another product, person, or institution. Contrasts with good.
Maturity	Maturity refers to the final payment date of a loan or other financial instrument, after which point no further interest or principal need be paid.
Yield curve	In finance, the yield curve is the relation between the interest rate (or cost of borrowing) and the maturity of the debt for a given borrower in a given currency.
Credit	Credit refers to a recording as positive in the balance of payments, any transaction that gives rise to a payment into the country, such as an export, the sale of an asset, or borrowing from abroad.
Yield	The interest rate that equates a future value or an annuity to a given present value is a yield.

Go to **Cram101.com** for the Practice Tests for this Chapter.

Chapter 14. Interest Rate and Currency Swaps

Chapter 14. Interest Rate and Currency Swaps

Marketable securities	Marketable securities refer to securities that are readily traded in the secondary securities market.
Balance sheet	A statement of the assets, liabilities, and net worth of a firm or individual at some given time often at the end of its "fiscal year," is referred to as a balance sheet.
Portfolio	In finance, a portfolio is a collection of investments held by an institution or a private individual. Holding but not always a portfolio is part of an investment and risk-limiting strategy called diversification. By owning several assets, certain types of risk (in particular specific risk) can be reduced.
Security	Security refers to a claim on the borrower future income that is sold by the borrower to the lender. A security is a type of transferable interest representing financial value.
Balance	In banking and accountancy, the outstanding balance is the amount of money owned, (or due), that remains in a deposit account (or a loan account) at a given date, after all past remittances, payments and withdrawal have been accounted for. It can be positive (then, in the balance sheet of a firm, it is an asset) or negative (a liability).
Financial manager	Managers who make recommendations to top executives regarding strategies for improving the financial strength of a firm are referred to as a financial manager.
Instrument	Instrument refers to an economic variable that is controlled by policy makers and can be used to influence other variables, called targets. Examples are monetary and fiscal policies used to achieve external and internal balance.
Eurobond	A bond that is issued outside of the jurisdiction of any single country, denominated in a eurocurrency is referred to as eurobond.
Hedging	A technique for avoiding a risk by making a counteracting transaction is referred to as hedging.
Market	A market is, as defined in economics, a social arrangement that allows buyers and sellers to discover information and carry out a voluntary exchange of goods or services.
Union	A worker association that bargains with employers over wages and working conditions is called a union.
Notional principal	The amount on which interest is being paid in a swap arrangement is known as notional principal. In interest rate swaps the notional amounts are not exchanged, so any credit risk is limited to the net amount payable plus a potential future exposure factor.
Interest expense	The cost a business incurs to borrow money. With respect to bonds payable, the interest expense is calculated by multiplying the market rate of interest by the carrying value of the bonds on the date of the payment.
Principal	In agency law, one under whose direction an agent acts and for whose benefit that agent acts is a principal.
Contract	A contract is a "promise" or an "agreement" that is enforced or recognized by the law. In the civil law, a contract is considered to be part of the general law of obligations.
Expense	In accounting, an expense represents an event in which an asset is used up or a liability is incurred. In terms of the accounting equation, expenses reduce owners' equity.
Buyer	A buyer refers to a role in the buying center with formal authority and responsibility to select the supplier and negotiate the terms of the contract.
Investment	Investment refers to spending for the production and accumulation of capital and additions to inventories. In a financial sense, buying an asset with the expectation of making a return.
Economy	The income, expenditures, and resources that affect the cost of running a business and

Go to **Cram101.com** for the Practice Tests for this Chapter.

Chapter 14. Interest Rate and Currency Swaps

Chapter 14. Interest Rate and Currency Swaps

	household are called an economy.
Treasurer	In many governments, a treasurer is the person responsible for running the treasury. Treasurers are also employed by organizations to look after funds.
Futures	Futures refer to contracts for the sale and future delivery of stocks or commodities, wherein either party may waive delivery, and receive or pay, as the case may be, the difference in market price at the time set for delivery.
Currency futures contract	A futures contract that may be used for hedging or speculation in foreign exchange is called a currency futures contract.
Futures contract	In finance, a futures contract is a standardized contract, traded on a futures exchange, to buy or sell a certain underlying instrument at a certain date in the future, at a pre-set price. The
Chicago Mercantile Exchange	The Chicago Mercantile Exchange is the largest futures exchange in the United States. It has four major product areas: short term interest rates, stock market indexes, foreign exchange, and commodities. It has the largest options and futures contracts open interest (number of contracts outstanding) of any futures exchange in the world, which indicates a very high liquidity. This is vital to the success of any stock or futures exchange.
Bond	Bond refers to a debt instrument, issued by a borrower and promising a specified stream of payments to the purchaser, usually regular interest payments plus a final repayment of principal.
Interest payment	The payment to holders of bonds payable, calculated by multiplying the stated rate on the face of the bond by the par, or face, value of the bond. If bonds are issued at a discount or premium, the interest payment does not equal the interest expense.
Maturity date	The date on which the final payment on a bond is due from the bond issuer to the investor is a maturity date.
Future interest	Future interest refers to an interest that will come into being at some future time. It is distinguished from a present interest, which already exists. Assume that Dan transfers securities to a newly created trust.
Futures market	Futures market refers to a market for exchange in futures contracts. That is, participants contract to exchange currencies, not today, but at a specified calendar date in the future, and at a price that is agreed upon today.
Swap	In finance a swap is a derivative, where two counterparties exchange one stream of cash flows against another stream. These streams are called the legs of the swap. The cash flows are calculated over a notional principal amount. Swaps are often used to hedge certain risks, for instance interest rate risk. Another use is speculation.
Currency swap	Currency swap refers to the exchange of a set of payments in one currency for a set of payments in another currency.
Capital	Capital generally refers to financial wealth, especially that used to start or maintain a business. In classical economics, capital is one of four factors of production, the others being land and labor and entrepreneurship.
Standing	Standing refers to the legal requirement that anyone seeking to challenge a particular action in court must demonstrate that such action substantially affects his legitimate interests before he will be entitled to bring suit.
Forming	The first stage of team development, where the team is formed and the objectives for the team are set is referred to as forming.

Chapter 14. Interest Rate and Currency Swaps

Fixed interest rate — Interest rate that does not change over the life of the loan is called the fixed interest rate. A rate that does not fluctuate with general market conditions.

Fixed interest — A fixed interest rate loan is a loan where the interest rate doesn't fluctuate over the life of the loan. This allows the borrower to accurately predict their future payments. When the prevailing interest rate is very low, a fixed rate loan will be slightly higher than variable rate loans because the lender is taking a risk they he could get a higher interest rate by loaning money later.

Derivative — A derivative is a generic term for specific types of investments from which payoffs over time are derived from the performance of assets (such as commodities, shares or bonds), interest rates, exchange rates, or indices (such as a stock market index, consumer price index (CPI) or an index of weather conditions).

Coupon — In finance, a coupon is "attached" to a bond, either physically (as with old bonds) or electronically. Each coupon represents a predetermined payment promized to the bond-holder in return for his or her loan of money to the bond-issuer. .

Dealer — People who link buyers with sellers by buying and selling securities at stated prices are referred to as a dealer.

Gap — In December of 1995, Gap became the first major North American retailer to accept independent monitoring of the working conditions in a contract factory producing its garments. Gap is the largest specialty retailer in the United States.

Capital market — A financial market in which long-term debt and equity instruments are traded is referred to as a capital market. The capital market includes the stock market and the bond market.

Corporation — A legal entity chartered by a state or the Federal government that is distinct and separate from the individuals who own it is a corporation. This separation gives the corporation unique powers which other legal entities lack.

Bid — A bid price is a price offered by a buyer when he/she buys a good. In the context of stock trading on a stock exchange, the bid price is the highest price a buyer of a stock is willing to pay for a share of that given stock.

Exchange rate — Exchange rate refers to the price at which one country's currency trades for another, typically on the exchange market.

Net present value — Net present value is a standard method in finance of capital budgeting – the planning of long-term investments. Using this method a potential investment project should be undertaken if the present value of all cash inflows minus the present value of all cash outflows (which equals the net present value) is greater than zero.

Present value — The value today of a stream of payments and/or receipts over time in the future and/or the past, converted to the present using an interest rate. If X t is the amount in period t and r the interest rate, then present value at time t=0 is V = ?T /t.

Inception — The date and time on which coverage under an insurance policy takes effect is inception. Also refers to the date at which a stock or mutual fund was first traded.

Financial accounting — Financial accounting is the branch of accountancy concerned with the preparation of financial statements for external decision makers, such as stockholders, suppliers, banks and government agencies. The fundamental need for financial accounting is to reduce principal-agent problem by measuring and monitoring agents' performance.

Accounting — A system that collects and processes financial information about an organization and reports that information to decision makers is referred to as accounting.

Spot exchange — The exchange rate at which a foreign exchange dealer will convert one currency into another

Chapter 14. Interest Rate and Currency Swaps

Chapter 14. Interest Rate and Currency Swaps

rate	that particular day is the spot exchange rate.
Appreciation	Appreciation refers to a rise in the value of a country's currency on the exchange market, relative either to a particular other currency or to a weighted average of other currencies. The currency is said to appreciate. Opposite of 'depreciation.' Appreciation can also refer to the increase in value of any asset.
Hedge	Hedge refers to a process of offsetting risk. In the foreign exchange market, hedgers use the forward market to cover a transaction or open position and thereby reduce exchange risk. The term applies most commonly to trade.
Counterparty	A counterparty is a legal and financial term. It means a party to a contract. Any legal entity can be a counterparty.
Face value	The nominal or par value of an instrument as expressed on its face is referred to as the face value.
Authority	Authority in agency law, refers to an agent's ability to affect his principal's legal relations with third parties. Also used to refer to an actor's legal power or ability to do something. In addition, sometimes used to refer to a statute, case, or other legal source that justifies a particular result.
Profit	Profit refers to the return to the resource entrepreneurial ability; total revenue minus total cost.
Exchange market	Exchange market refers to the market on which national currencies are bought and sold.
Holder	A person in possession of a document of title or an instrument payable or indorsed to him, his order, or to bearer is a holder.
Default	In finance, default occurs when a debtor has not met its legal obligations according to the debt contract, e.g. it has not made a scheduled payment, or violated a covenant (condition) of the debt contract.
Financial derivatives	Instruments that have payoffs that are linked to previously issued securities, used as risk reduction tools are referred to as financial derivatives.
Derivatives market	The derivatives market is the financial market for derivatives. The market can be divided into two, that for exchange traded derivatives and that for over-the-counter derivatives. The legal nature of these products is very different as well as the way they are traded, though many market participants are active in both.
Stock exchange	A stock exchange is a corporation or mutual organization which provides facilities for stock brokers and traders, to trade company stocks and other securities.
Option	A contract that gives the purchaser the option to buy or sell the underlying financial instrument at a specified price, called the exercise price or strike price, within a specific period of time.
Stock	In financial terminology, stock is the capital raized by a corporation, through the issuance and sale of shares.
Insurance	Insurance refers to a system by which individuals can reduce their exposure to risk of large losses by spreading the risks among a large number of persons.
Fund	Independent accounting entity with a self-balancing set of accounts segregated for the purposes of carrying on specific activities is referred to as a fund.
Financial institution	A financial institution acts as an agent that provides financial services for its clients. Financial institutions generally fall under financial regulation from a government authority.
Holding	The holding is a court's determination of a matter of law based on the issue presented in the

Chapter 14. Interest Rate and Currency Swaps

	particular case. In other words: under this law, with these facts, this result.
Euro	The common currency of a subset of the countries of the EU, adopted January 1, 1999 is called euro.
Replacement cost	The current purchase price of replacing a property damaged or lost with similar property is the replacement cost.
Basis point	One one-hundredth of a percentage point is a basis point. Each one percent in interest is equal to 100 basis points.
Points	Loan origination fees that may be deductible as interest by a buyer of property. A seller of property who pays points reduces the selling price by the amount of the points paid for the buyer.
Export credit	Export credit refers to a loan to the buyer of an export, extended by the exporting firm when shipping the good prior to payment, or by a facility of the exporting country's government.
Export	In economics, an export is any good or commodity, shipped or otherwise transported out of a country, province, town to another part of the world in a legitimate fashion, typically for use in trade or sale.
Goldman Sachs	Goldman Sachs is widely respected as a financial advisor to some of the most important companies, largest governments, and wealthiest families in the world. It is a primary dealer in the U.S. Treasury securities market. It offers its clients mergers & acquisitions advisory, provides underwriting services, engages in proprietary trading, invests in private equity deals, and also manages the wealth of affluent individuals and families.
Negotiation	Negotiation is the process whereby interested parties resolve disputes, agree upon courses of action, bargain for individual or collective advantage, and/or attempt to craft outcomes which serve their mutual interests.
Swap rate	Swap rate is the difference between the spot and forward exchange rates.
Credit risk	The risk of loss due to a counterparty defaulting on a contract, or more generally the risk of loss due to some "credit event" is called credit risk.
Comparative advantage	The ability to produce a good at lower cost, relative to other goods, compared to another country is a comparative advantage.
Volatility	Volatility refers to the extent to which an economic variable, such as a price or an exchange rate, moves up and down over time.
Variable	A variable is something measured by a number; it is used to analyze what happens to other things when the size of that number changes.
Currency risk	Currency risk is a form of risk that arises from the change in price of one currency against another. Whenever investors or companies have assets or business operations across national borders, they face currency risk if their positions are not hedged.
Profit center	Responsibility center where the manager is accountable for revenues and costs is referred to as a profit center.
Cost center	A cost center is a division that adds to the cost of the organization, but only indirectly adds to the profit of the company. Examples include Research and Development, Marketing and Customer service. A cost center is often identified with a speed type number.
Lender	Suppliers and financial institutions that lend money to companies is referred to as a lender.
Competitor	Other organizations in the same industry or type of business that provide a good or service to the same set of customers is referred to as a competitor.

Go to **Cram101.com** for the Practice Tests for this Chapter.

Chapter 14. Interest Rate and Currency Swaps

Weighted average	The weighted average unit cost of the goods available for sale for both cost of goods sold and ending inventory.
Cost of capital	Cost of capital refers to the percentage cost of funds used for acquiring resources for an organization, typically a weighted average of the firms cost of equity and cost of debt.
Weighted average cost of capital	Weighted average cost of capital refers to the computed cost of capital determined by multiplying the cost of each item in the optimal capital structure by its weighted representation in the overall capital structure and summing up the results.
Average cost	Average cost is equal to total cost divided by the number of goods produced (Quantity-Q). It is also equal to the sum of average variable costs (total variable costs divided by Q) plus average fixed costs (total fixed costs divided by Q).
Compounded semiannually	A compounding period of every six months is called compounded semiannually.
Manufacturing	Production of goods primarily by the application of labor and capital to raw materials and other intermediate inputs, in contrast to agriculture, mining, forestry, fishing, and services a manufacturing.
Federal Reserve	The Federal Reserve System was created via the Federal Reserve Act of December 23rd, 1913. All national banks were required to join the system and other banks could join. The Reserve Banks opened for business on November 16th, 1914. Federal Reserve Notes were created as part of the legislation, to provide an elastic supply of currency.
Emerging markets	The term emerging markets is commonly used to describe business and market activity in industrializing or emerging regions of the world. It is sometimes loosely used as a replacement for emerging economies, but really signifies a business phenomenon that is not fully described by or constrained to geography or economic strength; such countries are considered to be in a transitional phase between developing and developed status.
Emerging market	The term emerging market is commonly used to describe business and market activity in industrializing or emerging regions of the world.
Operation	A standardized method or technique that is performed repetitively, often on different materials resulting in different finished goods is called an operation.
Foreign subsidiary	A company owned in a foreign country by another company is referred to as foreign subsidiary.
Equity investment	Equity investment generally refers to the buying and holding of shares of stock on a stock market by individuals and funds in anticipation of income from dividends and capital gain as the value of the stock rises.
Subsidiary	A company that is controlled by another company or corporation is a subsidiary.
Equity	Equity is the name given to the set of legal principles, in countries following the English common law tradition, which supplement strict rules of law where their application would operate harshly, so as to achieve what is sometimes referred to as "natural justice."
Parent company	Parent company refers to the entity that has a controlling influence over another company. It may have its own operations, or it may have been set up solely for the purpose of owning the Subject Company.
Equity capital	Equity capital refers to money raized from within the firm or through the sale of ownership in the firm.
Profit and loss statement	Profit and loss statement refers to another term for the income statement.

Chapter 14. Interest Rate and Currency Swaps

Chapter 14. Interest Rate and Currency Swaps

Gain	In finance, gain is a profit or an increase in value of an investment such as a stock or bond. Gain is calculated by fair market value or the proceeds from the sale of the investment minus the sum of the purchase price and all costs associated with it.
Functional currency	Functional currency refers to the currency of the economic environment in which the taxpayer carries on most of its activities, and in which the taxpayer transacts most of its business.
Consolidation	The combination of two or more firms, generally of equal size and market power, to form an entirely new entity is a consolidation.
Shareholder	A shareholder is an individual or company (including a corporation) that legally owns one or more shares of stock in a joined stock company.
Financial accounting standards board	Financial accounting standards board refers to the private sector body given the primary responsibility to work out the detailed rules that become generally accepted accounting principles.
Financial accounting Standards	Financial Accounting Standards refers to a set of standards that dictate accounting rules concerning financial reporting; establish generally accepted accounting principles.
Accounting Standards Board	The role of the Accounting Standards Board is to issue accounting standards in the United Kingdom. It is recognized for that purpose under the Companies Act 1985. It took over the task of setting accounting standards from the Accounting Standards Committee (ASC) in 1990.
Fiscal year	A fiscal year is a 12-month period used for calculating annual ("yearly") financial reports in businesses and other organizations. In many jurisdictions, regulatory laws regarding accounting require such reports once per twelve months, but do not require that the twelve months constitute a calendar year (i.e. January to December).
Complexity	The technical sophistication of the product and hence the amount of understanding required to use it is referred to as complexity. It is the opposite of simplicity.
Comprehensive income	Comprehensive income refers to net income plus unrealized gain or loss on securities, minimum pension liability adjustment, and foreign currency translation adjustment.
Financial statement	Financial statement refers to a summary of all the transactions that have occurred over a particular period.
Earnings per share	Earnings per share refers to annual profit of the corporation divided by the number of shares outstanding.
Comprehensive	A comprehensive refers to a layout accurate in size, color, scheme, and other necessary details to show how a final ad will look. For presentation only, never for reproduction.
Sensitivity analysis	A what-if technique that managers use to examine how a result will change if the original predicted data are not achieved or if an underlying assumption changes is sensitivity analysis.

Go to Cram101.com for the Practice Tests for this Chapter.

Chapter 14. Interest Rate and Currency Swaps

Chapter 15. Foreign Direct Investment Theory and Strategy

Protectionism	Protectionism refers to advocacy of protection. The word has a negative connotation, and few advocates of protection in particular situations will acknowledge being protectionists.
Host country	The country in which the parent-country organization seeks to locate or has already located a facility is a host country.
Policy	Similar to a script in that a policy can be a less than completely rational decision-making method. Involves the use of a pre-existing set of decision steps for any problem that presents itself.
Fund	Independent accounting entity with a self-balancing set of accounts segregated for the purposes of carrying on specific activities is referred to as a fund.
Acquisition	A company's purchase of the property and obligations of another company is an acquisition.
Corporate governance	Corporate governance is the set of processes, customs, policies, laws and institutions affecting the way a corporation is directed, administered or controlled.
Merger	Merger refers to the combination of two firms into a single firm.
Nestle	Nestle is the world's biggest food and beverage company. In the 1860s, a pharmacist, developed a food for babies who were unable to be breastfed. His first success was a premature infant who could not tolerate his own mother's milk nor any of the usual substitutes. The value of the new product was quickly recognized when his new formula saved the child's life.
Asset	An item of property, such as land, capital, money, a share in ownership, or a claim on others for future payment, such as a bond or a bank deposit is an asset.
Technology	The body of knowledge and techniques that can be used to combine economic resources to produce goods and services is called technology.
Differentiated product	A firm's product that is not identical to products of other firms in the same industry is a differentiated product.
Marketing	Promoting and selling products or services to customers, or prospective customers, is referred to as marketing.
Competitive advantage	A business is said to have a competitive advantage when its unique strengths, often based on cost, quality, time, and innovation, offer consumers a greater percieved value and there by differtiating it from its competitors.
Human capital	Human capital refers to the stock of knowledge and skill, embodied in an individual as a result of education, training, and experience that makes them more productive. The stock of knowledge and skill embodied in the population of an economy.
Proprietary	Proprietary indicates that a party, or proprietor, exercises private ownership, control or use over an item of property, usually to the exclusion of other parties. Where a party, holds or claims proprietary interests in relation to certain types of property (eg. a creative literary work, or software), that property may also be the subject of intellectual property law (eg. copyright or patents).
Possession	Possession refers to respecting real property, exclusive dominion and control such as owners of like property usually exercise over it. Manual control of personal property either as owner or as one having a qualified right in it.
Capital	Capital generally refers to financial wealth, especially that used to start or maintain a business. In classical economics, capital is one of four factors of production, the others being land and labor and entrepreneurship.
Firm	An organization that employs resources to produce a good or service for profit and owns and

Chapter 15. Foreign Direct Investment Theory and Strategy

	operates one or more plants is referred to as a firm.
Transactions cost	Any cost associated with bringing buyers and sellers together is referred to as transactions cost.
Financial institution	A financial institution acts as an agent that provides financial services for its clients. Financial institutions generally fall under financial regulation from a government authority.
Asymmetric information	Asymmetric information refers to the failure of two parties to a transaction to have the same relevant information. Examples are buyers who know less about product quality than sellers, and lenders who know less about likely default than borrowers.
Agency cost	An agency cost is the cost incurred by an organization that is associated with problems such as divergent management-shareholder objectives and information asymmetry.
Trust	An arrangement in which shareholders of independent firms agree to give up their stock in exchange for trust certificates that entitle them to a share of the trust's common profits.
Foreign subsidiary	A company owned in a foreign country by another company is referred to as foreign subsidiary.
Joint venture	Joint venture refers to an undertaking by two parties for a specific purpose and duration, taking any of several legal forms.
Subsidiary	A company that is controlled by another company or corporation is a subsidiary.
Covenant	A covenant is a signed written agreement between two or more parties. Also referred to as a contract.
Capital controls	Capital controls refer to restrictions on cross-border capital flows that segment different stock markets; limit amount of a firm's stock a foreigner can own; and limit a citizen's ability to invest outside the country.
Capital control	Any policy intended to restrict the free movement of capital, especially financial capital, into or out of a country is referred to as capital control.
Specific factor	Specific factor refers to a factor of production that is unable to move into or out of an industry. The term is used to describe both factors that would not be of any use in other industries and -- more loosely -- factors that could be used elsewhere but are not.
Investment	Investment refers to spending for the production and accumulation of capital and additions to inventories. In a financial sense, buying an asset with the expectation of making a return.
Distribution	Distribution in economics, the manner in which total output and income is distributed among individuals or factors.
Competitor	Other organizations in the same industry or type of business that provide a good or service to the same set of customers is referred to as a competitor.
Production	The creation of finished goods and services using the factors of production: land, labor, capital, entrepreneurship, and knowledge.
Market	A market is, as defined in economics, a social arrangement that allows buyers and sellers to discover information and carry out a voluntary exchange of goods or services.
Licensing	Licensing is a form of strategic alliance which involves the sale of a right to use certain proprietary knowledge (so called intellectual property) in a defined way.
Profit	Profit refers to the return to the resource entrepreneurial ability; total revenue minus total cost.
Strategic alliance	Strategic alliance refers to a long-term partnership between two or more companies established to help each company build competitive market advantages.

Chapter 15. Foreign Direct Investment Theory and Strategy

Union	A worker association that bargains with employers over wages and working conditions is called a union.
Exchange	The trade of things of value between buyer and seller so that each is better off after the trade is called the exchange.
Stock	In financial terminology, stock is the capital raized by a corporation, through the issuance and sale of shares.
Intellectual property	In law, intellectual property is an umbrella term for various legal entitlements which attach to certain types of information, ideas, or other intangibles in their expressed form. The holder of this legal entitlement is generally entitled to exercise various exclusive rights in relation to its subject matter.
Knowledge management	Sharing, organizing and disseminating information in the simplest and most relevant way possible for the users of the information is a knowledge management.
Core competency	A company's core competency are things that a firm can (alsosns) do well and that meet the following three conditions. 1. It provides customer benefits, 2. It is hard for competitors to imitate, and 3. it can be leveraged widely to many products and market. A core competency can take various forms, including technical/subject matter knowhow, a reliable process, and/or close relationships with customers and suppliers. It may also include product development or culture such as employee dedication. Modern business theories suggest that most activities that are not part of a company's core competency should be outsourced.
Management	Management characterizes the process of leading and directing all or part of an organization, often a business, through the deployment and manipulation of resources. Early twentieth-century management writer Mary Parker Follett defined management as "the art of getting things done through people."
Property	Assets defined in the broadest legal sense. Property includes the unrealized receivables of a cash basis taxpayer, but not services rendered.
Core	A core is the set of feasible allocations in an economy that cannot be improved upon by subset of the set of the economy's consumers (a coalition). In construction, when the force in an element is within a certain center section, the core, the element will only be under compression.
Contract	A contract is a "promise" or an "agreement" that is enforced or recognized by the law. In the civil law, a contract is considered to be part of the general law of obligations.
Brand	A name, symbol, or design that identifies the goods or services of one seller or group of sellers and distinguishes them from the goods and services of competitors is a brand.
Comparative advantage	The ability to produce a good at lower cost, relative to other goods, compared to another country is a comparative advantage.
Classical theory	The original theory about organizations that closely resembles military structures is called classical theory.
Economic theory	Economic theory refers to a statement of a cause-effect relationship; when accepted by all economists, an economic principle.
Theory of comparative advantage	Ricardo's theory that specialization and free trade will benefit all trading partners, even those that may be absolutely less efficient producers are theory of comparative advantage.
Productivity	Productivity refers to the total output of goods and services in a given period of time divided by work hours.
Competitiveness	Competitiveness usually refers to characteristics that permit a firm to compete effectively

Chapter 15. Foreign Direct Investment Theory and Strategy

	with other firms due to low cost or superior technology, perhaps internationally.
Shell	One of the original Seven Sisters, Royal Dutch/Shell is the world's third-largest oil company by revenue, and a major player in the petrochemical industry and the solar energy business. Shell has six core businesses: Exploration and Production, Gas and Power, Downstream, Chemicals, Renewables, and Trading/Shipping, and operates in more than 140 countries.
Production efficiency	A situation in which the economy cannot produce more of one good without producing less of some other good is referred to as production efficiency.
International capital flows	International capital flows are purchases and sales of financial assets across national borders. Flows of physical capital goods are typically treated as ordinary trade flows, not capital flows, in the balance of payments accounts.
Capital flow	International capital movement is referred to as capital flow.
Raw material	Raw material refers to a good that has not been transformed by production; a primary product.
Acer	Acer is one of the world's top five branded PC vendors. It owns the largest computer retail chain in Taiwan. Acer's product offering includes desktop and mobile PCs, servers and storage, displays, peripherals, and e-business solutions for business, government, education, and home users.
Emerging markets	The term emerging markets is commonly used to describe business and market activity in industrializing or emerging regions of the world. It is sometimes loosely used as a replacement for emerging economies, but really signifies a business phenomenon that is not fully described by or constrained to geography or economic strength; such countries are considered to be in a transitional phase between developing and developed status.
Emerging market	The term emerging market is commonly used to describe business and market activity in industrializing or emerging regions of the world.
Management consulting	Management consulting refers to both the practice of helping companies to improve performance through analysis of existing business problems and development of future plans, as well as to the firms that specialize in this sort of consulting.
Corporate Strategy	Corporate strategy is concerned with the firm's choice of business, markets and activities and thus it defines the overall scope and direction of the business.
Industry	A group of firms that produce identical or similar products is an industry. It is also used specifically to refer to an area of economic production focused on manufacturing which involves large amounts of capital investment before any profit can be realized, also called "heavy industry".
Free trade	Free trade refers to a situation in which there are no artificial barriers to trade, such as tariffs and quotas. Usually used, often only implicitly, with frictionless trade, so that it implies that there are no barriers to trade of any kind.
Labor	People's physical and mental talents and efforts that are used to help produce goods and services are called labor.
Export	In economics, an export is any good or commodity, shipped or otherwise transported out of a country, province, town to another part of the world in a legitimate fashion, typically for use in trade or sale.
Absolute advantage	A country has an absolute advantage economically over another when it can produce something more cheaply. This term is often used to differentiate between comparative advantage.
Licensing agreement	Detailed and comprehensive written agreement between the licensor and licensee that sets forth the express terms of their agreement is called a licensing agreement.

Chapter 15. Foreign Direct Investment Theory and Strategy

Novartis	Novartis was created in 1996 from the merger of Ciba-Geigy and Sandoz Laboratories, both Swiss companies with long individual histories. At the time of the merger, it was the largest corporate merger in history.
Negotiation	Negotiation is the process whereby interested parties resolve disputes, agree upon courses of action, bargain for individual or collective advantage, and/or attempt to craft outcomes which serve their mutual interests.
Supply	Supply is the aggregate amount of any material good that can be called into being at a certain price point; it comprises one half of the equation of supply and demand. In classical economic theory, a curve representing supply is one of the factors that produce price.
Product development	In business and engineering, new product development is the complete process of bringing a new product to market. There are two parallel aspects to this process : one involves product engineering ; the other marketing analysis. Marketers see new product development as the first stage in product life cycle management, engineers as part of Product Lifecycle Management.
Retail sale	The sale of goods and services to consumers for their own use is a retail sale.
Manufacturing	Production of goods primarily by the application of labor and capital to raw materials and other intermediate inputs, in contrast to agriculture, mining, forestry, fishing, and services a manufacturing.

Go to **Cram101.com** for the Practice Tests for this Chapter.

Chapter 16. Multinational Capital Budgeting

Financial analysis	Financial analysis is the analysis of the accounts and the economic prospects of a firm.
Investment	Investment refers to spending for the production and accumulation of capital and additions to inventories. In a financial sense, buying an asset with the expectation of making a return.
Capital budgeting	Capital budgeting is the planning process used to determine a firm's long term investments such as new machinery, replacement machinery, new plants, new products, and research and development projects.
Cash inflow	Cash coming into the company as the result of a previous investment is a cash inflow.
Domestic	From or in one's own country. A domestic producer is one that produces inside the home country. A domestic price is the price inside the home country. Opposite of 'foreign' or 'world.'.
Capital	Capital generally refers to financial wealth, especially that used to start or maintain a business. In classical economics, capital is one of four factors of production, the others being land and labor and entrepreneurship.
Mergers and acquisitions	The phrase mergers and acquisitions refers to the aspect of corporate finance strategy and management dealing with the merging and acquiring of different companies as well as other assets. Usually mergers occur in a friendly setting where executives from the respective companies participate in a due diligence process to ensure a successful combination of all parts.
Manufacturing	Production of goods primarily by the application of labor and capital to raw materials and other intermediate inputs, in contrast to agriculture, mining, forestry, fishing, and services a manufacturing.
Acquisition	A company's purchase of the property and obligations of another company is an acquisition.
Merger	Merger refers to the combination of two firms into a single firm.
Salvage value	In accounting, the salvage value of an asset is its remaining value after depreciation. The estimated value of an asset at the end of its useful life.
Cash flow	In finance, cash flow refers to the amounts of cash being received and spent by a business during a defined period of time, sometimes tied to a specific project. Most of the time they are being used to determine gaps in the liquid position of a company.
Present value	The value today of a stream of payments and/or receipts over time in the future and/or the past, converted to the present using an interest rate. If X t is the amount in period t and r the interest rate, then present value at time t=0 is V = ?T /t.
Discount rate	Discount rate refers to the rate, per year, at which future values are diminished to make them comparable to values in the present. Can be either subjective or objective .
Discount	The difference between the face value of a bond and its selling price, when a bond is sold for less than its face value it's referred to as a discount.
Internal rate of return	Internal rate of return refers to a discounted cash flow method for evaluating capital budgeting projects. The internal rate of return is a discount rate that makes the present value of the cash inflows equal to the present value of the cash outflows.
Net present value	Net present value is a standard method in finance of capital budgeting – the planning of long-term investments. Using this method a potential investment project should be undertaken if the present value of all cash inflows minus the present value of all cash outflows (which equals the net present value) is greater than zero.
Rate of return	A rate of return is a comparison of the money earned (or lost) on an investment to the amount

Chapter 16. Multinational Capital Budgeting

Chapter 16. Multinational Capital Budgeting

	of money invested.
Complexity	The technical sophistication of the product and hence the amount of understanding required to use it is referred to as complexity. It is the opposite of simplicity.
Foreign subsidiary	A company owned in a foreign country by another company is referred to as foreign subsidiary.
Subsidiary	A company that is controlled by another company or corporation is a subsidiary.
License	A license in the sphere of Intellectual Property Rights (IPR) is a document, contract or agreement giving permission or the 'right' to a legally-definable entity to do something (such as manufacture a product or to use a service), or to apply something (such as a trademark), with the objective of achieving commercial gain.
Inflation	An increase in the overall price level of an economy, usually as measured by the CPI or by the implicit price deflator is called inflation.
Foreign exchange	In finance, foreign exchange means currencies, such as U.S. Dollars and Euros. These are traded on foreign exchange markets.
Exchange rate	Exchange rate refers to the price at which one country's currency trades for another, typically on the exchange market.
Exchange	The trade of things of value between buyer and seller so that each is better off after the trade is called the exchange.
Capital structure	Capital Structure refers to the way a corporation finances itself through some combination of equity sales, equity options, bonds, and loans. Optimal capital structure refers to the particular combination that minimizes the cost of capital while maximizing the stock price.
Weighted average	The weighted average unit cost of the goods available for sale for both cost of goods sold and ending inventory.
Cost of capital	Cost of capital refers to the percentage cost of funds used for acquiring resources for an organization, typically a weighted average of the firms cost of equity and cost of debt.
Weighted average cost of capital	Weighted average cost of capital refers to the computed cost of capital determined by multiplying the cost of each item in the optimal capital structure by its weighted representation in the overall capital structure and summing up the results.
Average cost	Average cost is equal to total cost divided by the number of goods produced (Quantity-Q). It is also equal to the sum of average variable costs (total variable costs divided by Q) plus average fixed costs (total fixed costs divided by Q).
Political risk	Refers to the many different actions of people, subgroups, and whole countries that have the potential to affect the financial status of a firm is called political risk.
Terminal value	In finance, the terminal value of a security is the present value at a future point in time of all future cash flows. It is most often used in multi-stage discounted cash flow analysis, and allows for the limitation of cash flow projections to a several-year period.
Public sector	Public sector refers to the part of the economy that contains all government entities; government.
Firm	An organization that employs resources to produce a good or service for profit and owns and operates one or more plants is referred to as a firm.
Valuation	In finance, valuation is the process of estimating the market value of a financial asset or liability. They can be done on assets (for example, investments in marketable securities such as stocks, options, business enterprises, or intangible assets such as patents and trademarks) or on liabilities (e.g., Bonds issued by a company).

Chapter 16. Multinational Capital Budgeting

Argument	The discussion by counsel for the respective parties of their contentions on the law and the facts of the case being tried in order to aid the jury in arriving at a correct and just conclusion is called argument.
Stockholder	A stockholder is an individual or company (including a corporation) that legally owns one or more shares of stock in a joined stock company. The shareholders are the owners of a corporation. Companies listed at the stock market strive to enhance shareholder value.
Dividend	Amount of corporate profits paid out for each share of stock is referred to as dividend.
Interest	In finance and economics, interest is the price paid by a borrower for the use of a lender's money. In other words, interest is the amount of paid to "rent" money for a period of time.
Evaluation	The consumer's appraisal of the product or brand on important attributes is called evaluation.
Host country	The country in which the parent-country organization seeks to locate or has already located a facility is a host country.
Government bond	A government bond is a bond issued by a national government denominated in the country's own currency. Bonds issued by national governments in foreign currencies are normally referred to as sovereign bonds.
Free market	A free market is a market where price is determined by the unregulated interchange of supply and demand rather than set by artificial means.
Maturity	Maturity refers to the final payment date of a loan or other financial instrument, after which point no further interest or principal need be paid.
Market	A market is, as defined in economics, a social arrangement that allows buyers and sellers to discover information and carry out a voluntary exchange of goods or services.
Yield	The interest rate that equates a future value or an annuity to a given present value is a yield.
Bond	Bond refers to a debt instrument, issued by a borrower and promising a specified stream of payments to the purchaser, usually regular interest payments plus a final repayment of principal.
Premium	Premium refers to the fee charged by an insurance company for an insurance policy. The rate of losses must be relatively predictable: In order to set the premium (prices) insurers must be able to estimate them accurately.
Competitor	Other organizations in the same industry or type of business that provide a good or service to the same set of customers is referred to as a competitor.
Shares	Shares refer to an equity security, representing a shareholder's ownership of a corporation. Shares are one of a finite number of equal portions in the capital of a company, entitling the owner to a proportion of distributed, non-reinvested profits known as dividends and to a portion of the value of the company in case of liquidation.
Earnings per share	Earnings per share refers to annual profit of the corporation divided by the number of shares outstanding.
Net earnings	Another name for net income is net earnings. That part of a company's profits remaining after all expenses and taxes have been paid and out of which dividends may be paid.
Affiliates	Local television stations that are associated with a major network are called affiliates. Affiliates agree to preempt time during specified hours for programming provided by the network and carry the advertising contained in the program.
Pro rata	Proportionate is referred to as pro rata. A method of equally and proportionately allocating

Chapter 16. Multinational Capital Budgeting

	money, profits or liabilities by percentage.
Consideration	Consideration in contract law, a basic requirement for an enforceable agreement under traditional contract principles, defined in this text as legal value, bargained for and given in exchange for an act or promise. In corporation law, cash or property contributed to a corporation in exchange for shares, or a promise to contribute such cash or property.
Fund	Independent accounting entity with a self-balancing set of accounts segregated for the purposes of carrying on specific activities is referred to as a fund.
Required rate of return	Required rate of return refers to the rate of return that investors demand from an investment to compensate them for the amount of risk involved.
Portfolio	In finance, a portfolio is a collection of investments held by an institution or a private individual. Holding but not always a portfolio is part of an investment and risk-limiting strategy called diversification. By owning several assets, certain types of risk (in particular specific risk) can be reduced.
Liquidity	Liquidity refers to the capacity to turn assets into cash, or the amount of assets in a portfolio that have that capacity.
Foreign direct investment	Foreign direct investment refers to the buying of permanent property and businesses in foreign nations.
Direct investment	Direct investment refers to a domestic firm actually investing in and owning a foreign subsidiary or division.
Cemex	Although it is not a monopoly, Cemex, along with Holcim-Apasco, controls the Mexican cement market. This has given rise to allegations that because of the oligopolistic structure in the Mexican cement market (as in many other markets in Mexico) consumers pay a higher price for cement than in other countries. However given the peculiarities of the Mexican cement market, the fact that it is sold mostly in bags, and the fact that cement is not an easily transported commodity make this accuzation difficult, if not impossible to prove.
Emerging market	The term emerging market is commonly used to describe business and market activity in industrializing or emerging regions of the world.
Depreciation	Depreciation is an accounting and finance term for the method of attributing the cost of an asset across the useful life of the asset. Depreciation is a reduction in the value of a currency in floating exchange rate.
Market share	That fraction of an industry's output accounted for by an individual firm or group of firms is called market share.
Commodity	Could refer to any good, but in trade a commodity is usually a raw material or primary product that enters into international trade, such as metals or basic agricultural products.
Turnover	Turnover in a financial context refers to the rate at which a provider of goods cycles through its average inventory. Turnover in a human resources context refers to the characteristic of a given company or industry, relative to rate at which an employer gains and loses staff.
Foreign ownership	Foreign ownership refers to the complete or majority ownership/control of businesses or resources in a country, by individuals who are not citizens of that country, or by companies whose headquarters are not in that country.
Operation	A standardized method or technique that is performed repetitively, often on different materials resulting in different finished goods is called an operation.
Industry	A group of firms that produce identical or similar products is an industry. It is also used specifically to refer to an area of economic production focused on manufacturing which

Chapter 16. Multinational Capital Budgeting

Chapter 16. Multinational Capital Budgeting

	involves large amounts of capital investment before any profit can be realized, also called "heavy industry".
Inflation rate	The percentage increase in the price level per year is an inflation rate. Alternatively, the inflation rate is the rate of decrease in the purchasing power of money.
Spot exchange rate	The exchange rate at which a foreign exchange dealer will convert one currency into another that particular day is the spot exchange rate.
Spot rate	Spot rate refers to the rate at which the currency is traded for immediate delivery. It is the existing cash price.
Authority	Authority in agency law, refers to an agent's ability to affect his principal's legal relations with third parties. Also used to refer to an actor's legal power or ability to do something. In addition, sometimes used to refer to a statute, case, or other legal source that justifies a particular result.
Policy	Similar to a script in that a policy can be a less than completely rational decision-making method. Involves the use of a pre-existing set of decision steps for any problem that presents itself.
Interest payment	The payment to holders of bonds payable, calculated by multiplying the stated rate on the face of the bond by the par, or face, value of the bond. If bonds are issued at a discount or premium, the interest payment does not equal the interest expense.
Corporate tax	Corporate tax refers to a direct tax levied by various jurisdictions on the profits made by companies or associations. As a general principle, this varies substantially between jurisdictions.
Deductible	The dollar sum of costs that an insured individual must pay before the insurer begins to pay is called deductible.
Liability	A liability is a present obligation of the enterprise arizing from past events, the settlement of which is expected to result in an outflow from the enterprise of resources embodying economic benefits.
Parent company	Parent company refers to the entity that has a controlling influence over another company. It may have its own operations, or it may have been set up solely for the purpose of owning the Subject Company.
Purchasing power	The amount of goods that money will buy, usually measured by the CPI is referred to as purchasing power.
Purchasing	Purchasing refers to the function in a firm that searches for quality material resources, finds the best suppliers, and negotiates the best price for goods and services.
Financial statement	Financial statement refers to a summary of all the transactions that have occurred over a particular period.
Income statement	Income statement refers to a financial statement that presents the revenues and expenses and resulting net income or net loss of a company for a specific period of time.
Pro forma income	Pro forma income refers to a measure of income that usually excludes items that a company thinks are unusual or nonrecurring; forecast income.
Pro forma financial statements	Pro forma financial statements refer to a series of projected financial statements. Of major importance are the pro forma income statement, the pro forma balance sheet, and the cash budget.
Pro forma income	A projection of anticipated sales, expenses, and income is called pro forma income statement. If the projections predict a downturn in profitability, you can make operational changes

Chapter 16. Multinational Capital Budgeting

Chapter 16. Multinational Capital Budgeting

statement	such as increasing prices or decreasing costs before these projections become reality.
Interest rate	The rate of return on bonds, loans, or deposits. When one speaks of 'the' interest rate, it is usually in a model where there is only one.
Enterprise	Enterprise refers to another name for a business organization. Other similar terms are business firm, sometimes simply business, sometimes simply firm, as well as company, and entity.
Export	In economics, an export is any good or commodity, shipped or otherwise transported out of a country, province, town to another part of the world in a legitimate fashion, typically for use in trade or sale.
Principal	In agency law, one under whose direction an agent acts and for whose benefit that agent acts is a principal.
Purchasing power parity	purchasing power parity is a theory based on the law of one price which says that the long-run equilibrium exchange rate of two currencies is the rate that equalizes the currencies' purchasing power.
Depreciate	A nation's currency is said to depreciate when exchange rates change so that a unit of its currency can buy fewer units of foreign currency.
Debt service	The payments made by a borrower on their debt, usually including both interest payments and partial repayment of principal, are called debt service.
Service	Service refers to a "non tangible product" that is not embodied in a physical good and that typically effects some change in another product, person, or institution. Contrasts with good.
Labor	People's physical and mental talents and efforts that are used to help produce goods and services are called labor.
Production	The creation of finished goods and services using the factors of production: land, labor, capital, entrepreneurship, and knowledge.
Tax credit	Allows a firm to reduce the taxes paid to the home government by the amount of taxes paid to the foreign government is referred to as tax credit.
Credit	Credit refers to a recording as positive in the balance of payments, any transaction that gives rise to a payment into the country, such as an export, the sale of an asset, or borrowing from abroad.
Management	Management characterizes the process of leading and directing all or part of an organization, often a business, through the deployment and manipulation of resources. Early twentieth-century management writer Mary Parker Follett defined management as "the art of getting things done through people."
Amortization	Systematic and rational allocation of the acquisition cost of an intangible asset over its useful life is referred to as amortization.
Expense	In accounting, an expense represents an event in which an asset is used up or a liability is incurred. In terms of the accounting equation, expenses reduce owners' equity.
Capital budget	A long-term budget that shows planned acquisition and disposal of capital assets, such as land, building, and equipment is a capital budget. Also a separate budget used by state governments for items such as new construction, major renovations, and acquisition of physical property.
Cost of debt	The cost of debt is the cost of borrowing money (usually denoted by Kd). It is derived by dividing debt's interest payments on the total market value of the debts.

Chapter 16. Multinational Capital Budgeting

Budget	Budget refers to an account, usually for a year, of the planned expenditures and the expected receipts of an entity. For a government, the receipts are tax revenues.
Interest expense	The cost a business incurs to borrow money. With respect to bonds payable, the interest expense is calculated by multiplying the market rate of interest by the carrying value of the bonds on the date of the payment.
Days Sales Outstanding	Days Sales Outstanding is a company's average collection period. A low figure indicates that the company collects its outstanding receivables quickly. Typically it is looked at either quarterly or yearly. It's a great leading indicator of impending trouble at a company particularly with product support and customer service.
Trade credit	Trade credit refers to an amount that is loaned to an exporter to be repaid when the exports are paid for by the foreign importer.
Inventory	Tangible property held for sale in the normal course of business or used in producing goods or services for sale is an inventory.
Payables	Obligations to make future economic sacrifices, usually cash payments, are referred to as payables. Same as current liabilities.
Tax treaty	Tax treaty refers to an agreement between the U.S. Department of State and another country, designed to alleviate double taxation of income and asset transfers, and to share administrative information useful to tax agencies in both countries.
Treaties	The first source of international law, consisting of agreements or contracts between two or more nations that are formally signed by an authorized representative and ratified by the supreme power of each nation are called treaties.
Levy	Levy refers to imposing and collecting a tax or tariff.
Free cash flow	Cash provided by operating activities adjusted for capital expenditures and dividends paid is referred to as free cash flow.
Equity	Equity is the name given to the set of legal principles, in countries following the English common law tradition, which supplement strict rules of law where their application would operate harshly, so as to achieve what is sometimes referred to as "natural justice."
Functional currency	Functional currency refers to the currency of the economic environment in which the taxpayer carries on most of its activities, and in which the taxpayer transacts most of its business.
Corporation	A legal entity chartered by a state or the Federal government that is distinct and separate from the individuals who own it is a corporation. This separation gives the corporation unique powers which other legal entities lack.
Hurdle rate	The minimum acceptable rate of return in a capital budgeting decision is the hurdle rate. The hurdle rate should reflect the riskiness of the investment, typically measured by volatility of cash flows, and must take into account the financing mix.
Sensitivity analysis	A what-if technique that managers use to examine how a result will change if the original predicted data are not achieved or if an underlying assumption changes is sensitivity analysis.
Financial risk	The risk related to the inability of the firm to meet its debt obligations as they come due is called financial risk.
Expropriation	Expropriation is the act of removing from control the owner of an item of property. The term is used to both refer to acts by a government or by any group of people.
Lender	Suppliers and financial institutions that lend money to companies is referred to as a lender.
Default	In finance, default occurs when a debtor has not met its legal obligations according to the

Chapter 16. Multinational Capital Budgeting

Chapter 16. Multinational Capital Budgeting

	debt contract, e.g. it has not made a scheduled payment, or violated a covenant (condition) of the debt contract.
Capital loss	Capital loss refers to the loss in value that the owner of an asset experiences when the price of the asset falls, including when the currency in which the asset is denominated depreciates. Contrasts with capital gain.
Book value	The book value of an asset or group of assets is sometimes the price at which they were originally acquired, in many cases equal to purchase price.
Negotiation	Negotiation is the process whereby interested parties resolve disputes, agree upon courses of action, bargain for individual or collective advantage, and/or attempt to craft outcomes which serve their mutual interests.
Hedge	Hedge refers to a process of offsetting risk. In the foreign exchange market, hedgers use the forward market to cover a transaction or open position and thereby reduce exchange risk. The term applies most commonly to trade.
Capacity utilization	Capacity utilization is a concept in Economics which refers to the extent to which an enterprise or a nation actually uses its installed productive capacity. Thus, it refers to the relationship between actual output produced and potential output that could be produced with installed equipment, if capacity was fully used.
Capacity utilization rate	In economics, the capacity utilization rate is the percentage of a company, industry, or country's production capacity that is actually or currently used. It is sometimes called the operating rate.
Working capital	The dollar difference between total current assets and total current liabilities is called working capital.
Variable	A variable is something measured by a number; it is used to analyze what happens to other things when the size of that number changes.
Discounted cash flow	In finance, the discounted cash flow approach describes a method to value a project or an entire company. The DCF methods determine the present value of future cash flows by discounting them using the appropriate cost of capital.
Option	A contract that gives the purchaser the option to buy or sell the underlying financial instrument at a specified price, called the exercise price or strike price, within a specific period of time.
Core	A core is the set of feasible allocations in an economy that cannot be improved upon by subset of the set of the economy's consumers (a coalition). In construction, when the force in an element is within a certain center section, the core, the element will only be under compression.
Points	Loan origination fees that may be deductible as interest by a buyer of property. A seller of property who pays points reduces the selling price by the amount of the points paid for the buyer.
Scenario analysis	Scenario analysis is a process of analyzing possible future events by considering alternative possible outcomes. The analysis is designed to allow improved decision-making by allowing more complete consideration of outcomes and their implications.
Discount factor	The discounted price is the original price multiplied by the discount factor.
Risk premium	In finance, the risk premium can be the expected rate of return above the risk-free interest rate.
Complement	A good that is used in conjunction with another good is a complement. For example, cameras and film would complement eachother.

Chapter 16. Multinational Capital Budgeting

Operating cash flows	Operating cash flows refers to the cash inflows and cash outflows from the general operating activities of the business; one of the three sections in the statement of cash flows.
Cost of equity	In finance, the cost of equity is the minimum rate of return a firm must offer shareholders to compensate for waiting for their returns, and for bearing some risk.
Joint venture	Joint venture refers to an undertaking by two parties for a specific purpose and duration, taking any of several legal forms.
Cash dividend	A pro rata distribution of cash to stockholders of corporate stock is called a cash dividend.
Operating expense	In throughput accounting, the cost accounting aspect of Theory of Constraints (TOC), operating expense is the money spent turning inventory into throughput. In TOC, operating expense is limited to costs that vary strictly with the quantity produced, like raw materials and purchased components.
Accounting income	The accountant's concept of income is generally based upon the realization principle. Financial accounting income may differ from taxable income. Differences are included in a reconciliation of taxable and accounting income on Schedule M-1 of Form 1120.
Accounting	A system that collects and processes financial information about an organization and reports that information to decision makers is referred to as accounting.
Capital gain	Capital gain refers to the gain in value that the owner of an asset experiences when the price of the asset rises, including when the currency in which the asset is denominated appreciates.
Gain	In finance, gain is a profit or an increase in value of an investment such as a stock or bond. Gain is calculated by fair market value or the proceeds from the sale of the investment minus the sum of the purchase price and all costs associated with it.
Quality control	The measurement of products and services against set standards is referred to as quality control.
Fixed asset	Fixed asset, also known as property, plant, and equipment (PP&E), is a term used in accountancy for assets and property which cannot easily be converted into cash. This can be compared with current assets such as cash or bank accounts, which are described as liquid assets. In most cases, only tangible assets are referred to as fixed.
Asset	An item of property, such as land, capital, money, a share in ownership, or a claim on others for future payment, such as a bond or a bank deposit is an asset.
Profit	Profit refers to the return to the resource entrepreneurial ability; total revenue minus total cost.
Depreciation expense	Depreciation expense refers to the amount recognized as an expense in one period resulting from the periodic recognition of the used portion of the cost of a long-term tangible asset over its life.
Administration	Administration refers to the management and direction of the affairs of governments and institutions; a collective term for all policymaking officials of a government; the execution and implementation of public policy.
Open market	In economics, the open market is the term used to refer to the environment in which bonds are bought and sold.
Economy	The income, expenditures, and resources that affect the cost of running a business and household are called an economy.
Pluralism	A theory of government that attempts to reaffirm the democratic character of society by asserting that open, multiple, competing, and responsive groups preserve traditional

Chapter 16. Multinational Capital Budgeting

	democratic values in a mass industrial state. Pluralism assumes that power will shift from group to group as elements in the mass public transfer their allegiance in response to their perceptions of their individual interests.
Economics	The social science dealing with the use of scarce resources to obtain the maximum satisfaction of society's virtually unlimited economic wants is an economics.
Labor relations	The field of labor relations looks at the relationship between management and workers, particularly groups of workers represented by a labor union.
Property	Assets defined in the broadest legal sense. Property includes the unrealized receivables of a cash basis taxpayer, but not services rendered.
Penetration strategy	Strategy in which a product is priced low to attract many customers and discourage competition is referred to as penetration strategy.
Market penetration	A strategy of increasing sales of present products in their existing markets is called market penetration.
Senior management	Senior management is generally a team of individuals at the highest level of organizational management who have the day-to-day responsibilities of managing a corporation.
Management team	A management team is directly responsible for managing the day-to-day operations (and profitability) of a company.
Corporate finance	Corporate finance is a specific area of finance dealing with the financial decisions corporations make and the tools as well as analyses used to make these decisions. The discipline as a whole may be divided among long-term and short-term decisions and techniques with the primary goal being the enhancing of corporate value by ensuring that return on capital exceeds cost of capital, without taking excessive financial risks.
Consultant	A professional that provides expert advice in a particular field or area in which customers occassionaly require this type of knowledge is a consultant.
Expected value	A representative value from a probability distribution arrived at by multiplying each outcome by the associated probability and summing up the values is called the expected value.
Value analysis	Value analysis refers to a systematic appraisal of the design, quality, and performance of a product to reduce purchasing costs.
Revenue	Revenue is a U.S. business term for the amount of money that a company receives from its activities, mostly from sales of products and/or services to customers.
Research and development	The use of resources for the deliberate discovery of new information and ways of doing things, together with the application of that information in inventing new products or processes is referred to as research and development.
Market development	Selling existing products to new markets is called market development.
Gross profit	Net sales less cost of goods sold is called gross profit.
Business risk	The risk related to the inability of the firm to hold its competitive position and maintain stability and growth in earnings is business risk.
Operating profit	Operating profit is a measure of a company's earning power from ongoing operations, equal to earnings before the deduction of interest payments and income taxes.
Call option	Call option refers to an option contract that provides the right to buy a security at a specified price within a certain time period.
Analyst	Analyst refers to a person or tool with a primary function of information analysis, generally

Go to Cram101.com for the Practice Tests for this Chapter.

	with a more limited, practical and short term set of goals than a researcher.
Expected return	Expected return refers to the return on an asset expected over the next period.

Chapter 16. Multinational Capital Budgeting

Chapter 17. Adjusting for Risk in Foreign Investment

Shareholder	A shareholder is an individual or company (including a corporation) that legally owns one or more shares of stock in a joined stock company.
Enterprise	Enterprise refers to another name for a business organization. Other similar terms are business firm, sometimes simply business, sometimes simply firm, as well as company, and entity.
Management	Management characterizes the process of leading and directing all or part of an organization, often a business, through the deployment and manipulation of resources. Early twentieth-century management writer Mary Parker Follett defined management as "the art of getting things done through people."
Economic policy	Economic policy refers to the actions that governments take in the economic field. It covers the systems for setting interest rates and government deficit as well as the labor market, national ownership, and many other areas of government.
Privatization	A process in which investment bankers take companies that were previously owned by the government to the public markets is referred to as privatization.
Openness	Openness refers to the extent to which an economy is open, often measured by the ratio of its trade to GDP.
Policy	Similar to a script in that a policy can be a less than completely rational decision-making method. Involves the use of a pre-existing set of decision steps for any problem that presents itself.
Capital	Capital generally refers to financial wealth, especially that used to start or maintain a business. In classical economics, capital is one of four factors of production, the others being land and labor and entrepreneurship.
Foreign exchange risk	Foreign exchange risk refers to a form of risk that refers to the possibility of experiencing a drop in revenue or an increase in cost in an international transaction due to a change in foreign exchange rates. Importers, exporters, investors, and multinational firms alike are exposed to this risk.
Foreign exchange	In finance, foreign exchange means currencies, such as U.S. Dollars and Euros. These are traded on foreign exchange markets.
Exchange	The trade of things of value between buyer and seller so that each is better off after the trade is called the exchange.
Competitive advantage	A business is said to have a competitive advantage when its unique strengths, often based on cost, quality, time, and innovation, offer consumers a greater percieved value and there by differtiating it from its competitors.
Foreign subsidiary	A company owned in a foreign country by another company is referred to as foreign subsidiary.
Manufacturing	Production of goods primarily by the application of labor and capital to raw materials and other intermediate inputs, in contrast to agriculture, mining, forestry, fishing, and services a manufacturing.
Subsidiary	A company that is controlled by another company or corporation is a subsidiary.
Market	A market is, as defined in economics, a social arrangement that allows buyers and sellers to discover information and carry out a voluntary exchange of goods or services.
Host country	The country in which the parent-country organization seeks to locate or has already located a facility is a host country.
Domestic	From or in one's own country. A domestic producer is one that produces inside the home

Chapter 17. Adjusting for Risk in Foreign Investment

	country. A domestic price is the price inside the home country. Opposite of 'foreign' or 'world.'.
Export	In economics, an export is any good or commodity, shipped or otherwise transported out of a country, province, town to another part of the world in a legitimate fashion, typically for use in trade or sale.
Firm	An organization that employs resources to produce a good or service for profit and owns and operates one or more plants is referred to as a firm.
Credit	Credit refers to a recording as positive in the balance of payments, any transaction that gives rise to a payment into the country, such as an export, the sale of an asset, or borrowing from abroad.
Emerging markets	The term emerging markets is commonly used to describe business and market activity in industrializing or emerging regions of the world. It is sometimes loosely used as a replacement for emerging economies, but really signifies a business phenomenon that is not fully described by or constrained to geography or economic strength; such countries are considered to be in a transitional phase between developing and developed status.
Emerging market	The term emerging market is commonly used to describe business and market activity in industrializing or emerging regions of the world.
Perceived risk	The anxieties felt because the consumer cannot anticipate the outcomes of a purchase but believes that there may be negative consequences is called a perceived risk.
Investment	Investment refers to spending for the production and accumulation of capital and additions to inventories. In a financial sense, buying an asset with the expectation of making a return.
Corporate level	Corporate level refers to level at which top management directs overall strategy for the entire organization.
Transaction exposure	Transaction exposure refers to foreign exchange gains and losses resulting from actual international transactions. These may be hedged through the foreign exchange market, the money market, or the currency futures market.
Human resources	Human resources refers to the individuals within the firm, and to the portion of the firm's organization that deals with hiring, firing, training, and other personnel issues.
Business risk	The risk related to the inability of the firm to hold its competitive position and maintain stability and growth in earnings is business risk.
Accounting	A system that collects and processes financial information about an organization and reports that information to decision makers is referred to as accounting.
Production	The creation of finished goods and services using the factors of production: land, labor, capital, entrepreneurship, and knowledge.
Portfolio	In finance, a portfolio is a collection of investments held by an institution or a private individual. Holding but not always a portfolio is part of an investment and risk-limiting strategy called diversification. By owning several assets, certain types of risk (in particular specific risk) can be reduced.
Marketing	Promoting and selling products or services to customers, or prospective customers, is referred to as marketing.
Asset	An item of property, such as land, capital, money, a share in ownership, or a claim on others for future payment, such as a bond or a bank deposit is an asset.
Diversification strategy	Diversification strategy is a corporate strategy that takes the organization away from both its current markets and products, as opposed to either market or product development.

Chapter 17. Adjusting for Risk in Foreign Investment

Chapter 17. Adjusting for Risk in Foreign Investment

Diversification	Investing in a collection of assets whose returns do not always move together, with the result that overall risk is lower than for individual assets is referred to as diversification.
Sensitivity analysis	A what-if technique that managers use to examine how a result will change if the original predicted data are not achieved or if an underlying assumption changes is sensitivity analysis.
Capital budgeting	Capital budgeting is the planning process used to determine a firm's long term investments such as new machinery, replacement machinery, new plants, new products, and research and development projects.
Political risk	Refers to the many different actions of people, subgroups, and whole countries that have the potential to affect the financial status of a firm is called political risk.
Expropriation	Expropriation is the act of removing from control the owner of an item of property. The term is used to both refer to acts by a government or by any group of people.
Fund	Independent accounting entity with a self-balancing set of accounts segregated for the purposes of carrying on specific activities is referred to as a fund.
Working capital	The dollar difference between total current assets and total current liabilities is called working capital.
Terminal value	In finance, the terminal value of a security is the present value at a future point in time of all future cash flows. It is most often used in multi-stage discounted cash flow analysis, and allows for the limitation of cash flow projections to a several-year period.
Discount rate	Discount rate refers to the rate, per year, at which future values are diminished to make them comparable to values in the present. Can be either subjective or objective .
Discount	The difference between the face value of a bond and its selling price, when a bond is sold for less than its face value it's referred to as a discount.
Exchange rate	Exchange rate refers to the price at which one country's currency trades for another, typically on the exchange market.
Cash flow	In finance, cash flow refers to the amounts of cash being received and spent by a business during a defined period of time, sometimes tied to a specific project. Most of the time they are being used to determine gaps in the liquid position of a company.
Cash inflow	Cash coming into the company as the result of a previous investment is a cash inflow.
Inputs	The inputs used by a firm or an economy are the labor, raw materials, electricity and other resources it uses to produce its outputs.
Currency depreciation	Currency depreciation occurs when currency falls in value on the foreign-exchange market, buying less on the foreign exchange
Depreciation	Depreciation is an accounting and finance term for the method of attributing the cost of an asset across the useful life of the asset. Depreciation is a reduction in the value of a currency in floating exchange rate.
Depreciate	A nation's currency is said to depreciate when exchange rates change so that a unit of its currency can buy fewer units of foreign currency.
Financial risk	The risk related to the inability of the firm to meet its debt obligations as they come due is called financial risk.
Assessment	Collecting information and providing feedback to employees about their behavior, communication style, or skills is an assessment.

Go to **Cram101.com** for the Practice Tests for this Chapter.

Chapter 17. Adjusting for Risk in Foreign Investment

Futures	Futures refer to contracts for the sale and future delivery of stocks or commodities, wherein either party may waive delivery, and receive or pay, as the case may be, the difference in market price at the time set for delivery.
Economic forces	Forces that affect the availability, production, and distribution of a society's resources among competing users are referred to as economic forces.
Complexity	The technical sophistication of the product and hence the amount of understanding required to use it is referred to as complexity. It is the opposite of simplicity.
Analyst	Analyst refers to a person or tool with a primary function of information analysis, generally with a more limited, practical and short term set of goals than a researcher.
Insurance	Insurance refers to a system by which individuals can reduce their exposure to risk of large losses by spreading the risks among a large number of persons.
Cost of capital	Cost of capital refers to the percentage cost of funds used for acquiring resources for an organization, typically a weighted average of the firms cost of equity and cost of debt.
Parent company	Parent company refers to the entity that has a controlling influence over another company. It may have its own operations, or it may have been set up solely for the purpose of owning the Subject Company.
Cemex	Although it is not a monopoly, Cemex, along with Holcim-Apasco, controls the Mexican cement market. This has given rise to allegations that because of the oligopolistic structure in the Mexican cement market (as in many other markets in Mexico) consumers pay a higher price for cement than in other countries. However given the peculiarities of the Mexican cement market, the fact that it is sold mostly in bags, and the fact that cement is not an easily transported commodity make this accuzation difficult, if not impossible to prove.
Rate of return	A rate of return is a comparison of the money earned (or lost) on an investment to the amount of money invested.
Discounted cash flow	In finance, the discounted cash flow approach describes a method to value a project or an entire company. The DCF methods determine the present value of future cash flows by discounting them using the appropriate cost of capital.
Corporate finance	Corporate finance is a specific area of finance dealing with the financial decisions corporations make and the tools as well as analyses used to make these decisions. The discipline as a whole may be divided among long-term and short-term decisions and techniques with the primary goal being the enhancing of corporate value by ensuring that return on capital exceeds cost of capital, without taking excessive financial risks.
Journal	Book of original entry, in which transactions are recorded in a general ledger system, is referred to as a journal.
Translation exposure	The foreign-located assets and liabilities of a multinational corporation, which are denominated in foreign currency units, and are exposed to losses and gains due to changing exchange rates is called accounting or translation exposure.
Disequilibrium	Inequality or imbalance of supply and demand is referred to as disequilibrium.
Credit risk	The risk of loss due to a counterparty defaulting on a contract, or more generally the risk of loss due to some "credit event" is called credit risk.
Stakeholder	A stakeholder is an individual or group with a vested interest in or expectation for organizational performance. Usually stakeholders can either have an effect on or are affected by an organization.
Economic development	Increase in the economic standard of living of a country's population, normally accomplished by increasing its stocks of physical and human capital and improving its technology is an

Chapter 17. Adjusting for Risk in Foreign Investment

	economic development.
Balance of payments	Balance of payments refers to a list, or accounting, of all of a country's international transactions for a given time period, usually one year.
Sovereignty	A country or region's power and ability to rule itself and manage its own affairs. Some feel that membership in international organizations such as the WTO is a threat to their sovereignty.
Industry	A group of firms that produce identical or similar products is an industry. It is also used specifically to refer to an area of economic production focused on manufacturing which involves large amounts of capital investment before any profit can be realized, also called "heavy industry".
Interest	In finance and economics, interest is the price paid by a borrower for the use of a lender's money. In other words, interest is the amount of paid to "rent" money for a period of time.
Balance	In banking and accountancy, the outstanding balance is the amount of money owned, (or due), that remains in a deposit account (or a loan account) at a given date, after all past remittances, payments and withdrawal have been accounted for. It can be positive (then, in the balance sheet of a firm, it is an asset) or negative (a liability).
Socialism	An economic system under which the state owns the resources and makes the economic decisions is called socialism.
Conflict management	Conflict management refers to the long-term management of intractable conflicts. It is the label for the variety of ways by which people handle grievances -- standing up for what they consider to be right and against what they consider to be wrong.
Administration	Administration refers to the management and direction of the affairs of governments and institutions; a collective term for all policymaking officials of a government; the execution and implementation of public policy.
Contract	A contract is a "promise" or an "agreement" that is enforced or recognized by the law. In the civil law, a contract is considered to be part of the general law of obligations.
Rate base	The circulation that magazines guarantee advertisers in computing advertising costs is called the rate base.
Capital market	A financial market in which long-term debt and equity instruments are traded is referred to as a capital market. The capital market includes the stock market and the bond market.
Foreign ownership	Foreign ownership refers to the complete or majority ownership/control of businesses or resources in a country, by individuals who are not citizens of that country, or by companies whose headquarters are not in that country.
Joint venture	Joint venture refers to an undertaking by two parties for a specific purpose and duration, taking any of several legal forms.
Raw material	Raw material refers to a good that has not been transformed by production; a primary product.
Expatriate	Employee sent by his or her company to live and manage operations in a different country is called an expatriate.
Possession	Possession refers to respecting real property, exclusive dominion and control such as owners of like property usually exercise over it. Manual control of personal property either as owner or as one having a qualified right in it.
Personnel	A collective term for all of the employees of an organization. Personnel is also commonly used to refer to the personnel management function or the organizational unit responsible for administering personnel programs.

Chapter 17. Adjusting for Risk in Foreign Investment

Going concern	A going concern describes a business that functions without the intention or threat of liquidation for the foreseeable future. Accountants and auditors may be required to evaluate and disclose whether a company is no longer a going concern, or is at risk of ceasing to be
Divestment	In finance and economics, divestment or divestiture is the reduction of some kind of asset, for either financial or social goals. A divestment is the opposite of an investment.
Developing country	Developing country refers to a country whose per capita income is low by world standards. Same as LDC. As usually used, it does not necessarily connote that the country's income is rising.
Developed country	A developed country is one that enjoys a relatively high standard of living derived through an industrialized, diversified economy. Countries with a very high Human Development Index are generally considered developed countries.
Corporation	A legal entity chartered by a state or the Federal government that is distinct and separate from the individuals who own it is a corporation. This separation gives the corporation unique powers which other legal entities lack.
Profit	Profit refers to the return to the resource entrepreneurial ability; total revenue minus total cost.
Property	Assets defined in the broadest legal sense. Property includes the unrealized receivables of a cash basis taxpayer, but not services rendered.
Consideration	Consideration in contract law, a basic requirement for an enforceable agreement under traditional contract principles, defined in this text as legal value, bargained for and given in exchange for an act or promise. In corporation law, cash or property contributed to a corporation in exchange for shares, or a promise to contribute such cash or property.
Logistics	Those activities that focus on getting the right amount of the right products to the right place at the right time at the lowest possible cost is referred to as logistics.
Value added	The value of output minus the value of all intermediate inputs, representing therefore the contribution of, and payments to, primary factors of production a value added.
Tradeoff	The sacrifice of some or all of one economic goal, good, or service to achieve some other goal, good, or service is a tradeoff.
Economies of scale	In economics, returns to scale and economies of scale are related terms that describe what happens as the scale of production increases. They are different terms and not to be used interchangeably.
Quality control	The measurement of products and services against set standards is referred to as quality control.
Operation	A standardized method or technique that is performed repetitively, often on different materials resulting in different finished goods is called an operation.
Economy	The income, expenditures, and resources that affect the cost of running a business and household are called an economy.
Strike	The withholding of labor services by an organized group of workers is referred to as a strike.
Patent	The legal right to the proceeds from and control over the use of an invented product or process, granted for a fixed period of time, usually 20 years. Patent is one form of intellectual property that is subject of the TRIPS agreement.
Technology	The body of knowledge and techniques that can be used to combine economic resources to produce goods and services is called technology.

Chapter 17. Adjusting for Risk in Foreign Investment

Cartel	Cartel refers to a group of firms that seeks to raise the price of a good by restricting its supply. The term is usually used for international groups, especially involving state-owned firms and/or governments.
Manufactured good	A manufactured good refers to goods that have been processed in any way.
Leverage	Leverage is using given resources in such a way that the potential positive or negative outcome is magnified. In finance, this generally refers to borrowing.
Tariff	A tax imposed by a nation on an imported good is called a tariff.
Market share	That fraction of an industry's output accounted for by an individual firm or group of firms is called market share.
Argument	The discussion by counsel for the respective parties of their contentions on the law and the facts of the case being tried in order to aid the jury in arriving at a correct and just conclusion is called argument.
Controlling	A management function that involves determining whether or not an organization is progressing toward its goals and objectives, and taking corrective action if it is not is called controlling.
Trademark	A distinctive word, name, symbol, device, or combination thereof, which enables consumers to identify favored products or services and which may find protection under state or federal law is a trademark.
Brand	A name, symbol, or design that identifies the goods or services of one seller or group of sellers and distinguishes them from the goods and services of competitors is a brand.
Monopoly	A monopoly is defined as a persistent market situation where there is only one provider of a kind of product or service.
Equity	Equity is the name given to the set of legal principles, in countries following the English common law tradition, which supplement strict rules of law where their application would operate harshly, so as to achieve what is sometimes referred to as "natural justice."
Creditor	A person to whom a debt or legal obligation is owed, and who has the right to enforce payment of that debt or obligation is referred to as creditor.
Protectionism	Protectionism refers to advocacy of protection. The word has a negative connotation, and few advocates of protection in particular situations will acknowledge being protectionists.
Amortization	Systematic and rational allocation of the acquisition cost of an intangible asset over its useful life is referred to as amortization.
Royalties	Remuneration paid to the owners of technology, patents, or trade names for the use of same name are called royalties.
Dividend	Amount of corporate profits paid out for each share of stock is referred to as dividend.
Service	Service refers to a "non tangible product" that is not embodied in a physical good and that typically effects some change in another product, person, or institution. Contrasts with good.
Return on investment	Return on investment refers to the return a businessperson gets on the money he and other owners invest in the firm; for example, a business that earned $100 on a $1,000 investment would have a ROI of 10 percent: 100 divided by 1000.
Expected return	Expected return refers to the return on an asset expected over the next period.
Repositioning	Changing the position an offering occupies in a consumer's mind relative to competitive

Chapter 17. Adjusting for Risk in Foreign Investment

	offerings and so expanding or otherwise altering its potential market is called repositioning.
Real value	Real value is the value of anything expressed in money of the day with the effects of inflation removed.
Inflation	An increase in the overall price level of an economy, usually as measured by the CPI or by the implicit price deflator is called inflation.
Required rate of return	Required rate of return refers to the rate of return that investors demand from an investment to compensate them for the amount of risk involved.
Expected rate of return	Expected rate of return refers to the increase in profit a firm anticipates it will obtain by purchasing capital ; expressed as a percentage of the total cost of the investment activity.
Rate of return on investment	The rate of return on investment refers to the benefits to an investor (the profit) relative to the cost of the initial investment.
Swap	In finance a swap is a derivative, where two counterparties exchange one stream of cash flows against another stream. These streams are called the legs of the swap. The cash flows are calculated over a notional principal amount. Swaps are often used to hedge certain risks, for instance interest rate risk. Another use is speculation.
Financial intermediary	Financial intermediary refers to a financial institution, such as a bank or a life insurance company, which directs other people's money into such investments as government and corporate securities.
Fronting loan	Fronting loan refers to a parent company's loan to a foreign subsidiary is channeled through a financial intermediary, usually a large international bank. The bank fronts for the parent in extending the loan to the foreign affiliate.
Principal	In agency law, one under whose direction an agent acts and for whose benefit that agent acts is a principal.
Collateral	Property that is pledged to the lender to guarantee payment in the event that the borrower is unable to make debt payments is called collateral.
Expense	In accounting, an expense represents an event in which an asset is used up or a liability is incurred. In terms of the accounting equation, expenses reduce owners' equity.
Margin	A deposit by a buyer in stocks with a seller or a stockbroker, as security to cover fluctuations in the market in reference to stocks that the buyer has purchased but for which he has not paid is a margin. Commodities are also traded on margin.
Jurisdiction	The power of a court to hear and decide a case is called jurisdiction. It is the practical authority granted to a formally constituted body or to a person to deal with and make pronouncements on legal matters and, by implication, to administer justice within a defined area of responsibility.
Lender	Suppliers and financial institutions that lend money to companies is referred to as a lender.
Authority	Authority in agency law, refers to an agent's ability to affect his principal's legal relations with third parties. Also used to refer to an actor's legal power or ability to do something. In addition, sometimes used to refer to a statute, case, or other legal source that justifies a particular result.
Parent corporation	Parent corporation refers to a corporation that owns a controlling interest of another corporation, called a subsidiary corporation.
Product line	A group of products that are physically similar or are intended for a similar market are called the product line.

Chapter 17. Adjusting for Risk in Foreign Investment

Preference	The act of a debtor in paying or securing one or more of his creditors in a manner more favorable to them than to other creditors or to the exclusion of such other creditors is a preference. In the absence of statute, a preference is perfectly good, but to be legal it must be bona fide, and not a mere subterfuge of the debtor to secure a future benefit to himself or to prevent the application of his property to his debts.
Money market	The money market, in macroeconomics and international finance, refers to the equilibration of demand for a country's domestic money to its money supply; market for short-term financial instruments.
Instrument	Instrument refers to an economic variable that is controlled by policy makers and can be used to influence other variables, called targets. Examples are monetary and fiscal policies used to achieve external and internal balance.
Liquidity	Liquidity refers to the capacity to turn assets into cash, or the amount of assets in a portfolio that have that capacity.
Treasury bills	Short-term obligations of the federal government are treasury bills. They are like zero coupon bonds in that they do not pay interest prior to maturity; instead they are sold at a discount of the par value to create a positive yield to maturity.
Yield	The interest rate that equates a future value or an annuity to a given present value is a yield.
Portfolio investment	Portfolio investment refers to the acquisition of portfolio capital. Usually refers to such transactions across national borders and/or across currencies.
Time deposit	The technical name for a savings account is a time deposit; the bank can require prior notice before the owner withdraws money from a time deposit.
Bond	Bond refers to a debt instrument, issued by a borrower and promising a specified stream of payments to the purchaser, usually regular interest payments plus a final repayment of principal.
Exchange control	Rationing of foreign exchange, typically used when the exchange rate is fixed and the central bank is unable or unwilling to enforce the rate by exchange-market intervention is an exchange control.
Commodity	Could refer to any good, but in trade a commodity is usually a raw material or primary product that enters into international trade, such as metals or basic agricultural products.
Opportunity cost	The cost of something in terms of opportunity foregone. The opportunity cost to a country of producing a unit more of a good, such as for export or to replace an import, is the quantity of some other good that could have been produced instead.
Stockpiling	The storage of something in order to have it available in the future if the need for it increases is stockpiling. In international economics, stockpiling occurs for speculative purposes, by governments to provide for national security, and by central banks managing international reserves.
Inventory	Tangible property held for sale in the normal course of business or used in producing goods or services for sale is an inventory.
Cost structure	The relative proportion of an organization's fixed, variable, and mixed costs is referred to as cost structure.
Exporter	A firm that sells its product in another country is an exporter.
Economic infrastructure	Economic infrastructure refers to a country's communications, transportation, financial, and distribution systems.

Go to Cram101.com for the Practice Tests for this Chapter.

Chapter 17. Adjusting for Risk in Foreign Investment

Chapter 17. Adjusting for Risk in Foreign Investment

Financial perspective	Financial perspective is one of the four standard perspectives used with the Balanced Scorecard. Financial perspective measures inform an organization whether strategy execution, which is detailed through measures in the other three perspectives, is leading to improved bottom line results.
Risk premium	In finance, the risk premium can be the expected rate of return above the risk-free interest rate.
Premium	Premium refers to the fee charged by an insurance company for an insurance policy. The rate of losses must be relatively predictable: In order to set the premium (prices) insurers must be able to estimate them accurately.
Interest rate	The rate of return on bonds, loans, or deposits. When one speaks of 'the' interest rate, it is usually in a model where there is only one.
Oppression	The officers, directors, or controlling shareholder's isolation of one group of shareholders for disadvantageous treatment to the benefit of another group of shareholders is oppression.
Intellectual property	In law, intellectual property is an umbrella term for various legal entitlements which attach to certain types of information, ideas, or other intangibles in their expressed form. The holder of this legal entitlement is generally entitled to exercise various exclusive rights in relation to its subject matter.
Property rights	Bundle of legal rights over the use to which a resource is put and over the use made of any income that may be derived from that resource are referred to as property rights.
Intellectual property rights	Intellectual property rights, such as patents, copyrights, trademarks, trade secrets, trade names, and domain names are very valuable business assets. Federal and state laws protect intellectual property rights from misappropriation and infringement.
Intellectual property right	Intellectual property right refers to the right to control and derive the benefits from something one has invented, discovered, or created.
Corruption	The unauthorized use of public office for private gain. The most common forms of corruption are bribery, extortion, and the misuse of inside information.
Nepotism	Nepotism means favoring relatives or personal friends because of their relationship rather than because of their abilities.
Boeing	Boeing is the world's largest aircraft manufacturer by revenue. Headquartered in Chicago, Illinois, Boeing is the second-largest defense contractor in the world. In 2005, the company was the world's largest civil aircraft manufacturer in terms of value.
Staffing	Staffing refers to a management function that includes hiring, motivating, and retaining the best people available to accomplish the company's objectives.
Labor law	Labor law is the body of laws, administrative rulings, and precedents which addresses the legal rights of, and restrictions on, workers and their organizations.
Labor	People's physical and mental talents and efforts that are used to help produce goods and services are called labor.
Union	A worker association that bargains with employers over wages and working conditions is called a union.
Staffing policy	Strategy concerned with selecting employees for particular jobs is called staffing policy.
Private sector	The households and business firms of the economy are referred to as private sector.
Infant industry	Infant industry refers to a young industry that may need temporary protection from competition from the established industries of other countries to develop an acquired comparative advantage.

Chapter 17. Adjusting for Risk in Foreign Investment

Infant industry argument	The theoretical rationale for infant industry protection is referred to as the infant industry argument.
Monetary policy	The use of the money supply and/or the interest rate to influence the level of economic activity and other policy objectives including the balance of payments or the exchange rate is called monetary policy.
Monetary union	An arrangement by which several nations adopt a common currency as a unit of account and medium of exchange. The European Monetary Union is scheduled to adopt the 'Euro' as the common currency in 1999.
Euro	The common currency of a subset of the countries of the EU, adopted January 1, 1999 is called euro.
Fiscal policy	Fiscal policy refers to any macroeconomic policy involving the levels of government purchases, transfers, or taxes, usually implicitly focused on domestic goods, residents, or firms.
Legal system	Legal system refers to system of rules that regulate behavior and the processes by which the laws of a country are enforced and through which redress of grievances is obtained.
Information system	An information system is a system whether automated or manual, that comprises people, machines, and/or methods organized to collect, process, transmit, and disseminate data that represent user information.
Antiglobaliz-tion	Antiglobalization is a term most commonly ascribed to the political stance of people and groups who oppose certain aspects of globalization in its current form, often including the domination of current global trade agreements and trade-governing bodies such as the World Trade Organization by powerful corporations.
Hedging	A technique for avoiding a risk by making a counteracting transaction is referred to as hedging.
Bureaucracy	Bureaucracy refers to an organization with many layers of managers who set rules and regulations and oversee all decisions.
World Trade Organization	The World Trade Organization is an international, multilateral organization, which sets the rules for the global trading system and resolves disputes between its member states, all of whom are signatories to its approximately 30 agreements.
Exporting	Selling products to another country is called exporting.
Income distribution	A description of the fractions of a population that are at various levels of income. The larger these differences in income, the 'worse' the income distribution is usually said to be, the smaller the 'better.'
Distribution	Distribution in economics, the manner in which total output and income is distributed among individuals or factors.
Disparity	Disparity refers to the regional and economic differences in a country, province, state, or continent
Competitor	Other organizations in the same industry or type of business that provide a good or service to the same set of customers is referred to as a competitor.
International strategy	Trying to create value by transferring core competencies to foreign markets where indigenous competitors lack those competencies is called international strategy.
Corporate governance	Corporate governance is the set of processes, customs, policies, laws and institutions affecting the way a corporation is directed, administered or controlled.
Ford Motor	Ford Motor Company introduced methods for large-scale manufacturing of cars, and large-scale

Chapter 17. Adjusting for Risk in Foreign Investment

Company	management of an industrial workforce, especially elaborately engineered manufacturing sequences typified by the moving assembly lines. Henry Ford's combination of highly efficient factories, highly paid workers, and low prices revolutionized manufacturing and came to be known around the world as Fordism by 1914.
Ford	Ford is an American company that manufactures and sells automobiles worldwide. Ford introduced methods for large-scale manufacturing of cars, and large-scale management of an industrial workforce, especially elaborately engineered manufacturing sequences typified by the moving assembly lines.
Revenue	Revenue is a U.S. business term for the amount of money that a company receives from its activities, mostly from sales of products and/or services to customers.
Points	Loan origination fees that may be deductible as interest by a buyer of property. A seller of property who pays points reduces the selling price by the amount of the points paid for the buyer.
Bribery	When one person gives another person money, property, favors, or anything else of value for a favor in return, we have bribery. Often referred to as a payoff or 'kickback.'
World Bank	The World Bank is a group of five international organizations responsible for providing finance and advice to countries for the purposes of economic development and poverty reduction, and for encouraging and safeguarding international investment.
Aid	Assistance provided by countries and by international institutions such as the World Bank to developing countries in the form of monetary grants, loans at low interest rates, in kind, or a combination of these is called aid. Aid can also refer to assistance of any type rendered to benefit some group or individual.
Transparency	Transparency refers to a concept that describes a company being so open to other companies working with it that the once-solid barriers between them become see-through and electronic information is shared as if the companies were one.
Transparency International	Transparency International is an international organization addressing corruption, including, but not limited to, political corruption.
Weighted average	The weighted average unit cost of the goods available for sale for both cost of goods sold and ending inventory.
Weighted average cost of capital	Weighted average cost of capital refers to the computed cost of capital determined by multiplying the cost of each item in the optimal capital structure by its weighted representation in the overall capital structure and summing up the results.
Average cost	Average cost is equal to total cost divided by the number of goods produced (Quantity-Q). It is also equal to the sum of average variable costs (total variable costs divided by Q) plus average fixed costs (total fixed costs divided by Q).
Evaluation	The consumer's appraisal of the product or brand on important attributes is called evaluation.
Growth strategy	A strategy based on investing in companies and sectors which are growing faster than their peers is a growth strategy. The benefits are usually in the form of capital gains rather than dividends.
Motorola	The Six Sigma quality system was developed at Motorola even though it became most well known because of its use by General Electric. It was created by engineer Bill Smith, under the direction of Bob Galvin (son of founder Paul Galvin) when he was running the company.
Startup	Any new company can be considered a startup, but the description is usually applied to aggressive young companies that are actively courting private financing from venture

Go to **Cram101.com** for the Practice Tests for this Chapter.

Chapter 17. Adjusting for Risk in Foreign Investment

	capitalists, including wealthy individuals and investment companies.
Nokia	Nokia Corporation is the world's largest manufacturer of mobile telephones (as of June 2006), with a global market share of approximately 34% in Q2 of 2006. It produces mobile phones for every major market and protocol, including GSM, CDMA, and W-CDMA (UMTS).
Siemens	Siemens is the world's largest conglomerate company. Worldwide, Siemens and its subsidiaries employs 461,000 people (2005) in 190 countries and reported global sales of €75.4 billion in fiscal year 2005.
Vendor	A person who sells property to a vendee is a vendor. The words vendor and vendee are more commonly applied to the seller and purchaser of real estate, and the words seller and buyer are more commonly applied to the seller and purchaser of personal property.
Users	Users refer to people in the organization who actually use the product or service purchased by the buying center.
Forbes	David Churbuck founded online Forbes in 1996. The site drew attention when it uncovered Stephen Glass' journalistic fraud in The New Republic in 1998, a scoop that gave credibility to internet journalism.
Political instability	Events such as riots, revolutions, or government upheavals that affect the operations of an international company is called political instability.
Economic growth	Economic growth refers to the increase over time in the capacity of an economy to produce goods and services and to improve the well-being of its citizens.
Fixed exchange rate	A fixed exchange rate, sometimes is a type of exchange rate regime wherein a currency's value is matched to the value of another single currency or to a basket of other currencies, or to another measure of value, such as gold.
Deficit	The deficit is the amount by which expenditure exceed revenue.
Purchasing power	The amount of goods that money will buy, usually measured by the CPI is referred to as purchasing power.
Purchasing	Purchasing refers to the function in a firm that searches for quality material resources, finds the best suppliers, and negotiates the best price for goods and services.
Option	A contract that gives the purchaser the option to buy or sell the underlying financial instrument at a specified price, called the exercise price or strike price, within a specific period of time.
Mistake	In contract law a mistake is incorrect understanding by one or more parties to a contract and may be used as grounds to invalidate the agreement. Common law has identified three different types of mistake in contract: unilateral mistake, mutual mistake, and common mistake.
Judiciary	The branch of government chosen to oversee the legal system through the court system is referred to as judiciary.

Chapter 18. Cross-Border Mergers, Acquisitions, and Valuation

Mergers and acquisitions	The phrase mergers and acquisitions refers to the aspect of corporate finance strategy and management dealing with the merging and acquiring of different companies as well as other assets. Usually mergers occur in a friendly setting where executives from the respective companies participate in a due diligence process to ensure a successful combination of all parts.
Acquisition	A company's purchase of the property and obligations of another company is an acquisition.
Merger	Merger refers to the combination of two firms into a single firm.
Discount rate	Discount rate refers to the rate, per year, at which future values are diminished to make them comparable to values in the present. Can be either subjective or objective.
Management	Management characterizes the process of leading and directing all or part of an organization, often a business, through the deployment and manipulation of resources. Early twentieth-century management writer Mary Parker Follett defined management as "the art of getting things done through people."
Investment	Investment refers to spending for the production and accumulation of capital and additions to inventories. In a financial sense, buying an asset with the expectation of making a return.
Valuation	In finance, valuation is the process of estimating the market value of a financial asset or liability. They can be done on assets (for example, investments in marketable securities such as stocks, options, business enterprises, or intangible assets such as patents and trademarks) or on liabilities (e.g., Bonds issued by a company).
Discount	The difference between the face value of a bond and its selling price, when a bond is sold for less than its face value it's referred to as a discount.
Strategic alliance	Strategic alliance refers to a long-term partnership between two or more companies established to help each company build competitive market advantages.
Enterprise	Enterprise refers to another name for a business organization. Other similar terms are business firm, sometimes simply business, sometimes simply firm, as well as company, and entity.
Market	A market is, as defined in economics, a social arrangement that allows buyers and sellers to discover information and carry out a voluntary exchange of goods or services.
Competitive advantage	A business is said to have a competitive advantage when its unique strengths, often based on cost, quality, time, and innovation, offer consumers a greater percieved value and there by diffetiating it from its competitors.
Core competency	A company's core competency are things that a firm can (alsosns) do well and that meet the following three conditions. 1. It provides customer benefits, 2. It is hard for competitors to imitate, and 3. it can be leveraged widely to many products and market. A core competency can take various forms, including technical/subject matter knowhow, a reliable process, and/or close relationships with customers and suppliers. It may also include product development or culture such as employee dedication. Modern business theories suggest that most activities that are not part of a company's core competency should be outsourced.
Target firm	The firm that is being studied or benchmarked against is referred to as target firm.
Core	A core is the set of feasible allocations in an economy that cannot be improved upon by subset of the set of the economy's consumers (a coalition). In construction, when the force in an element is within a certain center section, the core, the element will only be under compression.
Firm	An organization that employs resources to produce a good or service for profit and owns and operates one or more plants is referred to as a firm.

Go to **Cram101.com** for the Practice Tests for this Chapter.

Chapter 18. Cross-Border Mergers, Acquisitions, and Valuation

Chapter 18. Cross-Border Mergers, Acquisitions, and Valuation

Strategic plan	The formal document that presents the ways and means by which a strategic goal will be achieved is a strategic plan. A long-term flexible plan that does not regulate activities but rather outlines the means to achieve certain results, and provides the means to alter the course of action should the desired ends change.
Domestic	From or in one's own country. A domestic producer is one that produces inside the home country. A domestic price is the price inside the home country. Opposite of 'foreign' or 'world.'.
Market position	Market position is a measure of the position of a company or product on a market.
Takeover	A takeover in business refers to one company (the acquirer) purchasing another (the target). Such events resemble mergers, but without the formation of a new company.
Union	A worker association that bargains with employers over wages and working conditions is called a union.
DaimlerChrysler	In 2002, the merged company, DaimlerChrysler, appeared to run two independent product lines, with few signs of corporate integration. In 2003, however, it was alleged by the Detroit News that the "merger of equals" was, in fact, a takeover.
Exxon	Exxon formally replaced the Esso, Enco, and Humble brands on January 1, 1973, in the USA. The name Esso, pronounced S-O, attracted protests from other Standard Oil spinoffs because of its similarity to the name of the parent company, Standard Oil.
Emerging markets	The term emerging markets is commonly used to describe business and market activity in industrializing or emerging regions of the world. It is sometimes loosely used as a replacement for emerging economies, but really signifies a business phenomenon that is not fully described by or constrained to geography or economic strength; such countries are considered to be in a transitional phase between developing and developed status.
Emerging market	The term emerging market is commonly used to describe business and market activity in industrializing or emerging regions of the world.
Privatization	A process in which investment bankers take companies that were previously owned by the government to the public markets is referred to as privatization.
Gain	In finance, gain is a profit or an increase in value of an investment such as a stock or bond. Gain is calculated by fair market value or the proceeds from the sale of the investment minus the sum of the purchase price and all costs associated with it.
Developing country	Developing country refers to a country whose per capita income is low by world standards. Same as LDC. As usually used, it does not necessarily connote that the country's income is rising.
Developed country	A developed country is one that enjoys a relatively high standard of living derived through an industrialized, diversified economy. Countries with a very high Human Development Index are generally considered developed countries.
Trend	Trend refers to the long-term movement of an economic variable, such as its average rate of increase or decrease over enough years to encompass several business cycles.
Disparity	Disparity refers to the regional and economic differences in a country, province, state, or continent
Holding	The holding is a court's determination of a matter of law based on the issue presented in the particular case. In other words: under this law, with these facts, this result.
Asset	An item of property, such as land, capital, money, a share in ownership, or a claim on others for future payment, such as a bond or a bank deposit is an asset.

Chapter 18. Cross-Border Mergers, Acquisitions, and Valuation

Shareholder value	For a publicly traded company, shareholder value is the part of its capitalization that is equity as opposed to long-term debt. In the case of only one type of stock, this would roughly be the number of outstanding shares times current shareprice.
Shareholder	A shareholder is an individual or company (including a corporation) that legally owns one or more shares of stock in a joined stock company.
P/E ratio	In finance, the P/E ratio of a stock is used to measure how cheap or expensive share prices are. It is probably the single most consistent red flag to excessive optimism and over-investment.
Annual report	An annual report is prepared by corporate management that presents financial information including financial statements, footnotes, and the management discussion and analysis.
Advertisement	Advertisement is the promotion of goods, services, companies and ideas, usually by an identified sponsor. Marketers see advertising as part of an overall promotional strategy.
Stakeholder	A stakeholder is an individual or group with a vested interest in or expectation for organizational performance. Usually stakeholders can either have an effect on or are affected by an organization.
Stockholder	A stockholder is an individual or company (including a corporation) that legally owns one or more shares of stock in a joined stock company. The shareholders are the owners of a corporation. Companies listed at the stock market strive to enhance shareholder value.
Earnings per share	Earnings per share refers to annual profit of the corporation divided by the number of shares outstanding.
Margin	A deposit by a buyer in stocks with a seller or a stockbroker, as security to cover fluctuations in the market in reference to stocks that the buyer has purchased but for which he has not paid is a margin. Commodities are also traded on margin.
Market share	That fraction of an industry's output accounted for by an individual firm or group of firms is called market share.
Shares	Shares refer to an equity security, representing a shareholder's ownership of a corporation. Shares are one of a finite number of equal portions in the capital of a company, entitling the owner to a proportion of distributed, non-reinvested profits known as dividends and to a portion of the value of the company in case of liquidation.
Profit	Profit refers to the return to the resource entrepreneurial ability; total revenue minus total cost.
Greenfield investment	In foreign investment, direct investment in new facilities or the expansion of existing facilities is Greenfield investment.
Business opportunity	A business opportunity involves the sale or lease of any product, service, equipment, etc. that will enable the purchaser-licensee to begin a business
Capital market	A financial market in which long-term debt and equity instruments are traded is referred to as a capital market. The capital market includes the stock market and the bond market.
Capital	Capital generally refers to financial wealth, especially that used to start or maintain a business. In classical economics, capital is one of four factors of production, the others being land and labor and entrepreneurship.
Operation	A standardized method or technique that is performed repetitively, often on different materials resulting in different finished goods is called an operation.
Industry	A group of firms that produce identical or similar products is an industry. It is also used specifically to refer to an area of economic production focused on manufacturing which

Chapter 18. Cross-Border Mergers, Acquisitions, and Valuation

	involves large amounts of capital investment before any profit can be realized, also called "heavy industry".
Synergy	Corporate synergy occurs when corporations interact congruently. A corporate synergy refers to a financial benefit that a corporation expects to realize when it merges with or acquires another corporation.
Market power	The ability of a single economic actor to have a substantial influence on market prices is market power.
Proprietary	Proprietary indicates that a party, or proprietor, exercises private ownership, control or use over an item of property, usually to the exclusion of other parties. Where a party, holds or claims proprietary interests in relation to certain types of property (eg. a creative literary work, or software), that property may also be the subject of intellectual property law (eg. copyright or patents).
Organizational development	The application of behavioral science knowledge in a longrange effort to improve an organization's ability to cope with change in its external environment and increase its problem-solving capabilities is referred to as organizational development.
White knight	White knight refers to a firm that management calls on to help it avoid an unwanted takeover offer. It is an invited suitor.
Economies of scale	In economics, returns to scale and economies of scale are related terms that describe what happens as the scale of production increases. They are different terms and not to be used interchangeably.
Downsizing	The process of eliminating managerial and non-managerial positions are called downsizing.
Economy	The income, expenditures, and resources that affect the cost of running a business and household are called an economy.
Scope	Scope of a project is the sum total of all projects products and their requirements or features.
Market segmentation	The process of dividing the total market into several groups whose members have similar characteristics is market segmentation.
Tender	An unconditional offer of payment, consisting in the actual production in money or legal tender of a sum not less than the amount due.
Corporate Strategy	Corporate strategy is concerned with the firm's choice of business, markets and activities and thus it defines the overall scope and direction of the business.
Target market	One or more specific groups of potential consumers toward which an organization directs its marketing program are a target market.
Specialist	A specialist is a trader who makes a market in one or several stocks and holds the limit order book for those stocks.
Service	Service refers to a "non tangible product" that is not embodied in a physical good and that typically effects some change in another product, person, or institution. Contrasts with good.
Aid	Assistance provided by countries and by international institutions such as the World Bank to developing countries in the form of monetary grants, loans at low interest rates, in kind, or a combination of these is called aid. Aid can also refer to assistance of any type rendered to benefit some group or individual.
Discounted cash flow	In finance, the discounted cash flow approach describes a method to value a project or an entire company. The DCF methods determine the present value of future cash flows by

Chapter 18. Cross-Border Mergers, Acquisitions, and Valuation

	discounting them using the appropriate cost of capital.
Cash flow	In finance, cash flow refers to the amounts of cash being received and spent by a business during a defined period of time, sometimes tied to a specific project. Most of the time they are being used to determine gaps in the liquid position of a company.
Change management	Change management is the process of developing a planned approach to change in an organization. Typically the objective is to maximize the collective benefits for all people involved in the change and minimize the risk of failure of implementing the change.
General Electric	In 1876, Thomas Alva Edison opened a new laboratory in Menlo Park, New Jersey. Out of the laboratory was to come perhaps the most famous invention of all—a successful development of the incandescent electric lamp. By 1890, Edison had organized his various businesses into the Edison General Electric Company.
Honeywell	Honeywell is a major American multinational corporation that produces electronic control systems and automation equipment. It is a major supplier of engineering services and avionics for NASA, Boeing and the United States Department of Defense.
Antitrust	Government intervention to alter market structure or prevent abuse of market power is called antitrust.
Chief executive officer	A chief executive officer is the highest-ranking corporate officer or executive officer of a corporation, or agency. In closely held corporations, it is general business culture that the office chief executive officer is also the chairman of the board.
Jack Welch	In 1986, GE acquired NBC. During the 90s, Jack Welch helped to modernize GE by emphasizing a shift from manufacturing to services. He also made hundreds of acquisitions and made a push to dominate markets abroad. Welch adopted the Six Sigma quality program in late 1995.
Authority	Authority in agency law, refers to an agent's ability to affect his principal's legal relations with third parties. Also used to refer to an actor's legal power or ability to do something. In addition, sometimes used to refer to a statute, case, or other legal source that justifies a particular result.
Liquidation	Liquidation refers to a process whereby the assets of a business are converted to money. The conversion may be coerced by a legal process to pay off the debt of the business, or to satisfy any other business obligation that the business has not voluntarily satisfied.
Share exchange	When one corporation acquires all the shares of another corporation and both corporations retain their separate legal existence, we have share exchange.
Acquirer	An acquirer is a company offering debit and credit card acceptance services for merchants. Often the company is partially or wholly owned by a bank, sometimes a bank itself offers acquiring services.
Exchange	The trade of things of value between buyer and seller so that each is better off after the trade is called the exchange.
A share	In finance the term A share has two distinct meanings, both relating to securities. The first is a designation for a 'class' of common or preferred stock. A share of common or preferred stock typically has enhanced voting rights or other benefits compared to the other forms of shares that may have been created. The equity structure, or how many types of shares are offered, is determined by the corporate charter.
Capital gain	Capital gain refers to the gain in value that the owner of an asset experiences when the price of the asset rises, including when the currency in which the asset is denominated appreciates.
Open market	In economics, the open market is the term used to refer to the environment in which bonds are

Chapter 18. Cross-Border Mergers, Acquisitions, and Valuation

	bought and sold.
Liability	A liability is a present obligation of the enterprise arizing from past events, the settlement of which is expected to result in an outflow from the enterprise of resources embodying economic benefits.
Swap	In finance a swap is a derivative, where two counterparties exchange one stream of cash flows against another stream. These streams are called the legs of the swap. The cash flows are calculated over a notional principal amount. Swaps are often used to hedge certain risks, for instance interest rate risk. Another use is speculation.
Equity	Equity is the name given to the set of legal principles, in countries following the English common law tradition, which supplement strict rules of law where their application would operate harshly, so as to achieve what is sometimes referred to as "natural justice."
Premium	Premium refers to the fee charged by an insurance company for an insurance policy. The rate of losses must be relatively predictable: In order to set the premium (prices) insurers must be able to estimate them accurately.
Amoco	Amoco was formed as Standard Oil (Indiana) in 1889 by John D. Rockefeller as part of the Standard Oil trust. In 1910, with the rise in popularity of the automobile, Amoco decided to specialize in providing gas to everyday families and their cars. In 1911, the year it became independent from the Standard Oil trust, the company sold 88% of the gasoline and kerosene sold in the midwest.
British Petroleum	British Petroleum, is a British energy company with headquarters in London, one of four vertically integrated private sector oil, natural gas, and petrol (gasoline) "supermajors" in the world, along with Royal Dutch Shell, ExxonMobil and Total.
Management control	That aspect of management concerned with the comparison of actual versus planned performance as well as the development and implementation of procedures to correct substandard performance is called management control.
Negotiation	Negotiation is the process whereby interested parties resolve disputes, agree upon courses of action, bargain for individual or collective advantage, and/or attempt to craft outcomes which serve their mutual interests.
Negotiable	A negotiable instrument is one that can be bought and sold after being issued - in other words, it is a tradable instrument.
Boardroom coup	A boardroom coup is the sudden overthrow of the management or governing body of a corporation by an individual or small group of individuals, usually from within the company.
Dividend	Amount of corporate profits paid out for each share of stock is referred to as dividend.
Restructuring	Restructuring is the corporate management term for the act of partially dismantling and reorganizing a company for the purpose of making it more efficient and therefore more profitable.
Bureaucracy	Bureaucracy refers to an organization with many layers of managers who set rules and regulations and oversee all decisions.
Contract	A contract is a "promise" or an "agreement" that is enforced or recognized by the law. In the civil law, a contract is considered to be part of the general law of obligations.
Complaint	The pleading in a civil case in which the plaintiff states his claim and requests relief is called complaint. In the common law, it is a formal legal document that sets out the basic facts and legal reasons that the filing party (the plaintiffs) believes are sufficient to support a claim against another person, persons, entity or entities (the defendants) that entitles the plaintiff(s) to a remedy (either money damages or injunctive relief).

Chapter 18. Cross-Border Mergers, Acquisitions, and Valuation

Chapter 18. Cross-Border Mergers, Acquisitions, and Valuation

Wall Street Journal	Dow Jones & Company was founded in 1882 by reporters Charles Dow, Edward Jones and Charles Bergstresser. Jones converted the small Customers' Afternoon Letter into The Wall Street Journal, first published in 1889, and began delivery of the Dow Jones News Service via telegraph. The Journal featured the Jones 'Average', the first of several indexes of stock and bond prices on the New York Stock Exchange.
Journal	Book of original entry, in which transactions are recorded in a general ledger system, is referred to as a journal.
Corporate culture	The whole collection of beliefs, values, and behaviors of a firm that send messages to those within and outside the company about how business is done is the corporate culture.
Corporate governance	Corporate governance is the set of processes, customs, policies, laws and institutions affecting the way a corporation is directed, administered or controlled.
Voting shares	Voting shares are shares that give the stockholder the right to vote on matters of corporate policy making as well as who will compose the members of the board of directors.
Tender offer	A public offer by a bidder to purchase a subject company's shares directly from its shareholders at a specified price for a fixed period of time is called tender offer.
Jurisdiction	The power of a court to hear and decide a case is called jurisdiction. It is the practical authority granted to a formally constituted body or to a person to deal with and make pronouncements on legal matters and, by implication, to administer justice within a defined area of responsibility.
Bid	A bid price is a price offered by a buyer when he/she buys a good. In the context of stock trading on a stock exchange, the bid price is the highest price a buyer of a stock is willing to pay for a share of that given stock.
International Business	International business refers to any firm that engages in international trade or investment.
Accumulation	The acquisition of an increasing quantity of something. The accumulation of factors, especially capital, is a primary mechanism for economic growth.
Publicly traded corporation	A corporation whose stock is traded on the stock exchanges is referred to as a publicly traded corporation.
Corporation	A legal entity chartered by a state or the Federal government that is distinct and separate from the individuals who own it is a corporation. This separation gives the corporation unique powers which other legal entities lack.
Regulation	Regulation refers to restrictions state and federal laws place on business with regard to the conduct of its activities.
Stock	In financial terminology, stock is the capital raized by a corporation, through the issuance and sale of shares.
Security	Security refers to a claim on the borrower future income that is sold by the borrower to the lender. A security is a type of transferable interest representing financial value.
Revocation	Revocation, in general, refers to the recalling or voiding of a prior action. In contract law, the withdrawal of an offer by the offeror prior to effective acceptance by the offeree.
Disclosure	Disclosure means the giving out of information, either voluntarily or to be in compliance with legal regulations or workplace rules.
Tactic	A short-term immediate decision that, in its totality, leads to the achievement of strategic goals is called a tactic.
Interest	In finance and economics, interest is the price paid by a borrower for the use of a lender's

Chapter 18. Cross-Border Mergers, Acquisitions, and Valuation

	money. In other words, interest is the amount of paid to "rent" money for a period of time.
Proration	The spreading of underallocated or overallocated overhead among ending work in process, finished goods, and cost of goods sold is a proration. Also known as an allocation. A temporary limit on the amount of product customers can purchase at the terminal usually based on contracts and used to protect inventories in time of shortage.
Board of directors	The group of individuals elected by the stockholders of a corporation to oversee its operations is a board of directors.
Federal government	Federal government refers to the government of the United States, as distinct from the state and local governments.
Gap	In December of 1995, Gap became the first major North American retailer to accept independent monitoring of the working conditions in a contract factory producing its garments. Gap is the largest specialty retailer in the United States.
Outstanding shares	Total number of shares of stock that are owned by stockholders on any particular date is referred to as outstanding shares.
Holding company	A corporation whose purpose or function is to own or otherwise hold the shares of other corporations either for investment or control is called holding company.
In kind	Referring to a payment made with goods instead of money is an in kind. An expression relating to the insurer's right in many Property contracts to replace damaged objects with new or equivalent (in kind) material, rather than to pay a cash benefit.
Debt capital	Debt capital refers to funds raized through various forms of borrowing to finance a company that must be repaid.
Controlling	A management function that involves determining whether or not an organization is progressing toward its goals and objectives, and taking corrective action if it is not is called controlling.
Capital expenditure	A substantial expenditure that is used by a company to acquire or upgrade physical assets such as equipment, property, industrial buildings, including those which improve the quality and life of an asset is referred to as a capital expenditure.
Competitor	Other organizations in the same industry or type of business that provide a good or service to the same set of customers is referred to as a competitor.
Benetton	Benetton has been known in the United States for producing a long-running series of controversial, sometimes offensive, advertisements that have caused a number of media critics to accuse the company of deliberately creating controversy in order to sell its products. This publicity campaign originated when photographer Oliviero Toscani was given carte blanche by the Benetton management.
Controlling interest	A firm has a controlling interest in another business entity when it owns more than 50 percent of that entity's voting stock.
Conglomerate	A conglomerate is a large company that consists of divisions of often seemingly unrelated businesses.
Due diligence	Due diligence is the effort made by an ordinarily prudent or reasonable party to avoid harm to another party or himself. Failure to make this effort is considered negligence. Failure to make this effort is considered negligence.
Compatibility	Compatibility refers to used to describe a product characteristic, it means a good fit with other products used by the consumer or with the consumer's lifestyle. Used in a technical context, it means the ability of systems to work together.

Go to **Cram101.com** for the Practice Tests for this Chapter.

Chapter 18. Cross-Border Mergers, Acquisitions, and Valuation

Rationalization	Rationalization in economics is an attempt to change a pre-existing ad-hoc workflow into one that is based on a set of published rules.
Balance sheet	A statement of the assets, liabilities, and net worth of a firm or individual at some given time often at the end of its "fiscal year," is referred to as a balance sheet.
Balance	In banking and accountancy, the outstanding balance is the amount of money owned, (or due), that remains in a deposit account (or a loan account) at a given date, after all past remittances, payments and withdrawal have been accounted for. It can be positive (then, in the balance sheet of a firm, it is an asset) or negative (a liability).
Contribution	In business organization law, the cash or property contributed to a business by its owners is referred to as contribution.
Credibility	The extent to which a source is perceived as having knowledge, skill, or experience relevant to a communication topic and can be trusted to give an unbiased opinion or present objective information on the issue is called credibility.
Cash value	The cash value of an insurance policy is the amount available to the policy holder in cash upon cancellation of the policy. This term is normally used with a whole life policy in which a portion of the premiums go toward an investment. The cash value is the value of this investment at any particular time.
Marketing	Promoting and selling products or services to customers, or prospective customers, is referred to as marketing.
Distribution	Distribution in economics, the manner in which total output and income is distributed among individuals or factors.
Exporter	A firm that sells its product in another country is an exporter.
Export	In economics, an export is any good or commodity, shipped or otherwise transported out of a country, province, town to another part of the world in a legitimate fashion, typically for use in trade or sale.
Competitive market	A market in which no buyer or seller has market power is called a competitive market.
Operational excellence	Operational excellence is a goal of conducting business in a manner that improves quality, obtains higher yields, faster throughput, and less waste.
Consolidation	The combination of two or more firms, generally of equal size and market power, to form an entirely new entity is a consolidation.
Consumption	In Keynesian economics consumption refers to personal consumption expenditure, i.e., the purchase of currently produced goods and services out of income, out of savings (net worth), or from borrowed funds. It refers to that part of disposable income that does not go to saving.
Per capita	Per capita refers to per person. Usually used to indicate the average per person of any given statistic, commonly income.
Market niche	A market niche or niche market is a focused, targetable portion of a market. By definition, then, a business that focuses on a niche market is addressing a need for a product or service that is not being addressed by mainstream providers.
Niche	In industry, a niche is a situation or an activity perfectly suited to a person. A niche can imply a working position or an area suited to a person who occupies it. Basically, a job where a person is able to succeed and thrive.
Capital	Major investments in long-term assets such as land, buildings, equipment, or research and

Chapter 18. Cross-Border Mergers, Acquisitions, and Valuation

expenditures	development are referred to as capital expenditures.
Operating margin	In business, operating margin is the ratio of operating income divided by net sales.
Price war	Price war refers to successive and continued decreases in the prices charged by firms in an oligopolistic industry. Each firm lowers its price below rivals' prices, hoping to increase its sales and revenues at its rivals' expense.
Working capital	The dollar difference between total current assets and total current liabilities is called working capital.
Operating results	Operating results refers to measures that are important to monitoring and tracking the effectiveness of a company's operations.
Business unit	The lowest level of the company which contains the set of functions that carry a product through its life span from concept through manufacture, distribution, sales and service is a business unit.
Profit margin	Profit margin is a measure of profitability. It is calculated using a formula and written as a percentage or a number. Profit margin = Net income before tax and interest / Revenue.
Gross profit margin	Gross Profit Margin equals Gross Profit divided by Revenue, expressed as a percentage. The percentage represents the amount of each dollar of Revenue that results in Gross Profit.
Return on sales	Return on sales refers to the percent of net income generated by each dollar of sales; computed by dividing net income before taxes by sales revenue.
Amortization	Systematic and rational allocation of the acquisition cost of an intangible asset over its useful life is referred to as amortization.
Depreciation	Depreciation is an accounting and finance term for the method of attributing the cost of an asset across the useful life of the asset. Depreciation is a reduction in the value of a currency in floating exchange rate.
Gross profit	Net sales less cost of goods sold is called gross profit.
Expense	In accounting, an expense represents an event in which an asset is used up or a liability is incurred. In terms of the accounting equation, expenses reduce owners' equity.
Present value	The value today of a stream of payments and/or receipts over time in the future and/or the past, converted to the present using an interest rate. If X_t is the amount in period t and r the interest rate, then present value at time $t=0$ is $V = ?T /t$.
Statement of cash flow	Reports inflows and outflows of cash during the accounting period in the categories of operating, investing, and financing is a statement of cash flow.
Financing activities	Cash flow activities that include obtaining cash from issuing debt and repaying the amounts borrowed and obtaining cash from stockholders and paying dividends is referred to as financing activities.
Investing activities	Investing activities refers to cash flow activities that include purchasing and disposing of investments and productive long-lived assets using cash and lending money and collecting on those loans.
Operating activities	Cash flow activities that include the cash effects of transactions that create revenues and expenses and thus enter into the determination of net income is an operating activities.
Inputs	The inputs used by a firm or an economy are the labor, raw materials, electricity and other resources it uses to produce its outputs.
Labor	People's physical and mental talents and efforts that are used to help produce goods and services are called labor.

Chapter 18. Cross-Border Mergers, Acquisitions, and Valuation

Chapter 18. Cross-Border Mergers, Acquisitions, and Valuation

Accounting	A system that collects and processes financial information about an organization and reports that information to decision makers is referred to as accounting.
Deductible	The dollar sum of costs that an insured individual must pay before the insurer begins to pay is called deductible.
Production	The creation of finished goods and services using the factors of production: land, labor, capital, entrepreneurship, and knowledge.
Accounts receivable	Accounts receivable is one of a series of accounting transactions dealing with the billing of customers which owe money to a person, company or organization for goods and services that have been provided to the customer. This is typically done in a one person organization by writing an invoice and mailing or delivering it to each customer.
Accounts payable	A written record of all vendors to whom the business firm owes money is referred to as accounts payable.
Inventory	Tangible property held for sale in the normal course of business or used in producing goods or services for sale is an inventory.
Analyst	Analyst refers to a person or tool with a primary function of information analysis, generally with a more limited, practical and short term set of goals than a researcher.
Payables	Obligations to make future economic sacrifices, usually cash payments, are referred to as payables. Same as current liabilities.
Financial analysis	Financial analysis is the analysis of the accounts and the economic prospects of a firm.
Financial measure	A financial measure is often used as a very simple mechanism to describe the performance of a business or investment. Because they are easily calculated they can not only be used to compare year on year results but also to compare and set norms for a particular type of business or investment.
Free cash flow	Cash provided by operating activities adjusted for capital expenditures and dividends paid is referred to as free cash flow.
Technology	The body of knowledge and techniques that can be used to combine economic resources to produce goods and services is called technology.
Cash flow forecast	Forecast that predicts the cash inflows and outflows in future periods is a cash flow forecast. It is a company's projected cash receipts and disbursements over a set time horizon.
Terminal value	In finance, the terminal value of a security is the present value at a future point in time of all future cash flows. It is most often used in multi-stage discounted cash flow analysis, and allows for the limitation of cash flow projections to a several-year period.
Operating profit	Operating profit is a measure of a company's earning power from ongoing operations, equal to earnings before the deduction of interest payments and income taxes.
Innovation	Innovation refers to the first commercially successful introduction of a new product, the use of a new method of production, or the creation of a new form of business organization.
Property	Assets defined in the broadest legal sense. Property includes the unrealized receivables of a cash basis taxpayer, but not services rendered.
Weighted average	The weighted average unit cost of the goods available for sale for both cost of goods sold and ending inventory.
Cost of capital	Cost of capital refers to the percentage cost of funds used for acquiring resources for an organization, typically a weighted average of the firms cost of equity and cost of debt.

Chapter 18. Cross-Border Mergers, Acquisitions, and Valuation

Chapter 18. Cross-Border Mergers, Acquisitions, and Valuation

Weighted average cost of capital	Weighted average cost of capital refers to the computed cost of capital determined by multiplying the cost of each item in the optimal capital structure by its weighted representation in the overall capital structure and summing up the results.
Average cost	Average cost is equal to total cost divided by the number of goods produced (Quantity-Q). It is also equal to the sum of average variable costs (total variable costs divided by Q) plus average fixed costs (total fixed costs divided by Q).
Corporate tax	Corporate tax refers to a direct tax levied by various jurisdictions on the profits made by companies or associations. As a general principle, this varies substantially between jurisdictions.
Cost of debt	The cost of debt is the cost of borrowing money (usually denoted by K_d). It is derived by dividing debt's interest payments on the total market value of the debts.
Capital asset pricing model	The capital asset pricing model is used in finance to determine a theoretically appropriate required rate of return (and thus the price if expected cash flows can be estimated) of an asset, if that asset is to be added to an already well-diversified portfolio, given that asset's non-diversifiable risk.
Cost of equity	In finance, the cost of equity is the minimum rate of return a firm must offer shareholders to compensate for waiting for their returns, and for bearing some risk.
Capital asset	In accounting, a capital asset is an asset that is recorded as property that creates more property, e.g. a factory that creates shoes, or a forest that yields a quantity of wood.
Capital structure	Capital Structure refers to the way a corporation finances itself through some combination of equity sales, equity options, bonds, and loans. Optimal capital structure refers to the particular combination that minimizes the cost of capital while maximizing the stock price.
Stock exchange	A stock exchange is a corporation or mutual organization which provides facilities for stock brokers and traders, to trade company stocks and other securities.
Risk premium	In finance, the risk premium can be the expected rate of return above the risk-free interest rate.
Equity capital	Equity capital refers to money raized from within the firm or through the sale of ownership in the firm.
Leverage	Leverage is using given resources in such a way that the potential positive or negative outcome is magnified. In finance, this generally refers to borrowing.
Enterprise value	Enterprise value is a market-based measure of a company's value. It's mainly market cap + debt. If you buy the company you buy the debt load.
Creditor	A person to whom a debt or legal obligation is owed, and who has the right to enforce payment of that debt or obligation is referred to as creditor.
Fair value	Fair value is a concept used in finance and economics, defined as a rational and unbiased estimate of the potential market price of a good, service, or asset.
Stock market	An organized marketplace in which common stocks are traded. In the United States, the largest stock market is the New York Stock Exchange, on which are traded the stocks of the largest U.S. companies.
Sensitivity analysis	A what-if technique that managers use to examine how a result will change if the original predicted data are not achieved or if an underlying assumption changes is sensitivity analysis.
Ratio analysis	Ratio analysis refers to an analytical tool designed to identify significant relationships; measures the proportional relationship between two financial statement amounts.

Go to **Cram101.com** for the Practice Tests for this Chapter.

Chapter 18. Cross-Border Mergers, Acquisitions, and Valuation

Chapter 18. Cross-Border Mergers, Acquisitions, and Valuation

Market capitalization	Market capitalization is a business term that refers to the aggregate value of a firm's outstanding common shares. In essence, market capitalization reflects the total value of a firm's equity currently available on the market. This measure differs from equity value to the extent that a firm has outstanding stock options or other securities convertible to common shares. The size and growth of a firm's market capitalization is often one of the critical measurements of a public company's success or failure.
Long position	In finance, a long position in a security, such as a stock or a bond, means the holder of the position owns the security.
Purchasing	Purchasing refers to the function in a firm that searches for quality material resources, finds the best suppliers, and negotiates the best price for goods and services.
Exchange rate	Exchange rate refers to the price at which one country's currency trades for another, typically on the exchange market.
Closing	The finalization of a real estate sales transaction that passes title to the property from the seller to the buyer is referred to as a closing. Closing is a sales term which refers to the process of making a sale. It refers to reaching the final step, which may be an exchange of money or acquiring a signature.
Assessment	Collecting information and providing feedback to employees about their behavior, communication style, or skills is an assessment.
Book value of a firm	The book value of a firm is the amount of owner's equity or stockholders' equity reported on a company's balance sheet. This is not an indication of the firm's fair market value.
Retained earnings	Cumulative earnings of a company that are not distributed to the owners and are reinvested in the business are called retained earnings.
Common stock	Common stock refers to the basic, normal, voting stock issued by a corporation; called residual equity because it ranks after preferred stock for dividend and liquidation distributions.
Book value	The book value of an asset or group of assets is sometimes the price at which they were originally acquired, in many cases equal to purchase price.
Book value per share	Total shareholders' equity divided by the number of outstanding common shares is referred to as book value per share.
Market value	Market value refers to the price of an asset agreed on between a willing buyer and a willing seller; the price an asset could demand if it is sold on the open market.
Historical cost	In accounting terminology, historical cost describes the original cost of an asset at the time of purchase or payment as opposed to its market value
Complexity	The technical sophistication of the product and hence the amount of understanding required to use it is referred to as complexity. It is the opposite of simplicity.
Holder	A person in possession of a document of title or an instrument payable or indorsed to him, his order, or to bearer is a holder.
Intellectual property	In law, intellectual property is an umbrella term for various legal entitlements which attach to certain types of information, ideas, or other intangibles in their expressed form. The holder of this legal entitlement is generally entitled to exercise various exclusive rights in relation to its subject matter.
Cemex	Although it is not a monopoly, Cemex, along with Holcim-Apasco, controls the Mexican cement market. This has given rise to allegations that because of the oligopolistic structure in the Mexican cement market (as in many other markets in Mexico) consumers pay a higher price for cement than in other countries. However given the peculiarities of the Mexican cement market,

Chapter 18. Cross-Border Mergers, Acquisitions, and Valuation

	the fact that it is sold mostly in bags, and the fact that cement is not an easily transported commodity make this accuzation difficult, if not impossible to prove.
Tesoro	Tesoro was founded in 1968 as a company primarily engaged in petroleum exploration and production. In 1969, Tesoro began operating Alaska's first refinery, near Kenai. As of 2005, Tesoro is a FORTUNE 200 company and one of the largest independent petroleum refiners and marketers in the United States
International Monetary Fund	The International Monetary Fund is the international organization entrusted with overseeing the global financial system by monitoring exchange rates and balance of payments, as well as offering technical and financial assistance when asked.
Fund	Independent accounting entity with a self-balancing set of accounts segregated for the purposes of carrying on specific activities is referred to as a fund.
World Bank	The World Bank is a group of five international organizations responsible for providing finance and advice to countries for the purposes of economic development and poverty reduction, and for encouraging and safeguarding international investment.
Gross domestic product	Gross domestic product refers to the total value of new goods and services produced in a given year within the borders of a country, regardless of by whom.
Market leader	The market leader is dominant in its industry. It has substantial market share and often extensive distribution arrangements with retailers. It typically is the industry leader in developing innovative new business models and new products (although not always).
Devaluation	Lowering the value of a nation's currency relative to other currencies is called devaluation.
Currency crisis	Occurs when a speculative attack on the exchange value of a currency results in a sharp depreciation in the value of the currency or forces authorities to expend large volumes of international currency reserves and sharply increase interest rates to defend the prevailing exchange rate are referred to as currency crisis.
Relative cost	Relative cost refers to the relationship between the price paid for advertising time or space and the size of the audience delivered; it is used to compare the prices of various media vehicles.
Distortion	Distortion refers to any departure from the ideal of perfect competition that interferes with economic agents maximizing social welfare when they maximize their own.
Concession	A concession is a business operated under a contract or license associated with a degree of exclusivity in exploiting a business within a certain geographical area. For example, sports arenas or public parks may have concession stands; and public services such as water supply may be operated as concessions.

Go to **Cram101.com** for the Practice Tests for this Chapter.

Chapter 19. International Portfolio Theory and Diversification

Portfolio	In finance, a portfolio is a collection of investments held by an institution or a private individual. Holding but not always a portfolio is part of an investment and risk-limiting strategy called diversification. By owning several assets, certain types of risk (in particular specific risk) can be reduced.
Variance	Variance refers to a measure of how much an economic or statistical variable varies across values or observations. Its calculation is the same as that of the covariance, being the covariance of the variable with itself.
Market	A market is, as defined in economics, a social arrangement that allows buyers and sellers to discover information and carry out a voluntary exchange of goods or services.
Systematic risk	Movements in a stock portfolio's value that are attributable to macroeconomic forces affecting all firms in an economy, rather than factors specific to an individual firm are referred to as systematic risk.
Security	Security refers to a claim on the borrower future income that is sold by the borrower to the lender. A security is a type of transferable interest representing financial value.
Stock	In financial terminology, stock is the capital raized by a corporation, through the issuance and sale of shares.
Diversification	Investing in a collection of assets whose returns do not always move together, with the result that overall risk is lower than for individual assets is referred to as diversification.
Foreign exchange risk	Foreign exchange risk refers to a form of risk that refers to the possibility of experiencing a drop in revenue or an increase in cost in an international transaction due to a change in foreign exchange rates. Importers, exporters, investors, and multinational firms alike are exposed to this risk.
Foreign exchange	In finance, foreign exchange means currencies, such as U.S. Dollars and Euros. These are traded on foreign exchange markets.
International diversification	Achieving diversification through many different foreign investments that are influenced by a variety of factors is referred to as international diversification. By diversifying across nations whose economic cycles are not perfectly correlated, investors can typically reduce the variability of their returns.
Exchange	The trade of things of value between buyer and seller so that each is better off after the trade is called the exchange.
Diversified portfolio	Diversified portfolio refers to a portfolio that includes a variety of assets whose prices are not likely all to change together. In international economics, this usually means holding assets denominated in different currencies.
Domestic	From or in one's own country. A domestic producer is one that produces inside the home country. A domestic price is the price inside the home country. Opposite of 'foreign' or 'world.'.
Investment	Investment refers to spending for the production and accumulation of capital and additions to inventories. In a financial sense, buying an asset with the expectation of making a return.
Asset	An item of property, such as land, capital, money, a share in ownership, or a claim on others for future payment, such as a bond or a bank deposit is an asset.
Expected return	Expected return refers to the return on an asset expected over the next period.
Currency risk	Currency risk is a form of risk that arises from the change in price of one currency against another. Whenever investors or companies have assets or business operations across national borders, they face currency risk if their positions are not hedged.

Go to **Cram101.com** for the Practice Tests for this Chapter.

Chapter 19. International Portfolio Theory and Diversification

Chapter 19. International Portfolio Theory and Diversification

Spot exchange rate	The exchange rate at which a foreign exchange dealer will convert one currency into another that particular day is the spot exchange rate.
Stock exchange	A stock exchange is a corporation or mutual organization which provides facilities for stock brokers and traders, to trade company stocks and other securities.
Exchange rate	Exchange rate refers to the price at which one country's currency trades for another, typically on the exchange market.
A share	In finance the term A share has two distinct meanings, both relating to securities. The first is a designation for a 'class' of common or preferred stock. A share of common or preferred stock typically has enhanced voting rights or other benefits compared to the other forms of shares that may have been created. The equity structure, or how many types of shares are offered, is determined by the corporate charter.
Shares	Shares refer to an equity security, representing a shareholder's ownership of a corporation. Shares are one of a finite number of equal portions in the capital of a company, entitling the owner to a proportion of distributed, non-reinvested profits known as dividends and to a portion of the value of the company in case of liquidation.
Yield	The interest rate that equates a future value or an annuity to a given present value is a yield.
Market price	Market price is an economic concept with commonplace familiarity; it is the price that a good or service is offered at, or will fetch, in the marketplace; it is of interest mainly in the study of microeconomics.
Spot rate	Spot rate refers to the rate at which the currency is traded for immediate delivery. It is the existing cash price.
Aid	Assistance provided by countries and by international institutions such as the World Bank to developing countries in the form of monetary grants, loans at low interest rates, in kind, or a combination of these is called aid. Aid can also refer to assistance of any type rendered to benefit some group or individual.
Cost of capital	Cost of capital refers to the percentage cost of funds used for acquiring resources for an organization, typically a weighted average of the firms cost of equity and cost of debt.
Capital	Capital generally refers to financial wealth, especially that used to start or maintain a business. In classical economics, capital is one of four factors of production, the others being land and labor and entrepreneurship.
Supply	Supply is the aggregate amount of any material good that can be called into being at a certain price point; it comprises one half of the equation of supply and demand. In classical economic theory, a curve representing supply is one of the factors that produce price.
Firm	An organization that employs resources to produce a good or service for profit and owns and operates one or more plants is referred to as a firm.
Bid	A bid price is a price offered by a buyer when he/she buys a good. In the context of stock trading on a stock exchange, the bid price is the highest price a buyer of a stock is willing to pay for a share of that given stock.
Portfolio theory	Portfolio theory refers to an economic theory that describes how rational investors allocate their wealth among different financial assets-that is, how they put their wealth into a 'portfolio.'
Efficient frontier	A line drawn through the optimum point selections in a risk-return trade-off diagram is referred to as efficient frontier.
Capital market	A financial market in which long-term debt and equity instruments are traded is referred to

Chapter 19. International Portfolio Theory and Diversification

	as a capital market. The capital market includes the stock market and the bond market.
Correlation	A correlation is the measure of the extent to which two economic or statistical variables move together, normalized so that its values range from -1 to +1. It is defined as the covariance of the two variables divided by the square root of the product of their variances.
Gain	In finance, gain is a profit or an increase in value of an investment such as a stock or bond. Gain is calculated by fair market value or the proceeds from the sale of the investment minus the sum of the purchase price and all costs associated with it.
Sony	Sony is a multinational corporation and one of the world's largest media conglomerates founded in Tokyo, Japan. One of its divisions Sony Electronics is one of the leading manufacturers of electronics, video, communications, and information technology products for the consumer and professional markets.
Portfolio capital	Financial assets, including stocks, bonds, deposits, and currencies are referred to as portfolio capital.
Holding	The holding is a court's determination of a matter of law based on the issue presented in the particular case. In other words: under this law, with these facts, this result.
Positively correlated	Positively correlated refers to values or amounts of two items that move in the same direction. In accounting and finance, the amount of risk and the amount of return on an investment move in the same direction.
Equity	Equity is the name given to the set of legal principles, in countries following the English common law tradition, which supplement strict rules of law where their application would operate harshly, so as to achieve what is sometimes referred to as "natural justice."
Composition	An out-of-court settlement in which creditors agree to accept a fractional settlement on their original claim is referred to as composition.
Business cycle	Business cycle refers to the pattern followed by macroeconommic variables, such as GDP and unemployment that rise and fall irregularly over time, relative to trend.
Economy	The income, expenditures, and resources that affect the cost of running a business and household are called an economy.
Stock market	An organized marketplace in which common stocks are traded. In the United States, the largest stock market is the New York Stock Exchange, on which are traded the stocks of the largest U.S. companies.
Securities market	The securities market is the market for securities, where companies and the government can raise long-term funds.
Union	A worker association that bargains with employers over wages and working conditions is called a union.
Euro	The common currency of a subset of the countries of the EU, adopted January 1, 1999 is called euro.
Hedging	A technique for avoiding a risk by making a counteracting transaction is referred to as hedging.
Fund	Independent accounting entity with a self-balancing set of accounts segregated for the purposes of carrying on specific activities is referred to as a fund.
Points	Loan origination fees that may be deductible as interest by a buyer of property. A seller of property who pays points reduces the selling price by the amount of the points paid for the buyer.
Transaction	Transaction exposure refers to foreign exchange gains and losses resulting from actual

Chapter 19. International Portfolio Theory and Diversification

exposure	international transactions. These may be hedged through the foreign exchange market, the money market, or the currency futures market.
Financial manager	Managers who make recommendations to top executives regarding strategies for improving the financial strength of a firm are referred to as a financial manager.
Hedge	Hedge refers to a process of offsetting risk. In the foreign exchange market, hedgers use the forward market to cover a transaction or open position and thereby reduce exchange risk. The term applies most commonly to trade.
Capital asset pricing model	The capital asset pricing model is used in finance to determine a theoretically appropriate required rate of return (and thus the price if expected cash flows can be estimated) of an asset, if that asset is to be added to an already well-diversified portfolio, given that asset's non-diversifiable risk.
Capital asset	In accounting, a capital asset is an asset that is recorded as property that creates more property, e.g. a factory that creates shoes, or a forest that yields a quantity of wood.
Cost of equity	In finance, the cost of equity is the minimum rate of return a firm must offer shareholders to compensate for waiting for their returns, and for bearing some risk.
Standard deviation	A measure of the spread or dispersion of a series of numbers around the expected value is the standard deviation. The standard deviation tells us how well the expected value represents a series of values.
Nestle	Nestle is the world's biggest food and beverage company. In the 1860s, a pharmacist, developed a food for babies who were unable to be breastfed. His first success was a premature infant who could not tolerate his own mother's milk nor any of the usual substitutes. The value of the new product was quickly recognized when his new formula saved the child's life.
Government bond	A government bond is a bond issued by a national government denominated in the country's own currency. Bonds issued by national governments in foreign currencies are normally referred to as sovereign bonds.
Bond	Bond refers to a debt instrument, issued by a borrower and promising a specified stream of payments to the purchaser, usually regular interest payments plus a final repayment of principal.
Deregulation	The lessening or complete removal of government regulations on an industry, especially concerning the price that firms are allowed to charge and leaving price to be determined by market forces a deregulation.
Integration	Economic integration refers to reducing barriers among countries to transactions and to movements of goods, capital, and labor, including harmonization of laws, regulations, and standards. Integrated markets theoretically function as a unified market.
Trend	Trend refers to the long-term movement of an economic variable, such as its average rate of increase or decrease over enough years to encompass several business cycles.
Opportunity cost	The cost of something in terms of opportunity foregone. The opportunity cost to a country of producing a unit more of a good, such as for export or to replace an import, is the quantity of some other good that could have been produced instead.
Equity capital	Equity capital refers to money raized from within the firm or through the sale of ownership in the firm.
Purchasing power parity	purchasing power parity is a theory based on the law of one price which says that the long-run equilibrium exchange rate of two currencies is the rate that equalizes the currencies' purchasing power.

Chapter 19. International Portfolio Theory and Diversification

Perfect information	Perfect information is a term used in economics and game theory to describe a state of complete knowledge about the actions of other players that is instantaneously updated as new information arises.
Purchasing power	The amount of goods that money will buy, usually measured by the CPI is referred to as purchasing power.
Rate of return	A rate of return is a comparison of the money earned (or lost) on an investment to the amount of money invested.
Purchasing	Purchasing refers to the function in a firm that searches for quality material resources, finds the best suppliers, and negotiates the best price for goods and services.
Numeraire	The unit in which prices are measured. This may be a currency, but in real models, such as most trade models, the numeraire is usually one of the goods, whose price is then set at one.
Eurobond	A bond that is issued outside of the jurisdiction of any single country, denominated in a eurocurrency is referred to as eurobond.
Buyer	A buyer refers to a role in the buying center with formal authority and responsibility to select the supplier and negotiate the terms of the contract.
Slope	The slope of a line in the plane containing the x and y axes is generally represented by the letter m, and is defined as the change in the y coordinate divided by the corresponding change in the x coordinate, between two distinct points on the line.
Globalization	The increasing world-wide integration of markets for goods, services and capital that attracted special attention in the late 1990s is called globalization.
Asset allocation	Asset Allocation is a concept of determining and maintaining a plan of investment in terms of a chosen mix of investments in different assets. A large part of financial planning is finding an asset allocation that is appropriate for a given person in terms of their appetite for and ability to shoulder risk.
Assessment	Collecting information and providing feedback to employees about their behavior, communication style, or skills is an assessment.
Operation	A standardized method or technique that is performed repetitively, often on different materials resulting in different finished goods is called an operation.
Mutual fund	A mutual fund is a form of collective investment that pools money from many investors and invests the money in stocks, bonds, short-term money market instruments, and/or other securities. In a mutual fund, the fund manager trades the fund's underlying securities, realizing capital gains or loss, and collects the dividend or interest income.
Analyst	Analyst refers to a person or tool with a primary function of information analysis, generally with a more limited, practical and short term set of goals than a researcher.
Boeing	Boeing is the world's largest aircraft manufacturer by revenue. Headquartered in Chicago, Illinois, Boeing is the second-largest defense contractor in the world. In 2005, the company was the world's largest civil aircraft manufacturer in terms of value.
Market value	Market value refers to the price of an asset agreed on between a willing buyer and a willing seller; the price an asset could demand if it is sold on the open market.
Business operations	Business operations are those activities involved in the running of a business for the purpose of producing value for the stakeholders. The outcome of business operations is the harvesting of value from assets owned by a business.
Management	Management characterizes the process of leading and directing all or part of an organization, often a business, through the deployment and manipulation of resources. Early twentieth-

Chapter 19. International Portfolio Theory and Diversification

	century management writer Mary Parker Follett defined management as "the art of getting things done through people."
Financial statement	Financial statement refers to a summary of all the transactions that have occurred over a particular period.
Due diligence	Due diligence is the effort made by an ordinarily prudent or reasonable party to avoid harm to another party or himself. Failure to make this effort is considered negligence. Failure to make this effort is considered negligence.
Inventory	Tangible property held for sale in the normal course of business or used in producing goods or services for sale is an inventory.
Expected value	A representative value from a probability distribution arrived at by multiplying each outcome by the associated probability and summing up the values is called the expected value.
Valuation	In finance, valuation is the process of estimating the market value of a financial asset or liability. They can be done on assets (for example, investments in marketable securities such as stocks, options, business enterprises, or intangible assets such as patents and trademarks) or on liabilities (e.g., Bonds issued by a company).
Free cash flow	Cash provided by operating activities adjusted for capital expenditures and dividends paid is referred to as free cash flow.
Cash flow	In finance, cash flow refers to the amounts of cash being received and spent by a business during a defined period of time, sometimes tied to a specific project. Most of the time they are being used to determine gaps in the liquid position of a company.
Depreciation	Depreciation is an accounting and finance term for the method of attributing the cost of an asset across the useful life of the asset. Depreciation is a reduction in the value of a currency in floating exchange rate.
Direct cost	A direct cost is a cost that can be identified specifically with a particular sponsored project, an instructional activity, or any other institutional activity, or that can be directly assigned to such activities relatively easily with a high degree of accuracy.
Interest	In finance and economics, interest is the price paid by a borrower for the use of a lender's money. In other words, interest is the amount of paid to "rent" money for a period of time.
Expense	In accounting, an expense represents an event in which an asset is used up or a liability is incurred. In terms of the accounting equation, expenses reduce owners' equity.
Service	Service refers to a "non tangible product" that is not embodied in a physical good and that typically effects some change in another product, person, or institution. Contrasts with good.
Revenue	Revenue is a U.S. business term for the amount of money that a company receives from its activities, mostly from sales of products and/or services to customers.

Go to **Cram101.com** for the Practice Tests for this Chapter.

Chapter 20. Multinational Tax Management

Profit	Profit refers to the return to the resource entrepreneurial ability; total revenue minus total cost.
Incorporation	Incorporation is the forming of a new corporation. The corporation may be a business, a non-profit organization or even a government of a new city or town.
Host country	The country in which the parent-country organization seeks to locate or has already located a facility is a host country.
Authority	Authority in agency law, refers to an agent's ability to affect his principal's legal relations with third parties. Also used to refer to an actor's legal power or ability to do something. In addition, sometimes used to refer to a statute, case, or other legal source that justifies a particular result.
Domestic	From or in one's own country. A domestic producer is one that produces inside the home country. A domestic price is the price inside the home country. Opposite of 'foreign' or 'world.'.
Firm	An organization that employs resources to produce a good or service for profit and owns and operates one or more plants is referred to as a firm.
Levy	Levy refers to imposing and collecting a tax or tariff.
Jurisdiction	The power of a court to hear and decide a case is called jurisdiction. It is the practical authority granted to a formally constituted body or to a person to deal with and make pronouncements on legal matters and, by implication, to administer justice within a defined area of responsibility.
Gap	In December of 1995, Gap became the first major North American retailer to accept independent monitoring of the working conditions in a contract factory producing its garments. Gap is the largest specialty retailer in the United States.
Privilege	Generally, a legal right to engage in conduct that would otherwise result in legal liability is a privilege. Privileges are commonly classified as absolute or conditional. Occasionally, privilege is also used to denote a legal right to refrain from particular behavior.
Foreign subsidiary	A company owned in a foreign country by another company is referred to as foreign subsidiary.
Subsidiary	A company that is controlled by another company or corporation is a subsidiary.
Double taxation	The taxation of both corporate net income and the dividends paid from this net income when they become the personal income of households a double taxation.
Organization for economic cooperation and development	Organization for economic cooperation and development refers to Paris-based intergovernmental organization of 'wealthy' nations whose purpose is to provide its 29 member states with a forum in which governments can compare their experiences, discuss the problems they share, and seek solutions that can then be applied within their own national contexts.
Tax treaty	Tax treaty refers to an agreement between the U.S. Department of State and another country, designed to alleviate double taxation of income and asset transfers, and to share administrative information useful to tax agencies in both countries.
Treaties	The first source of international law, consisting of agreements or contracts between two or more nations that are formally signed by an authorized representative and ratified by the supreme power of each nation are called treaties.
Exporting	Selling products to another country is called exporting.
Manufacturing	Production of goods primarily by the application of labor and capital to raw materials and other intermediate inputs, in contrast to agriculture, mining, forestry, fishing, and

Chapter 20. Multinational Tax Management

Chapter 20. Multinational Tax Management

	services a manufacturing.
Operation	A standardized method or technique that is performed repetitively, often on different materials resulting in different finished goods is called an operation.
Export	In economics, an export is any good or commodity, shipped or otherwise transported out of a country, province, town to another part of the world in a legitimate fashion, typically for use in trade or sale.
Negotiation	Negotiation is the process whereby interested parties resolve disputes, agree upon courses of action, bargain for individual or collective advantage, and/or attempt to craft outcomes which serve their mutual interests.
Direct taxes	In the colloquial sense, a direct tax is one paid directly to the government by the persons (legal or natural) on whom it is imposed (often accompanied by a tax return filed by the taxpayer). In the United States, the term "direct tax" has a different meaning for the purposes of constitutional law. Traditionally a direct tax in the constitutional sense means a tax on property "by reason of its ownership" as well as a capitation (a "head tax").
Revenue	Revenue is a U.S. business term for the amount of money that a company receives from its activities, mostly from sales of products and/or services to customers.
Royalties	Remuneration paid to the owners of technology, patents, or trade names for the use of same name are called royalties.
Dividend	Amount of corporate profits paid out for each share of stock is referred to as dividend.
Interest	In finance and economics, interest is the price paid by a borrower for the use of a lender's money. In other words, interest is the amount of paid to "rent" money for a period of time.
Corporation	A legal entity chartered by a state or the Federal government that is distinct and separate from the individuals who own it is a corporation. This separation gives the corporation unique powers which other legal entities lack.
National sales tax	National sales tax intended as a replacement for the current Federal income tax. Unlike a value added tax, which is levied on the manufacturer, it would be imposed on the consumer upon the final sale of goods and services.
Value added	The value of output minus the value of all intermediate inputs, representing therefore the contribution of, and payments to, primary factors of production a value added.
Consumption	In Keynesian economics consumption refers to personal consumption expenditure, i.e., the purchase of currently produced goods and services out of income, out of savings (net worth), or from borrowed funds. It refers to that part of disposable income that does not go to saving.
Production	The creation of finished goods and services using the factors of production: land, labor, capital, entrepreneurship, and knowledge.
Sales tax	A sales tax is a tax on consumption. It is normally a certain percentage that is added onto the price of a good or service that is purchased.
Production goods	Items used in the manufacturing process that become part of the final product are called production goods.
Postal Service	The postal service was created in Philadelphia under Benjamin Franklin on July 26, 1775 by decree of the Second Continental Congress. Based on a clause in the United States Constitution empowering Congress "To establish Post Offices and post Roads."
Service	Service refers to a "non tangible product" that is not embodied in a physical good and that typically effects some change in another product, person, or institution. Contrasts with

Chapter 20. Multinational Tax Management

Chapter 20. Multinational Tax Management

	good.
Expense	In accounting, an expense represents an event in which an asset is used up or a liability is incurred. In terms of the accounting equation, expenses reduce owners' equity.
Exempt	Employees who are not covered by the Fair Labor Standards Act are exempt. Exempt employees are not eligible for overtime pay.
Union	A worker association that bargains with employers over wages and working conditions is called a union.
Stock market	An organized marketplace in which common stocks are traded. In the United States, the largest stock market is the New York Stock Exchange, on which are traded the stocks of the largest U.S. companies.
Turnover	Turnover in a financial context refers to the rate at which a provider of goods cycles through its average inventory. Turnover in a human resources context refers to the characteristic of a given company or industry, relative to rate at which an employer gains and loses staff.
Security	Security refers to a claim on the borrower future income that is sold by the borrower to the lender. A security is a type of transferable interest representing financial value.
Market	A market is, as defined in economics, a social arrangement that allows buyers and sellers to discover information and carry out a voluntary exchange of goods or services.
Stock	In financial terminology, stock is the capital raized by a corporation, through the issuance and sale of shares.
Property	Assets defined in the broadest legal sense. Property includes the unrealized receivables of a cash basis taxpayer, but not services rendered.
Balance of payments	Balance of payments refers to a list, or accounting, of all of a country's international transactions for a given time period, usually one year.
Foreign exchange	In finance, foreign exchange means currencies, such as U.S. Dollars and Euros. These are traded on foreign exchange markets.
Exchange	The trade of things of value between buyer and seller so that each is better off after the trade is called the exchange.
Balance	In banking and accountancy, the outstanding balance is the amount of money owned, (or due), that remains in a deposit account (or a loan account) at a given date, after all past remittances, payments and withdrawal have been accounted for. It can be positive (then, in the balance sheet of a firm, it is an asset) or negative (a liability).
Foreign tax credit	Foreign tax credit refers to a tax credit a U.S. citizen or resident who incurs or pays income taxes to a foreign country on income subject to U.S. tax may be able to claim against the U.S. income tax.
Tax credit	Allows a firm to reduce the taxes paid to the home government by the amount of taxes paid to the foreign government is referred to as tax credit.
Credit	Credit refers to a recording as positive in the balance of payments, any transaction that gives rise to a payment into the country, such as an export, the sale of an asset, or borrowing from abroad.
Grant	Grant refers to an intergovernmental transfer of funds . Since the New Deal, state and local governments have become increasingly dependent upon federal grants for an almost infinite variety of programs.
Channel	Channel, in communications (sometimes called communications channel), refers to the medium

Go to **Cram101.com** for the Practice Tests for this Chapter.

Chapter 20. Multinational Tax Management

Chapter 20. Multinational Tax Management

	used to convey information from a sender (or transmitter) to a receiver.
Capital	Capital generally refers to financial wealth, especially that used to start or maintain a business. In classical economics, capital is one of four factors of production, the others being land and labor and entrepreneurship.
Liability	A liability is a present obligation of the enterprise arizing from past events, the settlement of which is expected to result in an outflow from the enterprise of resources embodying economic benefits.
Distribution	Distribution in economics, the manner in which total output and income is distributed among individuals or factors.
Deductible	The dollar sum of costs that an insured individual must pay before the insurer begins to pay is called deductible.
Foreign corporation	Foreign corporation refers to a corporation incorporated in one state doing business in another state. A corporation doing business in a jurisdiction in which it was not formed.
Net profit	Net profit is an accounting term which is commonly used in business. It is equal to the gross revenue for a given time period minus associated expenses.
Parent corporation	Parent corporation refers to a corporation that owns a controlling interest of another corporation, called a subsidiary corporation.
Corporate tax	Corporate tax refers to a direct tax levied by various jurisdictions on the profits made by companies or associations. As a general principle, this varies substantially between jurisdictions.
Net income	Net income is equal to the income that a firm has after subtracting costs and expenses from the total revenue. Expenses will typically include tax expense.
Effective tax rate	The effective tax rate is the amount of income tax an individual or firm pays divided by the individual or firm's total taxable income. This ratio is usually expressed as a percentage.
Cash flow	In finance, cash flow refers to the amounts of cash being received and spent by a business during a defined period of time, sometimes tied to a specific project. Most of the time they are being used to determine gaps in the liquid position of a company.
Corporate income tax	A tax levied on the net income of corporations is called the corporate income tax.
Management	Management characterizes the process of leading and directing all or part of an organization, often a business, through the deployment and manipulation of resources. Early twentieth-century management writer Mary Parker Follett defined management as "the art of getting things done through people."
Basket	A basket is an economic term for a group of several securities created for the purpose of simultaneous buying or selling. Baskets are frequently used for program trading.
Shareholder	A shareholder is an individual or company (including a corporation) that legally owns one or more shares of stock in a joined stock company.
Tax haven	A country in which either locally sourced income or residents of the country are subject to a low rate of taxation is called a tax haven.
Insurance	Insurance refers to a system by which individuals can reduce their exposure to risk of large losses by spreading the risks among a large number of persons.
Commodity	Could refer to any good, but in trade a commodity is usually a raw material or primary product that enters into international trade, such as metals or basic agricultural products.

Go to Cram101.com for the Practice Tests for this Chapter.

Chapter 20. Multinational Tax Management

Chapter 20. Multinational Tax Management

Gain	In finance, gain is a profit or an increase in value of an investment such as a stock or bond. Gain is calculated by fair market value or the proceeds from the sale of the investment minus the sum of the purchase price and all costs associated with it.
Deferral	Deferred is any account where the asset or liability is not realized until a future date, e.g. annuities, charges, taxes, income, etc. The deferred item may be carried, dependent on type of deferral, as either an asset or liability.
Incentive	An incentive is any factor (financial or non-financial) that provides a motive for a particular course of action, or counts as a reason for preferring one choice to the alternatives.
Consideration	Consideration in contract law, a basic requirement for an enforceable agreement under traditional contract principles, defined in this text as legal value, bargained for and given in exchange for an act or promise. In corporation law, cash or property contributed to a corporation in exchange for shares, or a promise to contribute such cash or property.
Income statement	Income statement refers to a financial statement that presents the revenues and expenses and resulting net income or net loss of a company for a specific period of time.
Fund	Independent accounting entity with a self-balancing set of accounts segregated for the purposes of carrying on specific activities is referred to as a fund.
Conversion	Conversion refers to any distinct act of dominion wrongfully exerted over another's personal property in denial of or inconsistent with his rights therein. That tort committed by a person who deals with chattels not belonging to him in a manner that is inconsistent with the ownership of the lawful owner.
Common stock	Common stock refers to the basic, normal, voting stock issued by a corporation; called residual equity because it ranks after preferred stock for dividend and liquidation distributions.
Equity	Equity is the name given to the set of legal principles, in countries following the English common law tradition, which supplement strict rules of law where their application would operate harshly, so as to achieve what is sometimes referred to as "natural justice."
Tax avoidance	The minimization of one's tax liability by taking advantage of legally available tax planning opportunities. Tax avoidance can be contrasted with tax evasion, which entails the reduction of tax liability by illegal means.
Transfer price	Transfer price refers to the price one subunit charges for a product or service supplied to another subunit of the same organization.
Tax reform	Tax reform is the process of changing the way taxes are collected or managed by the government. Some seek to reduce the level of taxation of all people by the government. Some seek to make the tax system more/less progressive in its effect. Some may be trying to make the tax system more understandable, or more accountable.
Effectively connected	Effectively connected income of a nonresident alien or foreign corporation that is attributable to the operation of a U.S. trade or business under either the asset-use or businessactivities test.
Lease	A contract for the possession and use of land or other property, including goods, on one side, and a recompense of rent or other income on the other is the lease.
World Trade Organization	The World Trade Organization is an international, multilateral organization, which sets the rules for the global trading system and resolves disputes between its member states, all of whom are signatories to its approximately 30 agreements.
Exporter	A firm that sells its product in another country is an exporter.

Chapter 20. Multinational Tax Management

Chapter 20. Multinational Tax Management

Subsidy	Subsidy refers to government financial assistance to a domestic producer.
Deficit	The deficit is the amount by which expenditure exceed revenue.
Multinational enterprise	Multinational enterprise refers to a firm, usually a corporation, that operates in two or more countries.
Financial management	The job of managing a firm's resources so it can meet its goals and objectives is called financial management.
Shareholder value	For a publicly traded company, shareholder value is the part of its capitalization that is equity as opposed to long-term debt. In the case of only one type of stock, this would roughly be the number of outstanding shares times current shareprice.
Enterprise	Enterprise refers to another name for a business organization. Other similar terms are business firm, sometimes simply business, sometimes simply firm, as well as company, and entity.
Debit	Debit refers to recording as negative in the balance of payments, any transaction that gives rise to a payment out of the country, such as an import, the purchase of an asset, or lending to foreigners. Opposite of credit.
Organizational structure	Organizational structure is the way in which the interrelated groups of an organization are constructed. From a managerial point of view the main concerns are ensuring effective communication and coordination.
Competitor	Other organizations in the same industry or type of business that provide a good or service to the same set of customers is referred to as a competitor.
Holding company	A corporation whose purpose or function is to own or otherwise hold the shares of other corporations either for investment or control is called holding company.
Holding	The holding is a court's determination of a matter of law based on the issue presented in the particular case. In other words: under this law, with these facts, this result.
Treasury bills	Short-term obligations of the federal government are treasury bills. They are like zero coupon bonds in that they do not pay interest prior to maturity; instead they are sold at a discount of the par value to create a positive yield to maturity.
Liquidity	Liquidity refers to the capacity to turn assets into cash, or the amount of assets in a portfolio that have that capacity.
Wholly owned subsidiary	A subsidiary in which the firm owns 100 percent of the stock is a wholly owned subsidiary.
Operating income	Total revenues from operation minus cost of goods sold and operating costs are called operating income.
Excise tax	A tax levied on the production of a specific product or on the quantity of the product purchased is an excise tax.
Principal	In agency law, one under whose direction an agent acts and for whose benefit that agent acts is a principal.
Contribution	In business organization law, the cash or property contributed to a business by its owners is referred to as contribution.
Committee	A long-lasting, sometimes permanent team in the organization structure created to deal with tasks that recur regularly is the committee.
Deferred income	Deferred income is a liability. It is recorded when an asset (e.g. receivable) is recorded, but the related income (i.e. revenue) will be earned only in the future.

Chapter 20. Multinational Tax Management

Chapter 20. Multinational Tax Management

Net present value	Net present value is a standard method in finance of capital budgeting – the planning of long-term investments. Using this method a potential investment project should be undertaken if the present value of all cash inflows minus the present value of all cash outflows (which equals the net present value) is greater than zero.
Present value	The value today of a stream of payments and/or receipts over time in the future and/or the past, converted to the present using an interest rate. If X t is the amount in period t and r the interest rate, then present value at time t=0 is V = ?T /t.
BMW	BMW is an independent German company and manufacturer of automobiles and motorcycles. BMW is the world's largest premium carmaker and is the parent company of the BMW MINI and Rolls-Royce car brands, and, formerly, Rover.
Disclosure	Disclosure means the giving out of information, either voluntarily or to be in compliance with legal regulations or workplace rules.
Shares	Shares refer to an equity security, representing a shareholder's ownership of a corporation. Shares are one of a finite number of equal portions in the capital of a company, entitling the owner to a proportion of distributed, non-reinvested profits known as dividends and to a portion of the value of the company in case of liquidation.
Policy	Similar to a script in that a policy can be a less than completely rational decision-making method. Involves the use of a pre-existing set of decision steps for any problem that presents itself.
Retained earnings	Cumulative earnings of a company that are not distributed to the owners and are reinvested in the business are called retained earnings.
Interest expense	The cost a business incurs to borrow money. With respect to bonds payable, the interest expense is calculated by multiplying the market rate of interest by the carrying value of the bonds on the date of the payment.
Stockholder	A stockholder is an individual or company (including a corporation) that legally owns one or more shares of stock in a joined stock company. The shareholders are the owners of a corporation. Companies listed at the stock market strive to enhance shareholder value.
Inflation	An increase in the overall price level of an economy, usually as measured by the CPI or by the implicit price deflator is called inflation.
Parent company	Parent company refers to the entity that has a controlling influence over another company. It may have its own operations, or it may have been set up solely for the purpose of owning the Subject Company.
Exchange rate	Exchange rate refers to the price at which one country's currency trades for another, typically on the exchange market.
International Business	International business refers to any firm that engages in international trade or investment.
Accounting	A system that collects and processes financial information about an organization and reports that information to decision makers is referred to as accounting.
Business law	Business law is the body of law which governs business and commerce and is often considered to be a branch of civil law and deals both with issues of private law and public law. It regulates corporate contracts, hiring practices, and the manufacture and sales of consumer goods.
Investment	Investment refers to spending for the production and accumulation of capital and additions to inventories. In a financial sense, buying an asset with the expectation of making a return.
Lender	Suppliers and financial institutions that lend money to companies is referred to as a lender.

Chapter 20. Multinational Tax Management

Chapter 20. Multinational Tax Management

Vendor	A person who sells property to a vendee is a vendor. The words vendor and vendee are more commonly applied to the seller and purchaser of real estate, and the words seller and buyer are more commonly applied to the seller and purchaser of personal property.
Procurement	Procurement is the acquisition of goods or services at the best possible total cost of ownership, in the right quantity, at the right time, in the right place for the direct benefit or use of the governments, corporations, or individuals generally via, but not limited to a contract.
Invoice	The itemized bill for a transaction, stating the nature of the transaction and its cost. In international trade, the invoice price is often the preferred basis for levying an ad valorem tariff.
Intellectual property	In law, intellectual property is an umbrella term for various legal entitlements which attach to certain types of information, ideas, or other intangibles in their expressed form. The holder of this legal entitlement is generally entitled to exercise various exclusive rights in relation to its subject matter.
Systems design	Systems design is the process or art of defining the hardware and software architecture, components, modules, interfaces, and data for a computer system to satisfy specified requirements.

Chapter 21. Repositioning Funds

Profit	Profit refers to the return to the resource entrepreneurial ability; total revenue minus total cost.
Firm	An organization that employs resources to produce a good or service for profit and owns and operates one or more plants is referred to as a firm.
Transfer price	Transfer price refers to the price one subunit charges for a product or service supplied to another subunit of the same organization.
Foreign subsidiary	A company owned in a foreign country by another company is referred to as foreign subsidiary.
Subsidiary	A company that is controlled by another company or corporation is a subsidiary.
Capital	Capital generally refers to financial wealth, especially that used to start or maintain a business. In classical economics, capital is one of four factors of production, the others being land and labor and entrepreneurship.
Acquisition	A company's purchase of the property and obligations of another company is an acquisition.
Fixed exchange rate	A fixed exchange rate, sometimes is a type of exchange rate regime wherein a currency's value is matched to the value of another single currency or to a basket of other currencies, or to another measure of value, such as gold.
Joint venture	Joint venture refers to an undertaking by two parties for a specific purpose and duration, taking any of several legal forms.
Exchange rate	Exchange rate refers to the price at which one country's currency trades for another, typically on the exchange market.
Exchange	The trade of things of value between buyer and seller so that each is better off after the trade is called the exchange.
Long run	In economic models, the long run time frame assumes no fixed factors of production. Firms can enter or leave the marketplace, and the cost (and availability) of land, labor, raw materials, and capital goods can be assumed to vary.
Financial management	The job of managing a firm's resources so it can meet its goals and objectives is called financial management.
Senior management	Senior management is generally a team of individuals at the highest level of organizational management who have the day-to-day responsibilities of managing a corporation.
Parent company	Parent company refers to the entity that has a controlling influence over another company. It may have its own operations, or it may have been set up solely for the purpose of owning the Subject Company.
Repositioning	Changing the position an offering occupies in a consumer's mind relative to competitive offerings and so expanding or otherwise altering its potential market is called repositioning.
Management	Management characterizes the process of leading and directing all or part of an organization, often a business, through the deployment and manipulation of resources. Early twentieth-century management writer Mary Parker Follett defined management as "the art of getting things done through people."
Cash flow	In finance, cash flow refers to the amounts of cash being received and spent by a business during a defined period of time, sometimes tied to a specific project. Most of the time they are being used to determine gaps in the liquid position of a company.
Foreign exchange	In finance, foreign exchange means currencies, such as U.S. Dollars and Euros. These are traded on foreign exchange markets.

Chapter 21. Repositioning Funds

Consideration	Consideration in contract law, a basic requirement for an enforceable agreement under traditional contract principles, defined in this text as legal value, bargained for and given in exchange for an act or promise. In corporation law, cash or property contributed to a corporation in exchange for shares, or a promise to contribute such cash or property.
Liquidity	Liquidity refers to the capacity to turn assets into cash, or the amount of assets in a portfolio that have that capacity.
Fund	Independent accounting entity with a self-balancing set of accounts segregated for the purposes of carrying on specific activities is referred to as a fund.
Exchange control	Rationing of foreign exchange, typically used when the exchange rate is fixed and the central bank is unable or unwilling to enforce the rate by exchange-market intervention is an exchange control.
Dividend	Amount of corporate profits paid out for each share of stock is referred to as dividend.
Jurisdiction	The power of a court to hear and decide a case is called jurisdiction. It is the practical authority granted to a formally constituted body or to a person to deal with and make pronouncements on legal matters and, by implication, to administer justice within a defined area of responsibility.
In transit	A state in which goods are in the possession of a bailee or carrier and not in the hands of the buyer, seller, lessee, or lessor is referred to as in transit.
Operation	A standardized method or technique that is performed repetitively, often on different materials resulting in different finished goods is called an operation.
Transaction cost	A transaction cost is a cost incurred in making an economic exchange. For example, most people, when buying or selling a stock, must pay a commission to their broker; that commission is a transaction cost of doing the stock deal.
Warrant	A warrant is a security that entitles the holder to buy or sell a certain additional quantity of an underlying security at an agreed-upon price, at the holder's discretion.
Cash dividend	A pro rata distribution of cash to stockholders of corporate stock is called a cash dividend.
Balance	In banking and accountancy, the outstanding balance is the amount of money owned, (or due), that remains in a deposit account (or a loan account) at a given date, after all past remittances, payments and withdrawal have been accounted for. It can be positive (then, in the balance sheet of a firm, it is an asset) or negative (a liability).
Host country	The country in which the parent-country organization seeks to locate or has already located a facility is a host country.
Unbundling	Relying on more than one financial technique to transfer funds across borders is called unbundling.
Authority	Authority in agency law, refers to an agent's ability to affect his principal's legal relations with third parties. Also used to refer to an actor's legal power or ability to do something. In addition, sometimes used to refer to a statute, case, or other legal source that justifies a particular result.
Expense	In accounting, an expense represents an event in which an asset is used up or a liability is incurred. In terms of the accounting equation, expenses reduce owners' equity.
Intellectual property	In law, intellectual property is an umbrella term for various legal entitlements which attach to certain types of information, ideas, or other intangibles in their expressed form. The holder of this legal entitlement is generally entitled to exercise various exclusive rights in relation to its subject matter.

Go to **Cram101.com** for the Practice Tests for this Chapter.

Chapter 21. Repositioning Funds

Chapter 21. Repositioning Funds

Royalties	Remuneration paid to the owners of technology, patents, or trade names for the use of same name are called royalties.
Property	Assets defined in the broadest legal sense. Property includes the unrealized receivables of a cash basis taxpayer, but not services rendered.
Matching	Matching refers to an accounting concept that establishes when expenses are recognized. Expenses are matched with the revenues they helped to generate and are recognized when those revenues are recognized.
Patent	The legal right to the proceeds from and control over the use of an invented product or process, granted for a fixed period of time, usually 20 years. Patent is one form of intellectual property that is subject of the TRIPS agreement.
Investment	Investment refers to spending for the production and accumulation of capital and additions to inventories. In a financial sense, buying an asset with the expectation of making a return.
Residual	Residual payments can refer to an ongoing stream of payments in respect of the completion of past achievements.
Inputs	The inputs used by a firm or an economy are the labor, raw materials, electricity and other resources it uses to produce its outputs.
Transfer pricing	Transfer pricing refers to the pricing of goods and services within a multi-divisional organization. Goods from the production division may be sold to the marketing division, or goods from a parent company may be sold to a foreign subsidiary.
Technology	The body of knowledge and techniques that can be used to combine economic resources to produce goods and services is called technology.
Service	Service refers to a "non tangible product" that is not embodied in a physical good and that typically effects some change in another product, person, or institution. Contrasts with good.
Domestic	From or in one's own country. A domestic producer is one that produces inside the home country. A domestic price is the price inside the home country. Opposite of 'foreign' or 'world.'.
Positioning	The art and science of fitting the product or service to one or more segments of the market in such a way as to set it meaningfully apart from competition is called positioning.
Regulation	Regulation refers to restrictions state and federal laws place on business with regard to the conduct of its activities.
Corporation	A legal entity chartered by a state or the Federal government that is distinct and separate from the individuals who own it is a corporation. This separation gives the corporation unique powers which other legal entities lack.
Policy	Similar to a script in that a policy can be a less than completely rational decision-making method. Involves the use of a pre-existing set of decision steps for any problem that presents itself.
Net income	Net income is equal to the income that a firm has after subtracting costs and expenses from the total revenue. Expenses will typically include tax expense.
Revenue	Revenue is a U.S. business term for the amount of money that a company receives from its activities, mostly from sales of products and/or services to customers.
Internal Revenue Service	In 1862, during the Civil War, President Lincoln and Congress created the office of Commissioner of Internal Revenue and enacted an income tax to pay war expenses. The position of Commissioner still exists today. The Commissioner is the head of the Internal Revenue

Go to **Cram101.com** for the Practice Tests for this Chapter.

Chapter 21. Repositioning Funds

	Service.
Gross income	Income subject to the Federal income tax. Gross income does not include all economic income. That is, certain exclusions are allowed. For a manufacturing or merchandizing business, gross income usually means gross profit.
Allowance	Reduction in the selling price of goods extended to the buyer because the goods are defective or of lower quality than the buyer ordered and to encourage a buyer to keep merchandise that would otherwise be returned is the allowance.
Credit	Credit refers to a recording as positive in the balance of payments, any transaction that gives rise to a payment into the country, such as an export, the sale of an asset, or borrowing from abroad.
Burden of proof	Used to refer both to the necessity or obligation of proving the facts needed to support a party's claim, and the persuasiveness of the evidence used to do so is a burden of proof. Regarding the second sense of the term, the usual burden of proof in a civil case is a preponderance of the evidence.
Organization for economic cooperation and development	Organization for economic cooperation and development refers to Paris-based intergovernmental organization of 'wealthy' nations whose purpose is to provide its 29 member states with a forum in which governments can compare their experiences, discuss the problems they share, and seek solutions that can then be applied within their own national contexts.
Committee	A long-lasting, sometimes permanent team in the organization structure created to deal with tasks that recur regularly is the committee.
Proprietary	Proprietary indicates that a party, or proprietor, exercises private ownership, control or use over an item of property, usually to the exclusion of other parties. Where a party, holds or claims proprietary interests in relation to certain types of property (eg. a creative literary work, or software), that property may also be the subject of intellectual property law (eg. copyright or patents).
Trademark	A distinctive word, name, symbol, device, or combination thereof, which enables consumers to identify favored products or services and which may find protection under state or federal law is a trademark.
Market	A market is, as defined in economics, a social arrangement that allows buyers and sellers to discover information and carry out a voluntary exchange of goods or services.
General Motors	General Motors is the world's largest automaker. Founded in 1908, today it employs about 327,000 people around the world. With global headquarters in Detroit, it manufactures its cars and trucks in 33 countries.
Ford	Ford is an American company that manufactures and sells automobiles worldwide. Ford introduced methods for large-scale manufacturing of cars, and large-scale management of an industrial workforce, especially elaborately engineered manufacturing sequences typified by the moving assembly lines.
Distribution	Distribution in economics, the manner in which total output and income is distributed among individuals or factors.
Markup	Markup is a term used in marketing to indicate how much the price of a product is above the cost of producing and distributing the product.
Direct cost	A direct cost is a cost that can be identified specifically with a particular sponsored project, an instructional activity, or any other institutional activity, or that can be directly assigned to such activities relatively easily with a high degree of accuracy.
Accounting	A system that collects and processes financial information about an organization and reports

Chapter 21. Repositioning Funds

Chapter 21. Repositioning Funds

	that information to decision makers is referred to as accounting.
Appeal	Appeal refers to the act of asking an appellate court to overturn a decision after the trial court's final judgment has been entered.
Incentive	An incentive is any factor (financial or non-financial) that provides a motive for a particular course of action, or counts as a reason for preferring one choice to the alternatives.
Profit center	Responsibility center where the manager is accountable for revenues and costs is referred to as a profit center.
Evaluation	The consumer's appraisal of the product or brand on important attributes is called evaluation.
Corporate level	Corporate level refers to level at which top management directs overall strategy for the entire organization.
Distortion	Distortion refers to any departure from the ideal of perfect competition that interferes with economic agents maximizing social welfare when they maximize their own.
Retained earnings	Cumulative earnings of a company that are not distributed to the owners and are reinvested in the business are called retained earnings.
Ownership equity	Ownership equity is the difference in value between the assets and the claims on them (liabilities), which accrues to the owner(s).
Payout ratio	A measure of the percentage of earnings distributed in the form of cash dividends to common stockholders is referred to as the payout ratio. More specifically, the firm's cash dividend divided by the firm's earnings in the same reporting period.
Stockholder	A stockholder is an individual or company (including a corporation) that legally owns one or more shares of stock in a joined stock company. The shareholders are the owners of a corporation. Companies listed at the stock market strive to enhance shareholder value.
Interest	In finance and economics, interest is the price paid by a borrower for the use of a lender's money. In other words, interest is the amount of paid to "rent" money for a period of time.
Equity	Equity is the name given to the set of legal principles, in countries following the English common law tradition, which supplement strict rules of law where their application would operate harshly, so as to achieve what is sometimes referred to as "natural justice."
Exporting	Selling products to another country is called exporting.
Administration	Administration refers to the management and direction of the affairs of governments and institutions; a collective term for all policymaking officials of a government; the execution and implementation of public policy.
Goodyear	Goodyear was founded in 1898 by German immigrants Charles and Frank Seiberling. Today it is the third largest tire and rubber company in the world.
Allegation	An allegation is a statement of a fact by a party in a pleading, which the party claims it will prove. Allegations remain assertions without proof, only claims until they are proved.
Logo	Logo refers to device or other brand name that cannot be spoken.
Manufacturing	Production of goods primarily by the application of labor and capital to raw materials and other intermediate inputs, in contrast to agriculture, mining, forestry, fishing, and services a manufacturing.
Marketing	Promoting and selling products or services to customers, or prospective customers, is referred to as marketing.

Chapter 21. Repositioning Funds

Chapter 21. Repositioning Funds

Open market	In economics, the open market is the term used to refer to the environment in which bonds are bought and sold.
Trade name	A commercial legal name under which a company does business is referred to as the trade name.
Production	The creation of finished goods and services using the factors of production: land, labor, capital, entrepreneurship, and knowledge.
License	A license in the sphere of Intellectual Property Rights (IPR) is a document, contract or agreement giving permission or the 'right' to a legally-definable entity to do something (such as manufacture a product or to use a service), or to apply something (such as a trademark), with the objective of achieving commercial gain.
Research and development	The use of resources for the deliberate discovery of new information and ways of doing things, together with the application of that information in inventing new products or processes is referred to as research and development.
Public relations	Public relations refers to the management function that evaluates public attitudes, changes policies and procedures in response to the public's requests, and executes a program of action and information to earn public understanding and acceptance.
Organizational development	The application of behavioral science knowledge in a longrange effort to improve an organization's ability to cope with change in its external environment and increase its problem-solving capabilities is referred to as organizational development.
Enterprise	Enterprise refers to another name for a business organization. Other similar terms are business firm, sometimes simply business, sometimes simply firm, as well as company, and entity.
A share	In finance the term A share has two distinct meanings, both relating to securities. The first is a designation for a 'class' of common or preferred stock. A share of common or preferred stock typically has enhanced voting rights or other benefits compared to the other forms of shares that may have been created. The equity structure, or how many types of shares are offered, is determined by the corporate charter.
Direct labor	The earnings of employees who work directly on the products being manufactured are direct labor.
Labor	People's physical and mental talents and efforts that are used to help produce goods and services are called labor.
Levy	Levy refers to imposing and collecting a tax or tariff.
Licensing	Licensing is a form of strategic alliance which involves the sale of a right to use certain proprietary knowledge (so called intellectual property) in a defined way.
Contract	A contract is a "promise" or an "agreement" that is enforced or recognized by the law. In the civil law, a contract is considered to be part of the general law of obligations.
Net sales	Gross sales less sales returns and allowances and sales discounts are referred to as net sales.
Invoice	The itemized bill for a transaction, stating the nature of the transaction and its cost. In international trade, the invoice price is often the preferred basis for levying an ad valorem tariff.
Trade discounts	Trade discounts refer to price reductions to reward wholesalers or retailers for marketing functions they will perform in the future.
Discount	The difference between the face value of a bond and its selling price, when a bond is sold for less than its face value it's referred to as a discount.

Go to **Cram101.com** for the Practice Tests for this Chapter.

Chapter 21. Repositioning Funds

Chapter 21. Repositioning Funds

Licensee	A person lawfully on land in possession of another for purposes unconnected with the business interests of the possessor is referred to as the licensee.
Foreign exchange risk	Foreign exchange risk refers to a form of risk that refers to the possibility of experiencing a drop in revenue or an increase in cost in an international transaction due to a change in foreign exchange rates. Importers, exporters, investors, and multinational firms alike are exposed to this risk.
Personnel	A collective term for all of the employees of an organization. Personnel is also commonly used to refer to the personnel management function or the organizational unit responsible for administering personnel programs.
Termination	The ending of a corporation that occurs only after the winding-up of the corporation's affairs, the liquidation of its assets, and the distribution of the proceeds to the claimants are referred to as a termination.
Arbitration	Arbitration is a form of mediation or conciliation, where the mediating party is given power by the disputant parties to settle the dispute by making a finding. In practice arbitration is generally used as a substitute for judicial systems, particularly when the judicial processes are viewed as too slow, expensive or biased. Arbitration is also used by communities which lack formal law, as a substitute for formal law.
Litigation	The process of bringing, maintaining, and defending a lawsuit is litigation.
Controlling	A management function that involves determining whether or not an organization is progressing toward its goals and objectives, and taking corrective action if it is not is called controlling.
Exporter	A firm that sells its product in another country is an exporter.
Import transaction	The purchase of a good or service that decreases the amount of foreign money held by citizens, firms, and governments of a nation is referred to as an import transaction.
Export transactions	A sale of a good or service that increases the amount of foreign currency flowing to a nation's citizens, firms, and government are called export transactions.
Export	In economics, an export is any good or commodity, shipped or otherwise transported out of a country, province, town to another part of the world in a legitimate fashion, typically for use in trade or sale.
Parent corporation	Parent corporation refers to a corporation that owns a controlling interest of another corporation, called a subsidiary corporation.
Shareholder	A shareholder is an individual or company (including a corporation) that legally owns one or more shares of stock in a joined stock company.
Liability	A liability is a present obligation of the enterprise arizing from past events, the settlement of which is expected to result in an outflow from the enterprise of resources embodying economic benefits.
Capitalism	Capitalism refers to an economic system in which capital is mostly owned by private individuals and corporations. Contrasts with communism.
Commodity	Could refer to any good, but in trade a commodity is usually a raw material or primary product that enters into international trade, such as metals or basic agricultural products.
Quartile	A quartile is any of the three values which divides sorted data set into four equal parts, so that each part represents 1/4th of the sample or population.
Political risk	Refers to the many different actions of people, subgroups, and whole countries that have the potential to affect the financial status of a firm is called political risk.

Go to **Cram101.com** for the Practice Tests for this Chapter.

Chapter 21. Repositioning Funds

Chapter 21. Repositioning Funds

Capital expenditures	Major investments in long-term assets such as land, buildings, equipment, or research and development are referred to as capital expenditures.
Capital expenditure	A substantial expenditure that is used by a company to acquire or upgrade physical assets such as equipment, property, industrial buildings, including those which improve the quality and life of an asset is referred to as a capital expenditure.
Capital requirement	The capital requirement is a bank regulation, which sets a framework on how banks and depository institutions must handle their capital. The categorization of assets and capital is highly standardized so that it can be risk weighted.
Working capital	The dollar difference between total current assets and total current liabilities is called working capital.
Dividend payout ratio	A measure of the percentage of earnings paid out in dividends; found by dividing cash dividends by the net income available to each class of stock is the dividend payout ratio.
Accounting profit	Total revenue minus total explicit cost is an accounting profit.
Inventory	Tangible property held for sale in the normal course of business or used in producing goods or services for sale is an inventory.
Transaction exposure	Transaction exposure refers to foreign exchange gains and losses resulting from actual international transactions. These may be hedged through the foreign exchange market, the money market, or the currency futures market.
Holding	The holding is a court's determination of a matter of law based on the issue presented in the particular case. In other words: under this law, with these facts, this result.
Payables	Obligations to make future economic sacrifices, usually cash payments, are referred to as payables. Same as current liabilities.
Foreign exchange exposure	The risk that future changes in a country's exchange rate will hurt the firm is a foreign exchange exposure.
Negotiation	Negotiation is the process whereby interested parties resolve disputes, agree upon courses of action, bargain for individual or collective advantage, and/or attempt to craft outcomes which serve their mutual interests.
Argument	The discussion by counsel for the respective parties of their contentions on the law and the facts of the case being tried in order to aid the jury in arriving at a correct and just conclusion is called argument.
Preference	The act of a debtor in paying or securing one or more of his creditors in a manner more favorable to them than to other creditors or to the exclusion of such other creditors is a preference. In the absence of statute, a preference is perfectly good, but to be legal it must be bona fide, and not a mere subterfuge of the debtor to secure a future benefit to himself or to prevent the application of his property to his debts.
Accounts payable	A written record of all vendors to whom the business firm owes money is referred to as accounts payable.
Interest rate	The rate of return on bonds, loans, or deposits. When one speaks of 'the' interest rate, it is usually in a model where there is only one.
Creditor	A person to whom a debt or legal obligation is owed, and who has the right to enforce payment of that debt or obligation is referred to as creditor.
Forward	The exchange rates governing forward exchange transactions is called the forward exchange

Go to **Cram101.com** for the Practice Tests for this Chapter.

Chapter 21. Repositioning Funds

Chapter 21. Repositioning Funds

exchange rate	rate.
Forward exchange	When two parties agree to exchange currency and execute a deal at some specific date in the future, we have forward exchange.
Buyer	A buyer refers to a role in the buying center with formal authority and responsibility to select the supplier and negotiate the terms of the contract.
Hedging	A technique for avoiding a risk by making a counteracting transaction is referred to as hedging.
Hedge	Hedge refers to a process of offsetting risk. In the foreign exchange market, hedgers use the forward market to cover a transaction or open position and thereby reduce exchange risk. The term applies most commonly to trade.
Setup cost	A setup cost is any cost necessary to prepare for production and to purchase inventory.
Customs duty	A customs duty is a tariff or tax on the import or export of goods.
Customs	Customs is an authority or agency in a country responsible for collecting customs duties and for controlling the flow of people, animals and goods (including personal effects and hazardous items) in and out of the country.
Tax haven	A country in which either locally sourced income or residents of the country are subject to a low rate of taxation is called a tax haven.
Multinational enterprise	Multinational enterprise refers to a firm, usually a corporation, that operates in two or more countries.
Cash inflow	Cash coming into the company as the result of a previous investment is a cash inflow.
Maturity	Maturity refers to the final payment date of a loan or other financial instrument, after which point no further interest or principal need be paid.
Alpha	Alpha is a risk-adjusted measure of the so-called "excess return" on an investment. It is a common measure of assessing active manager's performance as it is the return in excess of a benchmark index or "risk-free" investment.
Corporate tax	Corporate tax refers to a direct tax levied by various jurisdictions on the profits made by companies or associations. As a general principle, this varies substantially between jurisdictions.
Underpricing	When new or additional shares of stock are to be sold, investment bankers will generally set the price at slightly below the current market value to ensure a receptive market for the securities, we have underpricing.
Raw material	Raw material refers to a good that has not been transformed by production; a primary product.
Manufacturing overhead	Manufacturing overhead refers to all manufacturing costs other than direct-material and direct-labor costs.
Depreciation	Depreciation is an accounting and finance term for the method of attributing the cost of an asset across the useful life of the asset. Depreciation is a reduction in the value of a currency in floating exchange rate.
Fixed cost	The cost that a firm bears if it does not produce at all and that is independent of its output. The presence of a fixed cost tends to imply increasing returns to scale. Contrasts with variable cost.
Administrative cost	An administrative cost is all executive, organizational, and clerical costs associated with the general management of an organization rather than with manufacturing, marketing, or selling

Chapter 21. Repositioning Funds

Chapter 21. Repositioning Funds

Selling and administrative costs	Selling and administrative costs refer to costs that cannot be directly traced to products that are recognized as expenses in the period in which they are incurred. Examples include advertizing expense and rent expense.
Fixed expense	A fixed expense is an expense that remains constant as activity changes within the relevant range. Any costs not related directly to the production of your product or service.
Direct material costs	Acquisition costs of all materials that eventually become part of the cost object, and that can be traced to the cost object in an economically feasible way are direct material costs.
Corporate income tax	A tax levied on the net income of corporations is called the corporate income tax.
Financial manager	Managers who make recommendations to top executives regarding strategies for improving the financial strength of a firm are referred to as a financial manager.
Objection	In the trial of a case the formal remonstrance made by counsel to something that has been said or done, in order to obtain the court's ruling thereon is an objection.
Precedent	A previously decided court decision that is recognized as authority for the disposition of future decisions is a precedent.
Business unit	The lowest level of the company which contains the set of functions that carry a product through its life span from concept through manufacture, distribution, sales and service is a business unit.
Procurement	Procurement is the acquisition of goods or services at the best possible total cost of ownership, in the right quantity, at the right time, in the right place for the direct benefit or use of the governments, corporations, or individuals generally via, but not limited to a contract.
Value chain	The sequence of business functions in which usefulness is added to the products or services of a company is a value chain.

Go to **Cram101.com** for the Practice Tests for this Chapter.

Chapter 22. Working Capital Management in the MNE

Working capital	The dollar difference between total current assets and total current liabilities is called working capital.
Liquidity	Liquidity refers to the capacity to turn assets into cash, or the amount of assets in a portfolio that have that capacity.
Capital	Capital generally refers to financial wealth, especially that used to start or maintain a business. In classical economics, capital is one of four factors of production, the others being land and labor and entrepreneurship.
Fund	Independent accounting entity with a self-balancing set of accounts segregated for the purposes of carrying on specific activities is referred to as a fund.
Return on equity	Net profit after taxes per dollar of equity capital is referred to as return on equity.
Return on Assets	The Return on Assets percentage shows how profitable a company's assets are in generating revenue.
Working capital management	Working capital management refers to the financing and management of the current assets of the firm. The financial manager determines the mix between temporary and permanent 'current assets' and the nature of the financing arrangement.
Management	Management characterizes the process of leading and directing all or part of an organization, often a business, through the deployment and manipulation of resources. Early twentieth-century management writer Mary Parker Follett defined management as "the art of getting things done through people."
Equity	Equity is the name given to the set of legal principles, in countries following the English common law tradition, which supplement strict rules of law where their application would operate harshly, so as to achieve what is sometimes referred to as "natural justice."
Asset	An item of property, such as land, capital, money, a share in ownership, or a claim on others for future payment, such as a bond or a bank deposit is an asset.
Operating cycle	Operating cycle refers to the time it takes for a company to purchase goods or services from suppliers, sell those goods and services to customers, and collect cash from customers.
Cash conversion cycle	Cash conversion cycle, also known as asset conversion cycle, net operating cycle, working capital cycle or just cash cycle, is a figure used in the financial analysis of a business. The higher the number, the longer a firm's money is tied up in operations of the business and unavailable for other activities such as investing.
Conversion	Conversion refers to any distinct act of dominion wrongfully exerted over another's personal property in denial of or inconsistent with his rights therein. That tort committed by a person who deals with chattels not belonging to him in a manner that is inconsistent with the ownership of the lawful owner.
Foreign exchange	In finance, foreign exchange means currencies, such as U.S. Dollars and Euros. These are traded on foreign exchange markets.
Exchange rate	Exchange rate refers to the price at which one country's currency trades for another, typically on the exchange market.
Credit risk	The risk of loss due to a counterparty defaulting on a contract, or more generally the risk of loss due to some "credit event" is called credit risk.
Cash inflow	Cash coming into the company as the result of a previous investment is a cash inflow.
Exchange	The trade of things of value between buyer and seller so that each is better off after the trade is called the exchange.
Credit	Credit refers to a recording as positive in the balance of payments, any transaction that

Chapter 22. Working Capital Management in the MNE

	gives rise to a payment into the country, such as an export, the sale of an asset, or borrowing from abroad.
Firm	An organization that employs resources to produce a good or service for profit and owns and operates one or more plants is referred to as a firm.
Cash outflow	Cash flowing out of the business from all sources over a period of time is cash outflow.
Inputs	The inputs used by a firm or an economy are the labor, raw materials, electricity and other resources it uses to produce its outputs.
Transaction exposure	Transaction exposure refers to foreign exchange gains and losses resulting from actual international transactions. These may be hedged through the foreign exchange market, the money market, or the currency futures market.
Financial statement	Financial statement refers to a summary of all the transactions that have occurred over a particular period.
Contract	A contract is a "promise" or an "agreement" that is enforced or recognized by the law. In the civil law, a contract is considered to be part of the general law of obligations.
Buyer	A buyer refers to a role in the buying center with formal authority and responsibility to select the supplier and negotiate the terms of the contract.
Inventory	Tangible property held for sale in the normal course of business or used in producing goods or services for sale is an inventory.
Cash flow	In finance, cash flow refers to the amounts of cash being received and spent by a business during a defined period of time, sometimes tied to a specific project. Most of the time they are being used to determine gaps in the liquid position of a company.
Manufacturing	Production of goods primarily by the application of labor and capital to raw materials and other intermediate inputs, in contrast to agriculture, mining, forestry, fishing, and services a manufacturing.
Integration	Economic integration refers to reducing barriers among countries to transactions and to movements of goods, capital, and labor, including harmonization of laws, regulations, and standards. Integrated markets theoretically function as a unified market.
Technology	The body of knowledge and techniques that can be used to combine economic resources to produce goods and services is called technology.
Supply	Supply is the aggregate amount of any material good that can be called into being at a certain price point; it comprises one half of the equation of supply and demand. In classical economic theory, a curve representing supply is one of the factors that produce price.
Accounts payable	A written record of all vendors to whom the business firm owes money is referred to as accounts payable.
Balance sheet	A statement of the assets, liabilities, and net worth of a firm or individual at some given time often at the end of its "fiscal year," is referred to as a balance sheet.
Balance	In banking and accountancy, the outstanding balance is the amount of money owned, (or due), that remains in a deposit account (or a loan account) at a given date, after all past remittances, payments and withdrawal have been accounted for. It can be positive (then, in the balance sheet of a firm, it is an asset) or negative (a liability).
Corporation	A legal entity chartered by a state or the Federal government that is distinct and separate from the individuals who own it is a corporation. This separation gives the corporation unique powers which other legal entities lack.
Subsidiary	A company that is controlled by another company or corporation is a subsidiary.

Chapter 22. Working Capital Management in the MNE

Chapter 22. Working Capital Management in the MNE

Trade credit	Trade credit refers to an amount that is loaned to an exporter to be repaid when the exports are paid for by the foreign importer.
Income statement	Income statement refers to a financial statement that presents the revenues and expenses and resulting net income or net loss of a company for a specific period of time.
Invoice	The itemized bill for a transaction, stating the nature of the transaction and its cost. In international trade, the invoice price is often the preferred basis for levying an ad valorem tariff.
Spot exchange rate	The exchange rate at which a foreign exchange dealer will convert one currency into another that particular day is the spot exchange rate.
Accounts receivable	Accounts receivable is one of a series of accounting transactions dealing with the billing of customers which owe money to a person, company or organization for goods and services that have been provided to the customer. This is typically done in a one person organization by writing an invoice and mailing or delivering it to each customer.
Industry	A group of firms that produce identical or similar products is an industry. It is also used specifically to refer to an area of economic production focused on manufacturing which involves large amounts of capital investment before any profit can be realized, also called "heavy industry".
Accounting	A system that collects and processes financial information about an organization and reports that information to decision makers is referred to as accounting.
Current asset	A current asset is an asset on the balance sheet which is expected to be sold or otherwise used up in the near future, usually within one year.
Liability	A liability is a present obligation of the enterprise arizing from past events, the settlement of which is expected to result in an outflow from the enterprise of resources embodying economic benefits.
Finished goods	Completed products awaiting sale are called finished goods. An item considered a finished good in a supplying plant might be considered a component or raw material in a receiving plant.
Current liability	Current liability refers to a debt that can reasonably be expected to be paid from existing current assets or through the creation of other current liabilities, within one year or the operating cycle, whichever is longer.
Net worth	Net worth is the total assets minus total liabilities of an individual or company
Operation	A standardized method or technique that is performed repetitively, often on different materials resulting in different finished goods is called an operation.
Credit sale	A credit sale occurs when a customer does not pay cash at the time of the sale but instead agrees to pay later. The sale occurs now, with payment from the customer to follow at a later time.
Discount	The difference between the face value of a bond and its selling price, when a bond is sold for less than its face value it's referred to as a discount.
Cost of carry	The cost of carry refers to the lost opportunity cost of purchasing a particular security rather than an alternative.
Interest	In finance and economics, interest is the price paid by a borrower for the use of a lender's money. In other words, interest is the amount of paid to "rent" money for a period of time.
Parent company	Parent company refers to the entity that has a controlling influence over another company. It may have its own operations, or it may have been set up solely for the purpose of owning the

Go to **Cram101.com** for the Practice Tests for this Chapter.

Chapter 22. Working Capital Management in the MNE

Chapter 22. Working Capital Management in the MNE

	Subject Company.
Payables	Obligations to make future economic sacrifices, usually cash payments, are referred to as payables. Same as current liabilities.
Dell Computer	Dell Computer, formerly PC's Limited, was founded on the principle that by selling personal computer systems directly to customers, PC's Limited could best understand their needs and provide the most effective computing solutions to meet those needs.
Intel	Intel Corporation, founded in 1968 and based in Santa Clara, California, USA, is the world's largest semiconductor company. Intel is best known for its PC microprocessors, where it maintains roughly 80% market share.
Days in inventory	Days in inventory refers to measure of the average number of days inventory is held; calculated as 365 divided by inventory turnover ratio.
Apple Computer	Apple Computer has been a major player in the evolution of personal computing since its founding in 1976. The Apple II microcomputer, introduced in 1977, was a hit with home users.
Intermediate product	Intermediate product refers to product transferred from one subunit to another subunit of an organization. This product may either be further worked on by the receiving subunit or sold to an external customer.
Distribution	Distribution in economics, the manner in which total output and income is distributed among individuals or factors.
Domestic	From or in one's own country. A domestic producer is one that produces inside the home country. A domestic price is the price inside the home country. Opposite of 'foreign' or 'world.'.
Exporter	A firm that sells its product in another country is an exporter.
Export	In economics, an export is any good or commodity, shipped or otherwise transported out of a country, province, town to another part of the world in a legitimate fashion, typically for use in trade or sale.
Economy	The income, expenditures, and resources that affect the cost of running a business and household are called an economy.
Merchant	Under the Uniform Commercial Code, one who regularly deals in goods of the kind sold in the contract at issue, or holds himself out as having special knowledge or skill relevant to such goods, or who makes the sale through an agent who regularly deals in such goods or claims such knowledge or skill is referred to as merchant.
Negotiable	A negotiable instrument is one that can be bought and sold after being issued - in other words, it is a tradable instrument.
Security	Security refers to a claim on the borrower future income that is sold by the borrower to the lender. A security is a type of transferable interest representing financial value.
Commercial law	The law that relates to the rights of property and persons engaged in trade or commerce and regulates corporate contracts, hiring practices, and the manufacture and sales of consumer goods is called commercial law.
Inventory financing	The process of using inventory such as raw materials as collateral for a loan is inventory financing. Lenders may require additional collateral and may require an appraisal by a national appraisal firm acceptable to the lender. Depending on the type of inventory, the lender's advance rate can range from 35% to 80% of the orderly liquidation value of the inventory.
Interest rate	The rate of return on bonds, loans, or deposits. When one speaks of 'the' interest rate, it

Chapter 22. Working Capital Management in the MNE

	is usually in a model where there is only one.
Export credit	Export credit refers to a loan to the buyer of an export, extended by the exporting firm when shipping the good prior to payment, or by a facility of the exporting country's government.
Maturity	Maturity refers to the final payment date of a loan or other financial instrument, after which point no further interest or principal need be paid.
Aid	Assistance provided by countries and by international institutions such as the World Bank to developing countries in the form of monetary grants, loans at low interest rates, in kind, or a combination of these is called aid. Aid can also refer to assistance of any type rendered to benefit some group or individual.
Consideration	Consideration in contract law, a basic requirement for an enforceable agreement under traditional contract principles, defined in this text as legal value, bargained for and given in exchange for an act or promise. In corporation law, cash or property contributed to a corporation in exchange for shares, or a promise to contribute such cash or property.
Capital stock	The total amount of physical capital that has been accumulated, usually in a country is capital stock. Also refers to the total issued capital of a firm, including ordinary and preferred shares.
Subsidy	Subsidy refers to government financial assistance to a domestic producer.
Stock	In financial terminology, stock is the capital raized by a corporation, through the issuance and sale of shares.
Inventory management	The planning, coordinating, and controlling activities related to the flow of inventory into, through, and out of an organization is referred to as inventory management.
Devaluation	Lowering the value of a nation's currency relative to other currencies is called devaluation.
Anticipation	In finance, anticipation is where debts are paid off early, generally in order to pay less interest.
Holding	The holding is a court's determination of a matter of law based on the issue presented in the particular case. In other words: under this law, with these facts, this result.
Competitor	Other organizations in the same industry or type of business that provide a good or service to the same set of customers is referred to as a competitor.
Marketing mix	The marketing mix approach to marketing is a model of crafting and implementing marketing strategies. It stresses the "mixing" or blending of various factors in such a way that both organizational and consumer (target markets) objectives are attained.
Marketing	Promoting and selling products or services to customers, or prospective customers, is referred to as marketing.
Promotion	Promotion refers to all the techniques sellers use to motivate people to buy products or services. An attempt by marketers to inform people about products and to persuade them to participate in an exchange.
Commodity	Could refer to any good, but in trade a commodity is usually a raw material or primary product that enters into international trade, such as metals or basic agricultural products.
Option	A contract that gives the purchaser the option to buy or sell the underlying financial instrument at a specified price, called the exercise price or strike price, within a specific period of time.
Gain	In finance, gain is a profit or an increase in value of an investment such as a stock or bond. Gain is calculated by fair market value or the proceeds from the sale of the investment minus the sum of the purchase price and all costs associated with it.

Go to **Cram101.com** for the Practice Tests for this Chapter.

Chapter 22. Working Capital Management in the MNE

Customs duty	A customs duty is a tariff or tax on the import or export of goods.
Customs	Customs is an authority or agency in a country responsible for collecting customs duties and for controlling the flow of people, animals and goods (including personal effects and hazardous items) in and out of the country.
Duty free	Duty Free is the term that is often used to describe goods bought at ports and airports that do not attract the usual government taxes and customs duties.
Dealer	People who link buyers with sellers by buying and selling securities at stated prices are referred to as a dealer.
Point of Sale	Point of sale can mean a retail shop, a checkout counter in a shop, or a variable location where a transaction occurs.
Sony	Sony is a multinational corporation and one of the world's largest media conglomerates founded in Tokyo, Japan. One of its divisions Sony Electronics is one of the leading manufacturers of electronics, video, communications, and information technology products for the consumer and professional markets.
Production	The creation of finished goods and services using the factors of production: land, labor, capital, entrepreneurship, and knowledge.
Facilitation	Facilitation refers to helping a team or individual achieve a goal. Often used in meetings or with teams to help the teams achieve their objectives.
Marketable securities	Marketable securities refer to securities that are readily traded in the secondary securities market.
Cash disbursement	Cash disbursement is a transaction that is posted to a cardholder's credit card account in which the cardholder receives cash at an ATM, or cash or travelers checks at a branch of a member financial institution or at a qualified and approved agent of a member financial institution.
Capital turnover	Capital turnover refers to the productivity of capital or sales revenue divided by invested capital.
Turnover	Turnover in a financial context refers to the rate at which a provider of goods cycles through its average inventory. Turnover in a human resources context refers to the characteristic of a given company or industry, relative to rate at which an employer gains and loses staff.
Rate of return	A rate of return is a comparison of the money earned (or lost) on an investment to the amount of money invested.
Profit	Profit refers to the return to the resource entrepreneurial ability; total revenue minus total cost.
Financial manager	Managers who make recommendations to top executives regarding strategies for improving the financial strength of a firm are referred to as a financial manager.
Comprehensive	A comprehensive refers to a layout accurate in size, color, scheme, and other necessary details to show how a final ad will look. For presentation only, never for reproduction.
Cash budget	A projection of anticipated cash flows, usually over a one to two year period is called a cash budget.
Budget	Budget refers to an account, usually for a year, of the planned expenditures and the expected receipts of an entity. For a government, the receipts are tax revenues.
Variable	A variable is something measured by a number; it is used to analyze what happens to other things when the size of that number changes.

Chapter 22. Working Capital Management in the MNE

Average collection period	The average amount of time that a receivable is outstanding, calculated by dividing 365 days by the receivables turnover ratio is an average collection period.
Service	Service refers to a "non tangible product" that is not embodied in a physical good and that typically effects some change in another product, person, or institution. Contrasts with good.
Foreign subsidiary	A company owned in a foreign country by another company is referred to as foreign subsidiary.
Real interest rate	The real interest rate is the nominal interest rate minus the inflation rate. It is a better measure of the return that a lender receives (or the cost to the borrower) because it takes into account the fact that the value of money changes due to inflation over the course of the loan period.
Standing	Standing refers to the legal requirement that anyone seeking to challenge a particular action in court must demonstrate that such action substantially affects his legitimate interests before he will be entitled to bring suit.
Complexity	The technical sophistication of the product and hence the amount of understanding required to use it is referred to as complexity. It is the opposite of simplicity.
Payments system	The method of conducting transactions in the economy is referred to as the payments system. Collective term for mechanisms (both paper-backed and electronic) for moving funds, payments and money among financial institutions throughout the nation.
Federal reserve system	The central banking authority responsible for monetary policy in the United States is called federal reserve system or the Fed.
Federal Reserve	The Federal Reserve System was created via the Federal Reserve Act of December 23rd, 1913. All national banks were required to join the system and other banks could join. The Reserve Banks opened for business on November 16th, 1914. Federal Reserve Notes were created as part of the legislation, to provide an elastic supply of currency.
Euro	The common currency of a subset of the countries of the EU, adopted January 1, 1999 is called euro.
Transaction value	The actual price of a product, paid or payable, used for customs valuation purposes is called transaction value.
Financial institution	A financial institution acts as an agent that provides financial services for its clients. Financial institutions generally fall under financial regulation from a government authority.
Investment	Investment refers to spending for the production and accumulation of capital and additions to inventories. In a financial sense, buying an asset with the expectation of making a return.
Broker	In commerce, a broker is a party that mediates between a buyer and a seller. A broker who also acts as a seller or as a buyer becomes a principal party to the deal.
Derivative	A derivative is a generic term for specific types of investments from which payoffs over time are derived from the performance of assets (such as commodities, shares or bonds), interest rates, exchange rates, or indices (such as a stock market index, consumer price index (CPI) or an index of weather conditions).
Market	A market is, as defined in economics, a social arrangement that allows buyers and sellers to discover information and carry out a voluntary exchange of goods or services.
Electronic commerce	Electronic commerce or e-commerce, refers to any activity that uses some form of electronic communication in the inventory, exchange, advertisement, distribution, and payment of goods and services.

Chapter 22. Working Capital Management in the MNE

Commerce	Commerce is the exchange of something of value between two entities. It is the central mechanism from which capitalism is derived.
Centralized depository	The practice of centralizing corporate cash balances in a single depository is a centralized depository.
Affiliates	Local television stations that are associated with a major network are called affiliates. Affiliates agree to preempt time during specified hours for programming provided by the network and carry the advertising contained in the program.
Money market	The money market, in macroeconomics and international finance, refers to the equilibration of demand for a country's domestic money to its money supply; market for short-term financial instruments.
Instrument	Instrument refers to an economic variable that is controlled by policy makers and can be used to influence other variables, called targets. Examples are monetary and fiscal policies used to achieve external and internal balance.
Authority	Authority in agency law, refers to an agent's ability to affect his principal's legal relations with third parties. Also used to refer to an actor's legal power or ability to do something. In addition, sometimes used to refer to a statute, case, or other legal source that justifies a particular result.
Centralization	A structural policy in which decision-making authority is concentrated at the top of the organizational hierarchy is referred to as centralization.
Precautionary balances	Precautionary balances refers to cash balances held for emergency purposes. Precautionary cash balances are more likely to be important in seasonal or cyclical industries where cash inflows are more uncertain.
Quad	Quad refers to refers both to the Quadrilateral Meetings and to the participants in those meetings, the U.S., Canada, EU, and Japan. Their importance is due to the fact that these four economies are responsible for approximately 61% of world imports by value, and 71% of world exports.
Standard deviation	A measure of the spread or dispersion of a series of numbers around the expected value is the standard deviation. The standard deviation tells us how well the expected value represents a series of values.
Transaction cost	A transaction cost is a cost incurred in making an economic exchange. For example, most people, when buying or selling a stock, must pay a commission to their broker; that commission is a transaction cost of doing the stock deal.
Multilateral netting	A technique used to reduce the number of transactions between subsidiaries of the firm, thereby reducing the total transaction costs arising from foreign exchange dealings and transfer fees is multilateral netting.
Spot transaction	The predominant type of exchange rate transaction, involving the immediate exchange of bank deposits denominated in different currencies is a spot transaction.
Bilateral Netting	Bilateral netting refers to settlement in which the amount one subsidiary owes another can be canceled by the debt the second subsidiary owes the first.
Extension	Extension refers to an out-of-court settlement in which creditors agree to allow the firm more time to meet its financial obligations. A new repayment schedule will be developed, subject to the acceptance of creditors.
Remainder	A remainder in property law is a future interest created in a transferee that is capable of becoming possessory upon the natural termination of a prior estate created by the same instrument.

Chapter 22. Working Capital Management in the MNE

International Business	International business refers to any firm that engages in international trade or investment.
Notes payable	Notes payable refers to an obligation in the form of a written promissory note. It is a balance sheet term referring to a company's outstanding bank loans.
Creditor	A person to whom a debt or legal obligation is owed, and who has the right to enforce payment of that debt or obligation is referred to as creditor.
Overdraft	The withdrawal from a bank by a depositor of money in excess of the amount of money he or she has on deposit there is an overdraft.
Capital requirement	The capital requirement is a bank regulation, which sets a framework on how banks and depository institutions must handle their capital. The categorization of assets and capital is highly standardized so that it can be risk weighted.
Business unit	The lowest level of the company which contains the set of functions that carry a product through its life span from concept through manufacture, distribution, sales and service is a business unit.
Commercial bank	A firm that engages in the business of banking is a commercial bank.
Margin	A deposit by a buyer in stocks with a seller or a stockbroker, as security to cover fluctuations in the market in reference to stocks that the buyer has purchased but for which he has not paid is a margin. Commodities are also traded on margin.
Matching	Matching refers to an accounting concept that establishes when expenses are recognized. Expenses are matched with the revenues they helped to generate and are recognized when those revenues are recognized.
Economies of scale	In economics, returns to scale and economies of scale are related terms that describe what happens as the scale of production increases. They are different terms and not to be used interchangeably.
Points	Loan origination fees that may be deductible as interest by a buyer of property. A seller of property who pays points reduces the selling price by the amount of the points paid for the buyer.
Edge act corporation	Edge act corporation refers to a special subsidiary of a U.S. bank that is engaged primarily in international banking.
Draft	A signed, written order by which one party instructs another party to pay a specified sum to a third party, at sight or at a specific date is a draft.
Export transactions	A sale of a good or service that increases the amount of foreign currency flowing to a nation's citizens, firms, and government are called export transactions.
Personnel	A collective term for all of the employees of an organization. Personnel is also commonly used to refer to the personnel management function or the organizational unit responsible for administering personnel programs.
Eurocurrency	Eurocurrency is the term used to describe deposits residing in banks that are located outside the borders of the country that issues the currency the deposit is denominated in.
Host country	The country in which the parent-country organization seeks to locate or has already located a facility is a host country.
Board of directors	The group of individuals elected by the stockholders of a corporation to oversee its operations is a board of directors.
Charter	Charter refers to an instrument or authority from the sovereign power bestowing the right or power to do business under the corporate form of organization. Also, the organic law of a

Chapter 22. Working Capital Management in the MNE

	city or town, and representing a portion of the statute law of the state.
Shares	Shares refer to an equity security, representing a shareholder's ownership of a corporation. Shares are one of a finite number of equal portions in the capital of a company, entitling the owner to a proportion of distributed, non-reinvested profits known as dividends and to a portion of the value of the company in case of liquidation.
Regulation	Regulation refers to restrictions state and federal laws place on business with regard to the conduct of its activities.
Deductible	The dollar sum of costs that an insured individual must pay before the insurer begins to pay is called deductible.
Shell	One of the original Seven Sisters, Royal Dutch/Shell is the world's third-largest oil company by revenue, and a major player in the petrochemical industry and the solar energy business. Shell has six core businesses: Exploration and Production, Gas and Power, Downstream, Chemicals, Renewables, and Trading/Shipping, and operates in more than 140 countries.
Equity capital	Equity capital refers to money raized from within the firm or through the sale of ownership in the firm.
Appeal	Appeal refers to the act of asking an appellate court to overturn a decision after the trial court's final judgment has been entered.
Joint venture	Joint venture refers to an undertaking by two parties for a specific purpose and duration, taking any of several legal forms.
Policy	Similar to a script in that a policy can be a less than completely rational decision-making method. Involves the use of a pre-existing set of decision steps for any problem that presents itself.
Federal Reserve Act	The Federal Reserve Act, also known as the Act of December 23, 1913, is an act of Congress that created the Federal Reserve System, the central bank of the United States of America.
Money center banks	Large banks in key financial centers are referred to as money center banks.
Holding company	A corporation whose purpose or function is to own or otherwise hold the shares of other corporations either for investment or control is called holding company.
Time deposit	The technical name for a savings account is a time deposit; the bank can require prior notice before the owner withdraws money from a time deposit.
Just In Time	Just In Time is an inventory strategy implemented to improve the return on investment of a business by reducing in-process inventory and its associated costs. The process is driven by a series of signals, or Kanban that tell production processes to make the next part.
Raw material	Raw material refers to a good that has not been transformed by production; a primary product.
Operating expense	In throughput accounting, the cost accounting aspect of Theory of Constraints (TOC), operating expense is the money spent turning inventory into throughput. In TOC, operating expense is limited to costs that vary strictly with the quantity produced, like raw materials and purchased components.
Repositioning	Changing the position an offering occupies in a consumer's mind relative to competitive offerings and so expanding or otherwise altering its potential market is called repositioning.
Expense	In accounting, an expense represents an event in which an asset is used up or a liability is incurred. In terms of the accounting equation, expenses reduce owners' equity.
Vendor	A person who sells property to a vendee is a vendor. The words vendor and vendee are more

Chapter 22. Working Capital Management in the MNE

	commonly applied to the seller and purchaser of real estate, and the words seller and buyer are more commonly applied to the seller and purchaser of personal property.
Direct labor	The earnings of employees who work directly on the products being manufactured are direct labor.
Labor	People's physical and mental talents and efforts that are used to help produce goods and services are called labor.
Debit	Debit refers to recording as negative in the balance of payments, any transaction that gives rise to a payment out of the country, such as an import, the purchase of an asset, or lending to foreigners. Opposite of credit.
Volatility	Volatility refers to the extent to which an economic variable, such as a price or an exchange rate, moves up and down over time.
Wholly owned subsidiary	A subsidiary in which the firm owns 100 percent of the stock is a wholly owned subsidiary.
Government spending	Government spending refers to spending by all levels of government on goods and services.
International Monetary Fund	The International Monetary Fund is the international organization entrusted with overseeing the global financial system by monitoring exchange rates and balance of payments, as well as offering technical and financial assistance when asked.
Federal Aviation Administration	In 1967, a new U.S. Department of Transportation (DOT) combined major federal responsibilities for air and surface transport. The Federal Aviation Administration became one of several agencies within DOT. At the same time, a new National Transportation Safety Board took over the CAB's role of investigating aviation accidents.
Administration	Administration refers to the management and direction of the affairs of governments and institutions; a collective term for all policymaking officials of a government; the execution and implementation of public policy.
Compliance	A type of influence process where a receiver accepts the position advocated by a source to obtain favorable outcomes or to avoid punishment is the compliance.
Boeing	Boeing is the world's largest aircraft manufacturer by revenue. Headquartered in Chicago, Illinois, Boeing is the second-largest defense contractor in the world. In 2005, the company was the world's largest civil aircraft manufacturer in terms of value.
Control system	A control system is a device or set of devices that manage the behavior of other devices. Some devices or systems are not controllable.A control system is an interconnection of components connected or related in such a manner as to command, direct, or regulate itself or another system.
Concession	A concession is a business operated under a contract or license associated with a degree of exclusivity in exploiting a business within a certain geographical area. For example, sports arenas or public parks may have concession stands; and public services such as water supply may be operated as concessions.
Tactic	A short-term immediate decision that, in its totality, leads to the achievement of strategic goals is called a tactic.
Agent	A person who makes economic decisions for another economic actor. A hired manager operates as an agent for a firm's owner.
Honeywell	Honeywell is a major American multinational corporation that produces electronic control systems and automation equipment. It is a major supplier of engineering services and avionics for NASA, Boeing and the United States Department of Defense.

Go to **Cram101.com** for the Practice Tests for this Chapter.

Chapter 22. Working Capital Management in the MNE

Business opportunity	A business opportunity involves the sale or lease of any product, service, equipment, etc. that will enable the purchaser-licensee to begin a business
Currency risk	Currency risk is a form of risk that arises from the change in price of one currency against another. Whenever investors or companies have assets or business operations across national borders, they face currency risk if their positions are not hedged.
Confirmed	When the seller's bank agrees to assume liability on the letter of credit issued by the buyer's bank the transaction is confirmed. The term means that the credit is not only backed up by the issuing foreign bank, but that payment is also guaranteed by the notifying American bank.
Speculation	The purchase or sale of an asset in hopes that its price will rise or fall respectively, in order to make a profit is called speculation.
Dumping	Dumping refers to a practice of charging a very low price in a foreign market for such economic purposes as putting rival suppliers out of business.
Union	A worker association that bargains with employers over wages and working conditions is called a union.
Central Bank	Central bank refers to the institution in a country that is normally responsible for managing the supply of the country's money and the value of its currency on the foreign exchange market.
Forward market	A market for exchange of currencies in the future is the forward market. Participants in a forward market enter into a contract to exchange currencies, not today, but at a specified date in the future, typically 30, 60, or 90 days from now, and at a price that is agreed upon.
Fiscal year	A fiscal year is a 12-month period used for calculating annual ("yearly") financial reports in businesses and other organizations. In many jurisdictions, regulatory laws regarding accounting require such reports once per twelve months, but do not require that the twelve months constitute a calendar year (i.e. January to December).
Pay for Performance	A one-time cash payment to an investment center manager as a reward for meeting a predetermined criterion on a specified performance measure is referred to as pay for performance.
Performance target	A task established for an employee that provides the comparative basis for performance appraisal is a performance target.
Airbus	In 2003, for the first time in its 33-year history, Airbus delivered more jet-powered airliners than Boeing. Boeing states that the Boeing 777 has outsold its Airbus counterparts, which include the A340 family as well as the A330-300. The smaller A330-200 competes with the 767, outselling its Boeing counterpart.
Advance payment	An advance payment is the part of a contractually due sum that is paid in advance, while the balance will only follow after receipt on the counterpart in goods or services.
Profit center	Responsibility center where the manager is accountable for revenues and costs is referred to as a profit center.
Cost of capital	Cost of capital refers to the percentage cost of funds used for acquiring resources for an organization, typically a weighted average of the firms cost of equity and cost of debt.
Present value	The value today of a stream of payments and/or receipts over time in the future and/or the past, converted to the present using an interest rate. If X t is the amount in period t and r the interest rate, then present value at time t=0 is $V = ?T /t$.
Negotiation	Negotiation is the process whereby interested parties resolve disputes, agree upon courses of

action, bargain for individual or collective advantage, and/or attempt to craft outcomes which serve their mutual interests.

Buyer	A buyer refers to a role in the buying center with formal authority and responsibility to select the supplier and negotiate the terms of the contract.
Value chain activities	Value chain activities refer to Porter's chain of activities, including inbound logistics, production, and outbound logistics.
Value chain	The sequence of business functions in which usefulness is added to the products or services of a company is a value chain.
Shares	Shares refer to an equity security, representing a shareholder's ownership of a corporation. Shares are one of a finite number of equal portions in the capital of a company, entitling the owner to a proportion of distributed, non-reinvested profits known as dividends and to a portion of the value of the company in case of liquidation.
Firm	An organization that employs resources to produce a good or service for profit and owns and operates one or more plants is referred to as a firm.
Production	The creation of finished goods and services using the factors of production: land, labor, capital, entrepreneurship, and knowledge.
Service	Service refers to a "non tangible product" that is not embodied in a physical good and that typically effects some change in another product, person, or institution. Contrasts with good.
Inputs	The inputs used by a firm or an economy are the labor, raw materials, electricity and other resources it uses to produce its outputs.
Process improvement	Process improvement is the activity of elevating the performance of a process, especially that of a business process with regard to its goal.
Competitiveness	Competitiveness usually refers to characteristics that permit a firm to compete effectively with other firms due to low cost or superior technology, perhaps internationally.
Procurement	Procurement is the acquisition of goods or services at the best possible total cost of ownership, in the right quantity, at the right time, in the right place for the direct benefit or use of the governments, corporations, or individuals generally via, but not limited to a contract.
Purchasing	Purchasing refers to the function in a firm that searches for quality material resources, finds the best suppliers, and negotiates the best price for goods and services.
Exporter	A firm that sells its product in another country is an exporter.
Industry	A group of firms that produce identical or similar products is an industry. It is also used specifically to refer to an area of economic production focused on manufacturing which involves large amounts of capital investment before any profit can be realized, also called "heavy industry".
Business unit	The lowest level of the company which contains the set of functions that carry a product through its life span from concept through manufacture, distribution, sales and service is a business unit.
Corporation	A legal entity chartered by a state or the Federal government that is distinct and separate from the individuals who own it is a corporation. This separation gives the corporation unique powers which other legal entities lack.
Subsidiary	A company that is controlled by another company or corporation is a subsidiary.
Contract	A contract is a "promise" or an "agreement" that is enforced or recognized by the law. In the civil law, a contract is considered to be part of the general law of obligations.
Trust	An arrangement in which shareholders of independent firms agree to give up their stock in

Chapter 23. International Trade Finance

Chapter 23. International Trade Finance

	exchange for trust certificates that entitle them to a share of the trust's common profits.
International Business	International business refers to any firm that engages in international trade or investment.
Interest	In finance and economics, interest is the price paid by a borrower for the use of a lender's money. In other words, interest is the amount of paid to "rent" money for a period of time.
Composition	An out-of-court settlement in which creditors agree to accept a fractional settlement on their original claim is referred to as composition.
Legal system	Legal system refers to system of rules that regulate behavior and the processes by which the laws of a country are enforced and through which redress of grievances is obtained.
Exchange	The trade of things of value between buyer and seller so that each is better off after the trade is called the exchange.
Export	In economics, an export is any good or commodity, shipped or otherwise transported out of a country, province, town to another part of the world in a legitimate fashion, typically for use in trade or sale.
Interest payment	The payment to holders of bonds payable, calculated by multiplying the stated rate on the face of the bond by the par, or face, value of the bond. If bonds are issued at a discount or premium, the interest payment does not equal the interest expense.
Regulation	Regulation refers to restrictions state and federal laws place on business with regard to the conduct of its activities.
Quantity discounts	Quantity discounts refer to reductions in unit costs for a larger order.
Quantity discount	A quantity discount is a price reduction given for a large order.
Insurance	Insurance refers to a system by which individuals can reduce their exposure to risk of large losses by spreading the risks among a large number of persons.
Discount	The difference between the face value of a bond and its selling price, when a bond is sold for less than its face value it's referred to as a discount.
Financial management	The job of managing a firm's resources so it can meet its goals and objectives is called financial management.
Management	Management characterizes the process of leading and directing all or part of an organization, often a business, through the deployment and manipulation of resources. Early twentieth-century management writer Mary Parker Follett defined management as "the art of getting things done through people."
Possession	Possession refers to respecting real property, exclusive dominion and control such as owners of like property usually exercise over it. Manual control of personal property either as owner or as one having a qualified right in it.
Customs	Customs is an authority or agency in a country responsible for collecting customs duties and for controlling the flow of people, animals and goods (including personal effects and hazardous items) in and out of the country.
Bill of lading	Bill of lading refers to the receipt given by a transportation company to an exporter when the former accepts goods for transport. It includes the contract specifying what transport service will be provided and the limits of liability.
Common carrier	One who undertakes, for hire or reward, to transport the goods of such of the public as choose to employ him is a common carrier.

Go to **Cram101.com** for the Practice Tests for this Chapter.

Chapter 23. International Trade Finance

Chapter 23. International Trade Finance

Invoice	The itemized bill for a transaction, stating the nature of the transaction and its cost. In international trade, the invoice price is often the preferred basis for levying an ad valorem tariff.
Cost and Freight	Cost and Freight is an Incoterm. It means that the seller pays for transportation to the port of shipment, loading and freight. The buyer pays for the insurance and transportation of the goods from the port of destination to his factory. The passing of risk occurs when the goods pass the ship's rail at the port of shipment.
Free On Board	Free On Board is an Incoterm. It means that the seller pays for transportation of the goods to the port of shipment, plus loading costs. The buyer pays freight, insurance, unloading costs and transportation from the port of destination to his factory. The passing of risks occurs when the goods pass the ship's rail at the port of shipment.
Agent	A person who makes economic decisions for another economic actor. A hired manager operates as an agent for a firm's owner.
Policy	Similar to a script in that a policy can be a less than completely rational decision-making method. Involves the use of a pre-existing set of decision steps for any problem that presents itself.
Letter of credit	An instrument containing a request to pay to the bearer or person named money, or sell him or her some commodity on credit or give something of value and look to the drawer of the letter for recompense is called letter of credit.
Credit	Credit refers to a recording as positive in the balance of payments, any transaction that gives rise to a payment into the country, such as an export, the sale of an asset, or borrowing from abroad.
Exporting	Selling products to another country is called exporting.
Preparation	Preparation refers to usually the first stage in the creative process. It includes education and formal training.
Operation	A standardized method or technique that is performed repetitively, often on different materials resulting in different finished goods is called an operation.
Consignment	Consignment refers to a bailment for sale. The consignee does not undertake the absolute obligation to sell or pay for the goods.
Stipulation	A stipulation is an agreement made between two parties in legal proceedings. A stipulation removes points of contention so that progress can be made during the proceedings.
International trade	The export of goods and services from a country and the import of goods and services into a country is referred to as the international trade.
Credit report	Information about a person's credit history that can be secured from a credit bureau is referred to as credit report.
Domestic	From or in one's own country. A domestic producer is one that produces inside the home country. A domestic price is the price inside the home country. Opposite of 'foreign' or 'world.'.
Default	In finance, default occurs when a debtor has not met its legal obligations according to the debt contract, e.g. it has not made a scheduled payment, or violated a covenant (condition) of the debt contract.
Globalization	The increasing world-wide integration of markets for goods, services and capital that attracted special attention in the late 1990s is called globalization.
Market	A market is, as defined in economics, a social arrangement that allows buyers and sellers to

Chapter 23. International Trade Finance

Chapter 23. International Trade Finance

	discover information and carry out a voluntary exchange of goods or services.
Emerging markets	The term emerging markets is commonly used to describe business and market activity in industrializing or emerging regions of the world. It is sometimes loosely used as a replacement for emerging economies, but really signifies a business phenomenon that is not fully described by or constrained to geography or economic strength; such countries are considered to be in a transitional phase between developing and developed status.
Emerging market	The term emerging market is commonly used to describe business and market activity in industrializing or emerging regions of the world.
Trade flow	The quantity or value of a country's bilateral trade with another country is called trade flow.
Commodity	Could refer to any good, but in trade a commodity is usually a raw material or primary product that enters into international trade, such as metals or basic agricultural products.
Advance payment	An advance payment is the part of a contractually due sum that is paid in advance, while the balance will only follow after receipt on the counterpart in goods or services.
Multinational enterprise	Multinational enterprise refers to a firm, usually a corporation, that operates in two or more countries.
Enterprise	Enterprise refers to another name for a business organization. Other similar terms are business firm, sometimes simply business, sometimes simply firm, as well as company, and entity.
In transit	A state in which goods are in the possession of a bailee or carrier and not in the hands of the buyer, seller, lessee, or lessor is referred to as in transit.
Beneficiary	The person for whose benefit an insurance policy, trust, will, or contract is established is a beneficiary. In the case of a contract, the beneficiary is called a third-party beneficiary.
Collateral	Property that is pledged to the lender to guarantee payment in the event that the borrower is unable to make debt payments is called collateral.
Applicant	In many tribunal and administrative law suits, the person who initiates the claim is called the applicant.
Standing	Standing refers to the legal requirement that anyone seeking to challenge a particular action in court must demonstrate that such action substantially affects his legitimate interests before he will be entitled to bring suit.
Draft	A signed, written order by which one party instructs another party to pay a specified sum to a third party, at sight or at a specific date is a draft.
Compliance	A type of influence process where a receiver accepts the position advocated by a source to obtain favorable outcomes or to avoid punishment is the compliance.
Confirmed	When the seller's bank agrees to assume liability on the letter of credit issued by the buyer's bank the transaction is confirmed. The term means that the credit is not only backed up by the issuing foreign bank, but that payment is also guaranteed by the notifying American bank.
Foreign exchange	In finance, foreign exchange means currencies, such as U.S. Dollars and Euros. These are traded on foreign exchange markets.
Fund	Independent accounting entity with a self-balancing set of accounts segregated for the purposes of carrying on specific activities is referred to as a fund.
Bearer	A person in possession of a negotiable instrument that is payable to him, his order, or to

Go to **Cram101.com** for the Practice Tests for this Chapter.

Chapter 23. International Trade Finance

Chapter 23. International Trade Finance

	whoever is in possession of the instrument is referred to as bearer.
Line of credit	Line of credit refers to a given amount of unsecured short-term funds a bank will lend to a business, provided the funds are readily available.
Competitive disadvantage	A situation in which a firm is not implementing using strategies that are being used by competing organizations is competitive disadvantage.
Bill of exchange	Any negotiable or nonnegotiable document demanding payment to the drawer or to a third person is a bill of exchange.
Instrument	Instrument refers to an economic variable that is controlled by policy makers and can be used to influence other variables, called targets. Examples are monetary and fiscal policies used to achieve external and internal balance.
Commerce	Commerce is the exchange of something of value between two entities. It is the central mechanism from which capitalism is derived.
Drawee	The individual or firm on whom a draft is drawn and who owes the stated amount is the drawee.
Bearer instrument	A bearer instrument is a document that indicates that the bearer of the document has title to property, such as shares or bonds. Bearer instruments differ from normal registered instruments, in that no records are kept of who owns the underlying property, or of the transactions involving transfer of ownership. Whoever physically holds the bearer bond papers owns the property.
Negotiable instrument	A negotiable instrument is a specialized type of contract which obligates a party to pay a certain sum of money on specified terms.
Negotiable	A negotiable instrument is one that can be bought and sold after being issued - in other words, it is a tradable instrument.
Holder in due course	A holder in due course refers to a person who has acquired possession of a negotiable instrument through proper negotiation for value, in good faith, and without notice of any defenses to it.
Holder	A person in possession of a document of title or an instrument payable or indorsed to him, his order, or to bearer is a holder.
Sight draft	Sight draft refers to a draft or bill that is payable on demand or upon presentation.
Time draft	A draft payable at a designated future date is referred to as time draft.
Trade acceptance	Trade acceptance refers to a sight draft that arises when credit is extended with the sale of goods. The seller is both the drawer and the payee, and the buyer is the drawee.
Certificate of deposit	An acknowledgment by a bank of the receipt of money with an engagement to pay it back is referred to as certificate of deposit.
Money market	The money market, in macroeconomics and international finance, refers to the equilibration of demand for a country's domestic money to its money supply; market for short-term financial instruments.
Investment	Investment refers to spending for the production and accumulation of capital and additions to inventories. In a financial sense, buying an asset with the expectation of making a return.
Maturity	Maturity refers to the final payment date of a loan or other financial instrument, after which point no further interest or principal need be paid.
Securitization	Securitization is a financing technique that allows the corporation to separate credit origination and funding activities. The technique comes under the umbrella of structured finance as it applies to assets that typically are illiquid contracts.

Go to **Cram101.com** for the Practice Tests for this Chapter.

Chapter 23. International Trade Finance

Chapter 23. International Trade Finance

Balance sheet	A statement of the assets, liabilities, and net worth of a firm or individual at some given time often at the end of its "fiscal year," is referred to as a balance sheet.
Balance	In banking and accountancy, the outstanding balance is the amount of money owned, (or due), that remains in a deposit account (or a loan account) at a given date, after all past remittances, payments and withdrawal have been accounted for. It can be positive (then, in the balance sheet of a firm, it is an asset) or negative (a liability).
Cash flow	In finance, cash flow refers to the amounts of cash being received and spent by a business during a defined period of time, sometimes tied to a specific project. Most of the time they are being used to determine gaps in the liquid position of a company.
Setup cost	A setup cost is any cost necessary to prepare for production and to purchase inventory.
Financial institution	A financial institution acts as an agent that provides financial services for its clients. Financial institutions generally fall under financial regulation from a government authority.
Document of title	Document of title refers to an actual piece of paper, such as warehouse receipt or bill of lading or order for the delivery of goods, and also any other document which in the regular course of business is treated as proof that the person in possession of it is entitled to receive, hold and dispose of the document and the goods it covers.
Lien	In its most extensive meaning, it is a charge on property for the payment or discharge of a debt or duty is referred to as lien.
Negligence	The omission to do something that a reasonable person, guided by those considerations that ordinarily regulate human affairs, would do, or doing something that a prudent and reasonable person would not do is negligence.
Expense	In accounting, an expense represents an event in which an asset is used up or a liability is incurred. In terms of the accounting equation, expenses reduce owners' equity.
Consignee	A person to whom goods are consigned, shipped, or otherwise transmitted, either for sale or for safekeeping is the consignee.
Grant	Grant refers to an intergovernmental transfer of funds . Since the New Deal, state and local governments have become increasingly dependent upon federal grants for an almost infinite variety of programs.
Channel	Channel, in communications (sometimes called communications channel), refers to the medium used to convey information from a sender (or transmitter) to a receiver.
Open market	In economics, the open market is the term used to refer to the environment in which bonds are bought and sold.
Portfolio	In finance, a portfolio is a collection of investments held by an institution or a private individual. Holding but not always a portfolio is part of an investment and risk-limiting strategy called diversification. By owning several assets, certain types of risk (in particular specific risk) can be reduced.
Cash value	The cash value of an insurance policy is the amount available to the policy holder in cash upon cancellation of the policy. This term is normally used with a whole life policy in which a portion of the premiums go toward an investment. The cash value is the value of this investment at any particular time.
Face value	The nominal or par value of an instrument as expressed on its face is referred to as the face value.
Export credit insurance	A program to guarantee payment to exporting firms who extend export credits is called export credit insurance.

Chapter 23. International Trade Finance

Chapter 23. International Trade Finance

Export credit	Export credit refers to a loan to the buyer of an export, extended by the exporting firm when shipping the good prior to payment, or by a facility of the exporting country's government.
Supply chain	Supply chain refers to the flow of goods, services, and information from the initial sources of materials and services to the delivery of products to consumers.
Supply	Supply is the aggregate amount of any material good that can be called into being at a certain price point; it comprises one half of the equation of supply and demand. In classical economic theory, a curve representing supply is one of the factors that produce price.
Technology	The body of knowledge and techniques that can be used to combine economic resources to produce goods and services is called technology.
Competitor	Other organizations in the same industry or type of business that provide a good or service to the same set of customers is referred to as a competitor.
Commercial bank	A firm that engages in the business of banking is a commercial bank.
Insolvency	Insolvency is a financial condition experienced by a person or business entity when their assets no longer exceed their liabilities or when the person or entity can no longer meet its debt obligations when they come due.
Eximbank	An eximbank is the official export credit agency of the United States Government. It is an independent agency of the Executive Branch of The United States Governemnt established by the Congress of the United States in 1945 that finances or insures foreign purchases of U.S. goods for customers unable or unwilling to accept credit risk.
Aid	Assistance provided by countries and by international institutions such as the World Bank to developing countries in the form of monetary grants, loans at low interest rates, in kind, or a combination of these is called aid. Aid can also refer to assistance of any type rendered to benefit some group or individual.
Complement	A good that is used in conjunction with another good is a complement. For example, cameras and film would complement eachother.
Capital	Capital generally refers to financial wealth, especially that used to start or maintain a business. In classical economics, capital is one of four factors of production, the others being land and labor and entrepreneurship.
Lease	A contract for the possession and use of land or other property, including goods, on one side, and a recompense of rent or other income on the other is the lease.
Market penetration	A strategy of increasing sales of present products in their existing markets is called market penetration.
Transaction cost	A transaction cost is a cost incurred in making an economic exchange. For example, most people, when buying or selling a stock, must pay a commission to their broker; that commission is a transaction cost of doing the stock deal.
Distribution	Distribution in economics, the manner in which total output and income is distributed among individuals or factors.
Total cost	The sum of fixed cost and variable cost is referred to as total cost.
Inventory	Tangible property held for sale in the normal course of business or used in producing goods or services for sale is an inventory.
Tariff	A tax imposed by a nation on an imported good is called a tariff.
Foreign Credit Insurance Association	Foreign Credit Insurance Association refers to an agency established by a group of 60 U.S. insurance companies. It sells credit export insurance to interested exporters. The FCIA promises to pay for the exported merchandise if the foreign importer defaults on payment.

Chapter 23. International Trade Finance

Chapter 23. International Trade Finance

Weighted average	The weighted average unit cost of the goods available for sale for both cost of goods sold and ending inventory.
Cost of capital	Cost of capital refers to the percentage cost of funds used for acquiring resources for an organization, typically a weighted average of the firms cost of equity and cost of debt.
Weighted average cost of capital	Weighted average cost of capital refers to the computed cost of capital determined by multiplying the cost of each item in the optimal capital structure by its weighted representation in the overall capital structure and summing up the results.
Discount rate	Discount rate refers to the rate, per year, at which future values are diminished to make them comparable to values in the present. Can be either subjective or objective.
Average cost	Average cost is equal to total cost divided by the number of goods produced (Quantity-Q). It is also equal to the sum of average variable costs (total variable costs divided by Q) plus average fixed costs (total fixed costs divided by Q).
Market niche	A market niche or niche market is a focused, targetable portion of a market. By definition, then, a business that focuses on a niche market is addressing a need for a product or service that is not being addressed by mainstream providers.
Niche	In industry, a niche is a situation or an activity perfectly suited to a person. A niche can imply a working position or an area suited to a person who occupies it. Basically, a job where a person is able to succeed and thrive.
Merchant	Under the Uniform Commercial Code, one who regularly deals in goods of the kind sold in the contract at issue, or holds himself out as having special knowledge or skill relevant to such goods, or who makes the sale through an agent who regularly deals in such goods or claims such knowledge or skill is referred to as merchant.
License	A license in the sphere of Intellectual Property Rights (IPR) is a document, contract or agreement giving permission or the 'right' to a legally-definable entity to do something (such as manufacture a product or to use a service), or to apply something (such as a trademark), with the objective of achieving commercial gain.
Margin	A deposit by a buyer in stocks with a seller or a stockbroker, as security to cover fluctuations in the market in reference to stocks that the buyer has purchased but for which he has not paid is a margin. Commodities are also traded on margin.
Interest rate	The rate of return on bonds, loans, or deposits. When one speaks of 'the' interest rate, it is usually in a model where there is only one.
Currency risk	Currency risk is a form of risk that arises from the change in price of one currency against another. Whenever investors or companies have assets or business operations across national borders, they face currency risk if their positions are not hedged.

Go to Cram101.com for the Practice Tests for this Chapter.